M000313978

THIS OLD COOKBOOK

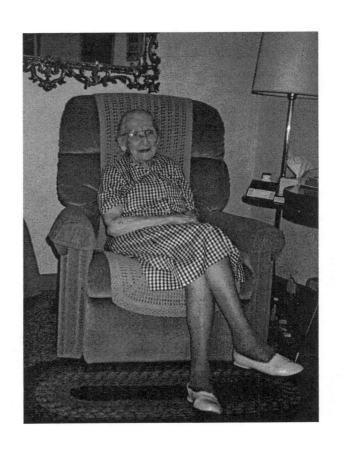

With my Love
Letha a Wiles

THIS OLD COOKBOOK

*Recipes from the kitchen of
99-year old Letha Grossnickel Wiles*

By
Yvonne Wiles Georg

**Published By
DYG Incorporated
1999**

Copyright © 1999 Yvonne Wiles Georg

First Edition

ISBN 0-9648521-1-X Hardcover
Library of Congress Catalog Card Number 94-12045

Published in the United States of America by DYG Incorporated.

All rights reserved. No part of this publication may be reproduced or distributed in any form or by any means, or stored in a database or retrieval system, or transmitted in any form, or by any means electronic, mechanical, photocopying, recording, or otherwise, without permission of the author, except for brief quotations in critical articles or reviews.

The DYG Incorporated disclaims all liability in connection with the use of this information.

Edited by
Anne Marie Gillen, Text
Daniel S. Patrell, Text
Rebecca A. Thompson, Recipes

Design by Philip H. Georg
Art by Alison Gregg Dowd
Cover Design by Shannon Haley at Diversions Publications, Inc.
Printed by BookCrafers, Inc. USA

Bulk purchases of this book may be made for education, business, or sales promotion use. For information please write:

DYG Incorporated
12428 LaPlata Street
Silver Spring, MD 20904

Cover photograph: Letha Grossnickel Wiles (1997) at her home in Middletown, Maryland.

Another book by the author: *So Many Mornings*
Published by DYG Incorporated, 1995

Publisher's Cataloging-in-Publication
(Provided by Quality Books, Inc.)

Georg, Yvonne Fay Wiles.
    This old cookbook : recipes from the kitchen of
99-year old Letha Grossnickel Wiles / by Yvonne
Wiles Georg. --
1st ed.
    p. cm.
    Preassigned LCCN: 94-12045
    ISBN: 0-9648521-1-X (hardcover)

    1. Cookery, American. 2. Cookery--Maryland--
Frederick County. I. Title.

TX7151999   641.59752'87
                  QBI98-1309

TABLE OF CONTENTS

Dedication
Introduction
Forward

ACKNOWLEDGMENTS

My special thanks to each of you!

Editor of Text - Anne Marie Gillen acquired her experience in technical and business writing and editing at the National Institutes of Health in Bethesda, MD where she has worked for 24 years. She is currently the Chief Administrative Officer for the Division of Engineering Services, Office of Research Services.

Editor of Text - Daniel S. Patrell is a writer who lives in Frederick. He is managing editor for *Frederick*, the magazine for mid-Maryland.

Editor of Recipes - Rebecca A. Thompson is a professional cook in the local area and is known for her cooking and baking skills, especially when making foods which are native to Maryland.

Art - Alison Gregg Dowd is an artist and calligrapher. She is pursuing a degree in Psychology. She currently resides in Frederick with her husband.

Design - Philip H. Georg is a systems engineer in the telecommunications industry.

Cover Design - Shannon Haley is art director for Diversions Publications, Inc. in Frederick.

Thanks, Doris!

A very special thanks to my husband, Darius, for all that you do for me. And to our son, Philip, who shared his expertise with so much love--*thanks!*

EDITOR'S PREFACE

The author has collected recipes used by 99-year old Letha Grossnickel Wiles. Letha makes no claim of being the originator of any. So many years have come and gone, her only intent is that you enjoy the recipes she used as a farmer's wife and mother of nine children.

The author has made every effort to ascertain the facts and to present events described in this cookbook in a truthful and complete manner to the best of her knowledge. It is the author's intent to lovingly remember the people mentioned in this book. While every attempt is made to provide accurate information, the author or her agents cannot be held responsible for errors or omissions. All recommendations are made without guarantee on the part of the author, editors or publisher. The author has made every effort to trace the ownership of all copyrighted material and to secure permission from copyright holders.

Yvonne Wiles Georg

It is my delight to share with you this picture of my dad, the late Russell Peter Wiles Sr., as a young man. He is driving Phil. He was a farmer who loved his family and truly knew the value of being so blessed. His father died at the age of 33, while Dad was but a 4-year old boy. Dad can be remembered for his gentle and wise traits. He was a man with a kind and tender heart.

DEDICATION

To my dear Mom,

My heart is turning home again, and it is my desire that these treasured recipes compiled for this cookbook will now be preserved as a heritage for family, friends, and whoever is interested in food that pleases the appetite of the young and the old. Down through the years you have been so very generous in sharing your food with so many wonderful folks throughout the great Middletown Valley in Maryland. The time has come for me to share with you the joy of producing *This Old Cookbook*.

Mom, in this cookbook, you not only instruct us how to prepare delicious food, but you tell us how you lived and cooked in the bygone years. Oft-repeated were the joys you and Dad brought to our family, and many of those were of you serving special foods. You never found a reason to hide behind a sham. You were proud of your and Dad's accomplishments, and rightfully so. A kiss and a hug vanished the hurts and worries of your children while we were little, and again today as adults we enjoy that same affection. By the same token, you always painted a rainbow of hope to the discouraged weary one ever since I can remember.

Mom, with Dad deceased, home is now the place over which you keep watch. Forever and forever, thanks for keeping the door open! Thanks for being a good wife to Dad and a wonderful mother to us children. Thanks for all the delicious meals you prepared over the years.

Dedication

If this book is worth anything at all, it is because you shared your knowledge of how to live by faith, hope, and love--even while cooking. In your kitchen, you worked with only the bare necessities of the day, if that. Still, tasty foods were prepared. Your entire life with Dad and family has been spent giving of yourself, beyond measure, as you cooked and cared for us. Little did you ever receive for you alone, so please enjoy the honor and pleasure that *This Old Cookbook* may bring you, as it is filled with love from my heart to yours.

Love forever,

Bonnie

Yvonne Wiles Georg

INTRODUCTION

This Old Cookbook is richly filled with love on each page and compiled due to numerous requests from family and friends for recipes used in Mom's country kitchen. You will delight in using these simple, yet delicious, recipes that have been tested with time and used for nearly a century by my mother, Letha Grossnickel Wiles, widow of Russell Peter Wiles Sr., of Middletown, Maryland. Russell passed away in 1977.

While writing *This Old Cookbook*, I sat by my mother's side. For hours she repeated to me from heart and memory recipe after recipe in detail, never missing a required step. She has no idea where some of the recipes had originated. Others have been stored on the backs of old envelopes or bits of paper, aged brown and brittle. These too have no ownership, to her knowledge. Some recipes in this cookbook have been passed to my mother by her friends; others date back to the kitchen of her mother, the late Clara Leatherman Grossnickel, and were used during the 1800s.

In the days gone by, in total ignorance, innocent blunders were made in following the instructions, and unfortunately the mistakes were passed onto the next person using the recipe. If the prepared food tasted good, however, who was ever to know the difference? The trial-and-error method produced many recipes in Mom's own kitchen! Rural living and finding herself in need of an ingredient often was the beginning of a favorite new dish right then and there. None of what I have stated changes the fact that the finished recipes remain delicious. Mom cooked and baked from her youth, so consequently, now into her golden years, adapting recipes is no big deal!

Introduction

Mom's original handwritten recipes which have aged with time, used a pinch, cupful (a teacup or coffee cup), and a "lump of lard the size of an egg or walnut" when giving the unit of measurement. Most recipes instructed to use enough flour to make a stiff or soft dough, not mentioning the amount to add. Throughout this cookbook references such as these have been converted to modern day measurements. We have come a long way in the precision of measuring the required ingredients!

It is with great pleasure that Mom and I share this assortment of interesting recipes and down-home cooking history. Please enjoy *This Old Cookbook*!

FOREWORD

Welcome to Letha Grossnickel Wiles' country kitchen! Here on an September day in 1998, my mother stands at age 99, and it seems impossible that after so many years of preparing food she would still enjoy cooking. One could consider concocting and serving food as Mom's way of saying you are welcome in her home. She has always tried to prepare food that satisfied the body while it delighted the soul of her large family and those seated around the table. Mom is now a frail 100 pounds, not from the lack of nourishment, but from her many trips around the sun. Mixed with that fragileness, the strength of a strong willpower can easily be found within her.

If I were summarizing Mom's pathway in life I would have to adamantly declare that it has not always been smooth or easy. But in the midst of this fact, she never forgot to look with a grateful heart for the good things that she enjoys. We too can alter our personality--and perhaps our lives--by changing our mental attitudes. For sure and certain, the more learned about Mom's life will set the record clear that she was not born with a silver spoon in her mouth.

I would have to say that the wisdom Mom and Dad gleaned through their years of life came with a high price most of the way. Together, they have been through lean and dark times but always lived in hope of the return of happy days. Mom believes not all wisdom is in the past, but new insight can be gained with each new experience life brings our way!

My mother absolutely never had the opportunity to be lazy, and certainly not so while in the kitchen. Nor does she care to achieve that trait anyway. No grass ever grew under her feet as a young woman. She has always lived a disciplined life and is eager to open the door to a new dawning.

To this day Mom can be found in her kitchen dressed in a simple checked gingham housedress. Many were the calico aprons she has worn in her lifetime. Each new morning found her slipping her head through the neck strap and wrapping a clean one around her waist with arms stretched to tie the side strings at her back. Believe me, fashion never got in her way!

Even in her elder years, Mom carries on in her home with a strong determination of keeping her independence. She never contemplated giving up, or quitting, at any point in her life, even at Dad's death on June 13, 1977. She always had an urgent and earnest will to carry on. She believes men and women were born to succeed and not to fail or to come up short in any good pleasure. God will grant the courage not to give up even though conditions and circumstances may appear hopeless or bleak. Mom believes this and has proven it true through the years of struggle that lie behind her.

After cooking for so many years for her large family, and with a bit of trial and error, making good food from scratch is old hat to Mom. Robust meals were prepared from foods that were grown at home on the farm she loves and dwells on today in Maryland's Middletown Valley.

With full knowledge that the preparation of a dish was time consuming, it was never determined too difficult when cooking for her family. It was a common occurrence for Mom to arise from bed before the morning sun ever peeped over the eastern mountain to start cooking and baking, spending hours to achieve a finished dish or special meal. She has tirelessly cooked, or seriously planned meals oftentimes while the rest of the world was slumbering in the dark. Neighbors can witness that even in her golden years, her 80s and 90s, lights could be seen glowing softly through the windows of home, and Mom could be found in those wee morning hours hustling about in the kitchen baking for a sick friend or someone very special. If the suggestion be made to her to spend that time resting, she would be quick to remind that we do not live successfully alone in this world. She believes that love given by doing kind deeds for others is eternal with reward--and you don't keep score of who did the last good deed for you! She has proven the only way to have a friend is to be a friend.

Mom has prepared 81 Christmas feasts in her home, the last one being Christmas Day 1997. When Mom married my dad in 1916, she cooked three meals a day from that point until his death in 1977. During their years of farming, throughout the busy seasons, she would cook for as many as 14 men or more, besides her family. I vividly remember every meal had dessert, and sometimes two varieties at that!

A million and one unforgettable memories have been made in Mom's kitchen. Whether good or bad, each has left its deeply marked impression on her mind and especially in her heart. The meaning of true values becomes clearer to me each day I live. Mom spent endless hours making the farmhouse a happy home for all to enjoy. Maybe it is the mixture of the pleasant and the tragic events we experienced as a family that spins a tapestry of life so rich and priceless. Never realizing our destination in this life, we are sure God held our family in His hands.

Little did Mom care about serving food on elegant china and costly silver platters. She owned no silver, then or now. Earthly riches and expensive things were not of importance to her. She cared more about fulfilling her family's needs and providing nourishment.

She liked pleasing our taste buds, and she still does. She cared about what went on in the kitchen but was concerned less about what was in the kitchen. In fact, during those early years of rearing the large family, we ate more often from chipped and cracked plates than from ones that were in perfect condition. And one never thought of coordinating colors while mismatched dime store *china* was placed on a table covered with a homemade printed chicken feed-bag tablecloth. Her guests never seemed to notice imperfections or the lack of brand names. She owned nothing material that was worth flaunting or showing off but served her meals with pride and grace. She could not afford to correct the needs and had no feeling of guilt or shame. Lack was just a fact of life back then. Mom was proud of what money could not buy--good character and pride in doing a job well. That alone brought my parents joy and contentment through the years. We children were taught that our processions are not important, it's the size and the motive of our heart that counts! We never need to drop our heads because we do not have what another may possess. We only need to drop our head in honor to the Lord when we pray.

Mom was never jealous or envious of others who had more than she. She knows nothing can spoil or ruin a life more quickly than jealousy. It can become a horrendous obstacle, and at the same time it is cruel and cold as death and the grave.

With so many years of preparing food, most of Mother's recipes were penciled on small scraps of paper or on the pages of a small composition-type notebook. To this day she owns only two cookbooks, and pays little attention to those! If we were to watch her prepare to cook at age 99, she would raise her arm to reach into a corner of a shelf in the oak kitchen cabinets, pull out a small bundle of scraps of paper, ragged but neatly contained with a rubber band, sort gently through the stack and carefully pull out the treasured hand-written recipe. Many are stored in her remarkable memory and are quick to come to mind when queried.

Mom has used many of the recipes in *This Old Cookbook* for nearly a century as she learned those from her mother and family. She recalls when she was a little country girl helping her mother prepare some of these dishes and learning the secrets to successful cooking while working at her side. Mom has never wandered far from simple country cooking. She remembers her mother baking in an outdoor bake oven, and over an open fireplace in the summer kitchen on her family's homestead on Harp Hill Road. She experienced living and cooking in these primitive conditions in the country home. Nevertheless, those memories of childhood days are near and dear to her heart. Looking back over her shoulder at the hard work and lack of modern conveniences makes cooking in a modern kitchen, with up-to-date appliances, a joy to Mom today. She has watched men and women climb to success, one great invention after another, only to share and reap the benefit of their success.

Back on January 1, 1916, Mom became a young housewife, and when mealtime came there was no money to buy prepared food items from the grocery store. In fact, there were no around-the-corner grocery stores to buy quick and easy packaged foods as we have available today. In preparation for the cold winter months, summertime was spent preserving food by canning, drying, and in recent years, freezing. Back then, Mom went to her pantry to survey the supply of food canned in glass jars and neatly lined up on the shelves. She knew the surplus vegetables and fruits she gathered during the harvest season would determine the quality of her meals once the garden had been gleaned. Mom dearly loved her family and made every effort to feed us well, never complaining about the demanding work involved. A large family cannot be fed well without good management in the kitchen and lots of energy, else it will wear you down before you ever have a chance to figure out what is happening!

Never was Mom's food exotic, but each dish was made with love and blessed by the Lord, who faithfully provided well for our family. Even at the worse moment in a terrible situation, it was with a grateful spirit that Mom prepared meals while never forgetting to remind her family of their many blessings.

Mom never wants to be found guilty of missing an opportunity to give or do something nice for others, especially if someone is in need. She has always been one to count on when a helping hand is needed, not to tell you what to do but to pitch in and help you out of your undesirable situation. She expects to pass this way but once, so she continues to strive with great diligence to make her house a home where love and goodwill abides. These days, when her middle-aged grandchildren visit she can still bring a quick and steady sparkle to their eyes as she offers them a bag of her scrumptious treats to take home.

It is Mom's belief that parents should be sincere, offer wise instructions while they dedicate themselves to their family, and be prepared to stand strong when the struggles that go along with living come their way. Hearts, both young and old, should be gently nurtured so to stay ablaze with zealous love--they are so fragile. Mom has learned that only God can provide the wisdom necessary to be a truly successful mother.

My mother, Letha Alice Grossnickel Wiles was born in 1899, the youngest of four children, and the only girl, the daughter of the late Charles Webster and Clara Leatherman Grossnickel. She grew up on a farm in Frederick County, in Ellerton, near Myersville, Maryland, a community of farming people who cultivate the rich land and enjoyed thriving crops along with herds of livestock. Steven and Joanne Leatherman presently own the farm that Mom grew up on. There is a tenderness in her heart for the old home ground and the home folks.

Eleven children were born to my parents, Russell and Letha Wiles. Two died in infancy, the other nine children live today and range in age from 53 to 81 years. Theodore Roosevelt once said that *a successful mother who has trained her children right holds a more important and honorable position than anyone in the community.* If there be any truth in that statement, Mom holds that honorable position!

My parents never had the opportunity to travel out of the United States but they did not feel cheated. Home was their treasure and pride and is still Mom's life and of most importance. The green, green grass from home can never be replaced--the farm and its soil are a part of her. No hill will ever appear greener to her eyes than those at home, likewise no friend dearer. That love runs deep into her soul!

For Mom, life is a race to be run with unshakeable strength and with a grand prize waiting at the end. She will tell you she faced all the raging seas and storms of life by truly standing in God's grace. And it was when the times were darkest that she realized this fact most. Mom clearly recognizes her weaknesses and believes she needs the strength that only God can provide to carry on. She believes we should not allow the cares of this life to drive us to doubt because God is sufficient for every need, every day. I have heard this old saying that encourages troubled folks and it goes like this: *Fear knocked at my door. Faith answered, but no one was there!*

Mom knows whatever she does in this world will no doubt go down as unnoticed history, but only what she does for God will be eternal and of importance. The characteristics of being honest, fair, and truthful will bring trust in all walks of life, she assures. So when all is said and done, the most valuable and costly inheritance a parent can give a child is a good example. We must never forget unsoiled character is much easier kept than recovered.

In the inheritance you leave behind, remember to include a collection of recipes to treasure. The recipes Mom and I selected to preserve are the ones she loved and served best. My mother's hope is that a recipe she has shared will become a favorite on your table. It delights me to avail them to you, so please enjoy, *This Old Cookbook.*

(The names Grossnickel and Grossnickle are used throughout this book. One of two German brothers changed the spelling of his name to clarify his descendants.)

A Farmer's Table Grace

Our Lord and our Heavenly Father, it is with grateful hearts that we sit around this family table, sharing the food grown on your sweet soil. You have blessed us with plenty and we would not forget to thank you. Forgive us if we should ever, in haste, forget to give thanks for what you have provided. We are enjoying a rich and good life together as a family and we ask for your constant guidance in all things. Now, bless each friend with each new day and protect our every step in this life's journey.

Amen

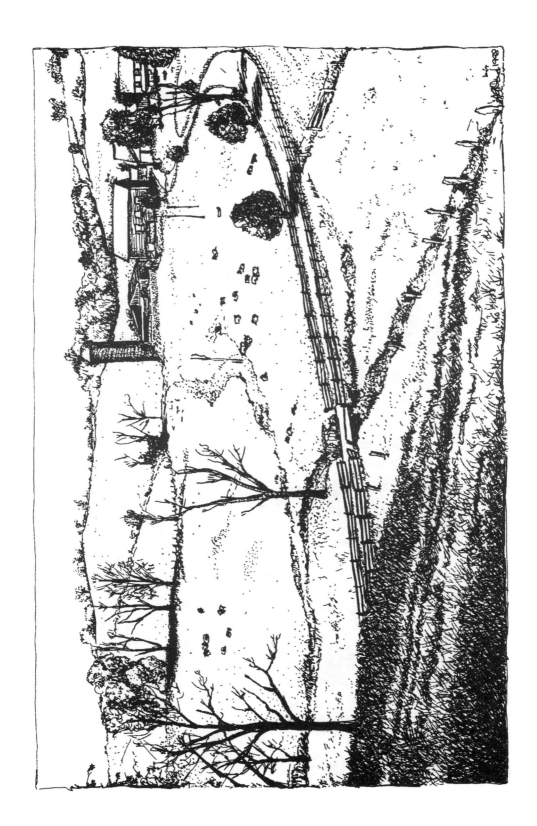

BREADS & QUICK BREADS

It seems to me, baking Bread-Dough Doughnuts is truly a labor of love. Mom will guarantee your reward from the family will be all smiles and praise when they get their first whiff of the fresh-baked fragrance. Faces will be certain to light up when they taste that airy freshness of the soft dough. Mom has a reputation of making wonderful, light doughnuts. The sensation to your mouth will be that of your fingers touching velvet. On February 11, 1997, with the help of her oldest daughter, she baked nine dozen doughnuts to share with folks she loves.

Today, we live in an "instant" society and most of us strive to produce methods where everything we do can be accomplished "quick and easy." When cooking and baking, some steps in a recipe cannot be bypassed or even shortened. Time must be allowed for reactions to take place with the ingredients, and the old-fashioned way of taking your time to follow each step closely and accurately is definitely encouraged, as it is best!

Only recently did Mom purchase a simple aluminum doughnut cutter. For years she cut the doughnuts with a large can that she washed and saved after it was opened and the food was used. She cut the hole in the middle of the dough with the thimble she used on her finger when sewing. In the young years of her and Dad's marriage, there was no extra cash for anything--not even a doughnut cutter.

There is an anonymous saying that is so very true and would have applied here in Mom and Dad's life. That saying is: *The poorest of all men is not the man without a cent; it is the man without a dream.* My parent's dream was to give their best to the family and their friends. Success has been all theirs!

Bread-Dough Doughnuts

1/2 cup butter, softened
1/2 cup granulated sugar
1 teaspoon salt
2 cups whole milk
2 eggs
1/2 cup warm water
2 tablespoons dry yeast
7 cups all-purpose flour

1. In a large mixing bowl combine the butter, sugar, and salt. Set aside.

2. In a heavy saucepan cook the milk over medium heat to almost a boil. A skim will form on top of the milk. *(NOTE: Do not allow to boil.)*

3. Pour the milk over the sugar, butter, and salt mixture. Stir with a spoon until sugar is dissolved and butter is melted.

4. Break the eggs into the mixture but do not stir. Set aside.

5. In a small saucepan stir and dissolve the dry yeast in the warm water. Pour into the above mixture and stir until well blended.

6. Add a cup of flour and beat with a spoon. Continue adding a cup or two and beating until flour is fully incorporated into the dough. Be sure to beat dough until very smooth after the last addition of flour.

7. Transfer dough to a large greased pan. Set in a warm place.
(NOTE: Dough pan may be placed over warm water to start the rising action but do not allow it to touch the water.)

8. Allow to rise to double in bulk.

9. Punch down and cover with a cloth. Allow to rise the second time.

10. Roll the dough on a floured surface to about 1/2 inch thick and cut with a doughnut cutter.

11. After doughnuts are cut out, allow them to rise for about 30 minutes.
(NOTE: Do not cover with a cloth.)

12. Heat cooking oil to 375 degrees in a deep skillet or heavy Dutch oven. Drop doughnuts carefully into the deep cooking oil and fry until lightly browned on one side. Then turn doughnut over with a fork and fry the other side until lightly browned.

13. Remove doughnuts from the oil and allow to drain on paper towels spread in a shallow pan.

When ready to serve, roll doughnut in powdered sugar or spread with jelly.

(NOTE: Store doughnuts in plastic bags. They will keep in the freezer for a few months.)

Yield: 3 dozen doughnuts.

❧   ❧   ❧

After all the cluttered years that have come and gone in Mom's long life, she has not forgotten the following story. I am sure you know marvelous memories linger long after the cook has put away her spoon, bowl, and pan!

As a young bride and farmer's wife, Mom forgot to bake doughnuts on Shrove Tuesday, as was the habit at her home. Her long-time good friend, Effie, was up early in the morning and in her kitchen baking fat cakes, a type of doughnut made without using yeast. So with the morning's work behind her, Effie decided to walk the several miles down a dirt and gravel road from her house to Mom's place to visit. Back in the early 1900s, folks did not have cars to jump into and ride wherever they wanted to go. They either walked or drove a horse and buggy. Most often the men rode horseback when going on an errand, especially when they did not need to carry something heavy with them.

Effie's Fat Cakes had turned out perfectly this day and so she brought a few along for my mother to taste. Eagerly entering the door of the farmhouse, Effie questioned if Mom had remembered the special day. Indeed, she had forgotten! But earlier in the day she had mixed up and baked a gingerbread that she had just removed from the wood stove oven. There in that modest country kitchen, the two young women chatted, enjoyed their visit, and an exchange of fat cakes for gingerbread was made right then and there. Food was a common element between them. They both found pleasure in cooking, and it was used to form a bond.

Effie was happy to share her fat cake recipe and Mom used it through the years. These two women provided verbal instructions and nearly always assumed some steps were understood by whoever used the recipe. There were few, if any, closely guarded secrets pertaining to cooking. It was their responsibility to cook, and these young women had a determination to develop and perfect whatever skills they needed to make a good home life. Sharing recipes brought them joy while trying to improve their culinary ability.

Mom not only remembers the day of nearly 80 years ago, but best of all her wonderful friend, Effie Delauter. Old friends have special memories buried deep in their innermost being, and these memories can't be stolen. Really and truly, there is no friend like an old friend.

Effie's Fat Cakes

8 cups all-purpose flour
2 teaspoons baking soda
1 teaspoon salt
2 cups granulated sugar
1/2 cup lard
(*NOTE: Solid vegetable shortening can be substituted for lard.*)
3 eggs
4 cups sour milk
(*NOTE: Make sour milk by adding 1 tablespoon of vinegar to 1 cup whole milk and stir.*)

1. In a large bowl sift together the flour, baking soda, and salt. Set aside.

2. In a separate mixing bowl cream together the sugar and lard with a spoon.

3. Add the eggs to the mixture and beat until well blended.

4. Add the sour milk and stir until blended.

5. Add a couple of cups of the flour mixture to the batter and beat until smooth with a spoon. Continue adding a few cups and beating until flour mixture is fully incorporated into the dough.

6. On a floured surface roll the dough to 1/2 inch thick and cut with a doughnut cutter.

7. In a deep, heavy pan heat the cooking oil over medium to high heat to about 375 degrees. Drop the doughnuts into the deep cooking oil and fry until lightly browned on one side. Then turn over with a fork and fry the other side until lightly browned.

8. Remove doughnuts from the oil and allow to drain on paper towels spread in a shallow pan.

When ready to serve, roll the doughnut in powdered sugar or spread with jelly.

Yield: 3 dozen doughnuts.

છ છ છ

Without hesitation, I can say yeast bread tastes good anytime! In the early 1950s, I remember that the bread man, Paul Shepley, delivered bakery bread to our kitchen door twice a week. His route took him through the countryside, and the convenience of "bread delivered to the doorstep" was certainly a timesaver for the farmer's wife. Upon arrival at our home, Paul jumped out of his truck carrying a basket filled with bags of potato chips, buns, candy bars, chewing gum, and, of course, bread. Holding it with one hand, the weight caused him to walk slightly bent to his side, the other arm he held out away from his body to keep a good balance.

Once, the youngest child in the family stood beside Mom and the bread man with the basket of goodies setting before them on the floor. The child looked straight into Mom's eyes and politely asked with great concern in the tone of his voice, "Mommy, I'd like to have a bag of potato chips, if you have the money."

The children quickly learned at a very early age that money was not always available to meet their wants. If Mom was going to treat, she usually told us ahead of the bread man's arrival. But even with time for thought, it seemed our big decision of the hour was always hurried! If we made up our fickle minds early, once that bountiful basket of goodies was displayed before us, we would be overwhelmed by the array, and the need to make another choice deemed necessary. It always seemed we spotted a candy bar that slipped our memory earlier but now appeared and was beyond our resistance. Although young, we were trained well, and we always wanted to get the most for our money!

Yeast Bread

Bake at 425 degrees.

1 3/4 cups warm water
2 tablespoons granulated sugar
1 teaspoon salt
2 tablespoons dry granulated yeast
1/2 cup warm water
2 tablespoons butter, softened
7 cups sifted all-purpose flour

1. In a large mixing bowl combine 1 3/4 cups of warm water, the sugar, and salt. Set aside.

2. In a saucepan stir and dissolve the yeast in 1/2 cup of warm water. Pour into the above mixture.

3. Add the softened butter. Add a cup of flour and stir. Continue adding a cup and stirring until flour is fully incorporated into the dough.

4. Place on a floured surface. Knead until the dough is smooth and no longer sticks to the surface.

5. Shape into loaves and place in greased loaf pans, either round or oblong. Set aside to rise double in bulk.

6. Bake for 15 to 20 minutes or until lightly browned. Baking time will vary with the size of the loaf.

Serve with plenty of butter spread on each slice.

Yield: 3 to 4 loaves.

&a &a &a

Egg White Glaze gives the bread's crust a nice shine. It is nice to use on dinner rolls when company is coming.

Egg White Glaze for Bread

1 egg white
1 tablespoons water

1. In a small bowl beat the egg white slightly with a rotary beater or wire whisk and combine with water.

2. Brush the mixture on top of the loaf of dough before baking.

ठ&   ठ&   ठ&

It seemed to me that time moved slowly when waiting for Mom's sticky buns to rise and then bake in the oven.

The walk-in pantry next to our kitchen in the old farmhouse had the look of a general store, clothes closet, and a woodshed! I remember a large chest-type woodbox sat on the right-hand side as one entered the pantry door. It was filled to the brim with dry wood for burning in the cookstove. When coming from the barn into the house, everyone pulled their dirty barn boots off their feet while standing on the porch, trying to keep the kitchen floor clean. Then we carried them to the pantry and lined them up, pair next to pair, on top of the wood in the woodbox.

This chest-type woodbox, which closed with a hinged lid, was six-foot long and was left behind in the kitchen at the Flora Wiles (Dad's mother) homestead in 1916. My parents claimed the relic and moved it with them whenever the time came for them to change farms and living quarters. A box such as this, served during this time period not only to store wood, but folks used it as a general storage area to keep dried corn, beans, fruit snits, etc. Still others piled articles that they frequently used there--blankets to throw over the children while napping, sewing supplies, and maybe a few books. Really, it was a "catch all," when not used as a woodbox. Often folks placed a chest behind the table, pushed it against the wall, and used it as a bench to seat the children at mealtime. Most couples had large families back then, and it could accommodate more little bodies than individual chairs since they could sit closer to one another.

In our pantry, clothes hooks were screwed to the wall, high above the woodbox, and on these we hung our barn coats and hats. I will never forget Mom's gingham checked sunbonnet and Dad's straw hat hanging on the metal clothes hooks or ten-penny nails. Back then these items were nothing more than a sunbonnet and hat. Today, they are symbols of "oh so sweet memories."

In warm weather Mom opened the small narrow window in the pantry. We could view the garden from there, and the fresh air was welcomed. She propped the sash up with a temporary expandable wooden-framed window screen. The window was covered with a "then modern" plastic curtain, pale aqua in color with gold embossed flowers. We used similar "fashionable" plastic drapes in the kitchen and living room. Those had a white background and were splattered with large, bright flowers. If we splashed food on the curtain hanging over the window above the kitchen sink, we just reached up with a wet cloth in hand and wiped it clean!

Rows of old stained wooden shelves lined the pantry's walls that were painted green from the floor to the tongue-groove board ceiling. Mom stored her large cooking pans and skillets on these. A heavy old steel food grinder was attached to the edge of one of the shelves at a prominent spot. It was in an area where Mom had room to stand and turn the handle while grinding food.

On still another shelf, a covered wooden bucket held sugar and reeked with a sweet scent. The flour was kept in a large bailed handled aluminum kettle with a tight lid that sported a tiny black knob in the center. A five-gallon tin can of lard made at the fall butchering was stored on the floor behind the door. The floor was covered with linoleum, and a few layers of old newspaper were placed under the lard can to collect any grease that escaped the container. Mom always kept a thin wooden slat half-bushel basket filled with corn cobs and a gallon tin can of kerosene in a handy spot to start the fire in the wood-burning cookstove. The flatirons for ironing the clothes were made of cast iron and rested on a clean shelf. A gallon gray earthenware vinegar jug with a cork jammed into the opening at the neck sat in the corner. And behind the door on the first shelf up from the floor was an old cardboard box filled with various little jars of nails, tacks and screws. That was Mom's handyman box of little treasures for doing emergency repair jobs around the house! Every farmer's wife declared ownership of an old worthless hammer and screw driver, confiscated from the blacksmith shop or tool shed!

The pantry had an aroma all its own, and I can make myself terribly homesick just thinking of it. I suppose no matter how hard she tried, Mom could never successfully hide ginger cookies or bananas when stored here. We children could track the scent of either one and end up at the right spot in nothing flat! The very top shelf in the pantry, which was far out of the children's reach, held a cigar box containing Dad's razor and shaving brush. The razor strop was hanging on a nail, down along side the door. Resting on that same shelf was a box of Ohio Red Tip wooden matches and anything that my parents thought might be harmful or get the little ones in trouble. As a matter of fact, the more I think about it, the pantry was the storehouse of family essentials!

I shall never forget, far up on the top shelf and nearly out of sight (since only a tip of the handle showed), laid a tiny wooden paddle or board of correction. A large rolling board with a little eye bolt that screwed in the narrow side hung over a nail driven into the edge of another shelf. Each item, in fact, had a story to tell: a walnut rolling pin; an old metal-blade slaw cutter mounted on a broad board; a tin flour sifter with a little red knob on the crank; a blue speckled enameled steel-ware coffee pot, and various battered pots and pans. Then again, so did the paddle Mom occasionally used to spank us! It was small in size but it sure made a big adjustment in our attitudes.

As regularly as Mom opened her eyes at the beginning of each new day, she opened the pantry door that was painted beige and covered with a top coat of dark varnish swirled in a design. One might ask, why do you write to tell these stories? In my mind countless citizens of the great Middletown Valley have shared in this same type of honest-to-goodness living. I will confess that this valley is more than just a valley to me. It is an open book, a story waiting to be told from the loftiness of the mountains that has cast an eye on each life from birth to death, to the greenish of green meadows in the low lands where children frolic and play while they grew to adulthood.

Sticky Buns

Bake at 350 degrees.

Dough Ingredients:

1/2 cup butter
1/2 cup granulated sugar
1 teaspoon salt
2 cups whole milk
2 eggs
1/2 cup warm water
2 tablespoons dry yeast
7 cups all-purpose flour

1. In a large mixing bowl combine the butter, sugar, and salt. Set aside.

2. In a heavy saucepan over medium heat bring the milk to almost a boil. A skim will form on top.
(NOTE: Do not allow to boil.)

3. Pour the milk over the sugar, butter, and salt mixture. Stir with a spoon until sugar is dissolved and butter is melted.

4. Break the eggs into the mixture but do not stir. Set aside.

5. In a small saucepan stir and dissolve the dry yeast in the warm water. Pour into the above mixture and stir until well blended.

6. Add a few cups of flour and stir until smooth. Continue adding a few cups until the flour is incorporated into the dough. Be sure to beat dough until very smooth after the last addition of flour.

7. Transfer to a large greased pan. Set in a warm place.
(NOTE: Dough pan may be placed over warm water to start the rising action, but do not allow it to touch the water.)

8. Allow to rise to double in bulk.

9. Punch dough down and cover with a cloth. Allow to rise the second time.
(NOTE: Prepare syrup for the bottom of baking pan before you are ready to roll the dough the last time.)

Syrup Ingredients:

2 cups brown sugar
1 stick butter
1/2 cup light corn syrup
1/2 cup water

10. In a heavy saucepan combine the syrup ingredients and bring to a boil over medium to high heat, stirring constantly. Pour syrup evenly over the bottom of a flat pan.

Spread Ingredients:

2 sticks butter
1 3/4 cups brown sugar
2 tablespoons ground cinnamon
raisins, if desired
nuts, if desired

11. Roll the dough on a floured surface to about 1/2 inch thick and spread with butter. Sprinkle with sugar and ground cinnamon. Sprinkle raisins and nuts on top, if desired.

12. Roll the dough like a jellyroll log, and cut into 1-inch thick slices with a sharp knife. Lay slices flat in the pan of syrup about 3/4 inch apart.

13. Allow to rise to double in bulk. Bake for 16 to 20 minutes.

14. Remove from the oven and turn pan upside down on a tray. Do not remove the pan for 3 minutes.

Yield: 3 dozen buns.

ཤ   ཤ   ཤ

Mom made Breakfast Milk Toast for her babies as soon as they were old enough to swallow a little bulk. She prepared it by using her home-baked bread but removed the hard crust, making the toast soft and smooth for the little one to swallow. I think of the many times she sat and patiently fed the babies, and there is no doubt in my mind, she did not take the time to enjoy her meal.

I believe so long as we love, we serve with "no strings attached." Mom holds each of us children, even in our years of adulthood, as her dearest worth. Is it any wonder my heart overflows with gratitude and thanks for all she has done for me.

Breakfast Milk Toast

2 slices buttered toast
2 cups whole milk
salt, to taste
ground cinnamon, to taste
granulated white or brown sugar, to taste

1. Prepare the buttered toast. Set aside.

2. In a small skillet, heat the milk to almost boiling.
(NOTE: Do not allow to boil.)

3. Add toast to the milk and allow to stand a few minutes on reduced heat before serving. Sprinkle with salt, cinnamon, and sugar. Serve immediately.

 è&   è&   è&

When Mom was cooking and a mishap occurred, we could be assured she would attempt to make it again soon. She hated to serve something she considered "not good." When it came to the quality of the finished product, she was extremely critical since she took great pleasure in trying to perfect her dishes. It is my desire to preserve these recipes that she has proven, treasured, and loved for most of her life. If a recipe fails, don't be disheartened. You too can make a new attempt on another day.

Lassie dumplings are a popular gooey dish which was served often in my mother's home on baking day. Grandmother Grossnickel thought it easier to make the dumplings and bake the bread on the same day, since both required the identical yeast dough. Lassie dumplings are cooked on top of the stove in a kettle of boiling syrup. While this is an unusual and time consuming method of making a delicious sweet treat, I am reminded of a lesson taken from my grandmother's and mother's dedication to their families that nothing they could do for them appeared to require too much work. We must all adjust to the changing times but still hold to their unchanging principals of love, dedication, and hard work.

In this recipe, use the desired amount of dough for dumplings and shape the excess into dinner rolls to bake for the next meal.

Lassie Dumplings

1 3/4 cups warm water
2 tablespoons granulated sugar
1 teaspoon salt
2 tablespoons dry granulated yeast

1/2 cup warm water
2 tablespoons butter, softened
7 cups sifted all-purpose flour

1. In a large mixing bowl combine 1 3/4 cups of warm water, the sugar, and salt. Set aside.

2. In a separate saucepan combine the yeast and 1/2 cup of warm water. Stir until dissolved. Pour into the above mixture.

3. Add the softened butter. Add a cup of flour at a time and stir after each addition. Continue until all the flour is incorporated into the dough.

4. Place dough on a floured surface. Knead the dough until smooth and no longer sticks to the surface.

5. Cut into pieces the size of a small egg and shape into a ball. Set aside to rise double in bulk.

Syrup Ingredients:

8 cups water
1 cup brown sugar
1 cup light molasses
1/2 teaspoon salt
1 tablespoon butter

6. In a heavy flat kettle combine all the syrup ingredients.

7. When syrup has boiled for 15 to 20 minutes, gently drop dumplings in, guarding to keep them apart, and cover pan with a tight lid. Cook 25 to 30 minutes over heat that will keep the syrup boiling.
(NOTE: Do not lift the lid or the dumpling will drop.)

8. Carefully lift each dumpling into an individual serving dish and pour the syrup over the top. If desired, cover with fresh milk.

Serve immediately at the beginning of the meal while dumplings are hot and plump.
(NOTE: Dumplings will drop if not served immediately, after transferring from the pan.)

ès   ès   ès

Dinner Rolls

To make dinner rolls or loaves of bread use the Lassie Dumpling recipe on Page 18.

Bake at 425 degrees for 15 to 20 minutes or until lightly browned.

ès   ès   ès

Communion bread is still made today by the deacons' wives for the Church of the Brethren Love Feasts. In Maryland, back in the mid-1800s the Love Feast and Communion Services were held in the farmers' barns. There were no large churches or convention centers to house largely attended events. The Love Feast lasted all day and was held on Saturday. Today the service lasts for an hour or so in the evening, usually on a Thursday or Saturday, according to the tradition of the congregation, and is held in the local church.

Back then, the afternoon service was a self-examination of one's spiritual condition. At this solemn and holy evening service church members washed each others feet and ate a meal together. The event ran late into the night. The meal consists of nothing more than a sandwich of buttered regular white bread and boiled sliced beef, plus beef broth poured in a bowl over broken pieces of bread. After the meal was over, the Communion Service begins. The communion bread, similar to that in this recipe, would be accompanied by unfermented grape juice.

During the horse and buggy days, those folks who lived a far distance from the location of the service, spent the night with families who were located near the site or at the church. Folks were often housed overnight in the attic of the Grossnickle Church of the Brethren when the Love Feast was in progress. Cots or beds and mattresses on the floor offered a place to lie down to sleep. Mom recalls going upstairs and seeing the heavy quilts and blankets folded neatly on the cots and a few cradles for the infants sat in the corner. The horses pulled buggies, surreys, spring or stick wagons and were boarded at a neighbor's barn. Everyone was willing to pitch in and help out.

The church kitchen offered a place to cook enough food to tide folks over and a fire to keep them warm when there was a chill in the air. Water was carried in buckets from Charlie Hoover's spring, which was located nearby on his property. The convenience of outdoor privies completed their needs!

On Sunday morning the hostess cooked breakfast for her guests, they gathered to worship, and a simple mid-day meal was served before they started for home. These folks found true happiness in giving and sharing.

The Brethren were sincere and dedicated to their belief. During the service no one so much as whispered to the person seated next to them. The stillness was broken only by the Elder or Reverend in charge of the service. Occasionally, a cricket chirped in the meadow or a frog croaked from the nearby stream, breaking the nearly silent night.

Mom bakes communion bread and serves it as a cracker, snack, or a replacement for bread with a meal.

Communion Bread

Bake at 350 degrees.

6 cups all-purpose flour
2 teaspoons granulated sugar
1/2 pound salt-free butter, softened
1 pint of whole milk
(NOTE: Use milk that is fresh.)

1. In a large mixing bowl combine the flour, sugar, and butter to make a dough. Work with your finger tips like you would a pie dough.

2. Add the milk to the flour mixture all at once.

3. Knead dough until smooth.

4. Roll the dough on a floured surface. Cut into 1/4-inch thick and 1-inch wide strips.

5. Place the strips of dough on an ungreased cookie sheet and punch holes in the top of each strip 1 inch apart with a fork.

6. Bake in the oven for 20 minutes or until lightly browned.

Variation: Add salt or salted butter for more flavor.

(NOTE: Communion bread can be baked and stored in a tight container in the freezer. It will keep for several weeks in the refrigerator.)

   ❦ ❦ ❦

One might consider homemade Cinnamon Buns a luxury today. There is no doubt, necessities and changes in lifestyle have altered the availability of an adult being in the home during daytime hours to bake and cook for the family.

Although Mom's education did not go beyond grade school, she is sharp as a tack when working with numbers and measurements. When required, it is no problem for her to increase or decrease fractions in a recipe, even though she accurately measures by sight much of the time. Today, most cooks have never cultivated the art of measuring by a pinch or handful.

When baking and cooking Mom reached into the can of flour and removed a handful, then dipped a coffee or tea cup into the old wooden sugar bucket and dumped those ingredients into her mixing bowl. Next she took a pinch of salt from the small earthenware pot that held about a pound. The amount of shortening needed was determined by the size of a nut or egg.

Mom determined how much of an ingredient to use by experience. Believe me, she had plenty of that! The kitchen was Mom's domain in which she was in control. It is a good habit to gather all ingredients before starting to mix a recipe.

Cinnamon Buns

Bake at 375 degrees.

1/2 cup butter
1/2 cup granulated sugar
1 teaspoon salt

2 cups whole milk
2 eggs
2 tablespoons dry yeast
1/2 cup warm water
7 cups all-purpose flour
sugar and ground cinnamon, to sprinkle on top of
    buttered dough

1. In a large mixing bowl combine the butter, sugar, and salt. Set aside.

2. In a heavy saucepan over medium heat bring the milk to almost a boil. A skim will form on top.
(NOTE: Do not allow to boil.)

3. Pour the milk over the sugar, butter, and salt mixture. Stir with a spoon until sugar is dissolved and butter is melted.

4. Break the eggs into the mixture but do not stir. Set aside.

5. In a small saucepan stir and dissolve the dry yeast in the warm water. Pour into the above mixture and stir until well blended.

6. Add a couple of cups of flour and beat until smooth with a spoon. Continue adding a few cups and beating until flour is fully incorporated into the dough. Be sure to beat dough until very smooth after the last addition of flour.

7. Transfer dough to a large greased pan. Set in a warm place.
(NOTE: Dough pan may be placed over warm water to start the rising action, but do not allow it to touch the water.)

8. Allow to rise to double in bulk.

9. Punch down and cover with a cloth. Allow to rise the second time.

10. Roll the dough on a floured surface to about 1/2 inch thick.

11. Spread thick with butter. Sprinkle generously with granulated sugar and cinnamon. Roll like a jellyroll log. Cut into 3/4- to 1-inch thick slices and lay down in a greased flat pan about 3/4 inch apart. Cover the pan with a cloth or piece of waxed paper and allow to rise double in bulk.

12. Uncover and bake in the oven for 35 to 45 minutes or until lightly browned.

13. Cool the buns and spread with a layer of your favorite icing. Or drizzle with a thin layer of White Drizzle Icing over warm buns.

White Drizzle Icing Ingredients:

1 cup powdered sugar
2 tablespoons hot cream
1 teaspoon vanilla

14. In a mixing bowl combine all the ingredients and beat until smooth. Drizzle over warm buns.

Variation: Sprinkle raisins on top of granulated sugar and ground cinnamon layer.

Yield: 3 dozen buns.

ॐ   ॐ   ॐ

In the early part of the 1900s, folks living in the rural areas of Frederick County traveled to gristmills to have wheat and corn ground into flour and cornmeal. Our family was no different. Oftentimes, Dad traveled to Wolfsville to Dick Grossnickle's Mill located near the intersection of Spruce Run and Route 17 with horse and stick wagon, loaded with barrels or bags of grain grown on the farm.

During the days of World War I, when the farmer visited the mill, if their wheat crop was scarce they purchased grain from the miller. At the same time, the customer was required to take a portion of cornmeal with his order of flour. The choice of most housewives was wheat flour since cornmeal produces a coarse dough and the end products are not as popular (or as tasty, in my opinion).

Dick's sons, Lester and Elmer Grossnickle, worked at the mill. They had a younger brother, Blaine. Most of the time Dad had wheat from the farm to grind, but when he ran short Lester filled Dad's order with all the flour he needed, asking him to take only a small portion of cornmeal. Mom used lots of flour since she baked bread for our large family and the hired farmhands, and she has never forgotten how much Lester helped the family! You see, he and Dad were about the same age and good friends. Recreational opportunities were limited, so as young single men, they went horseback riding around the community for fun. Mom remembers Lester and the kind manner he showed.

I believe, like Lester, we should all show the evidence of an earnest concern for others by doing something to help those who are in need. One should do that deed for the joy of giving alone, not expecting pay or something in return. We should count it a privilege to share our good fortune and blessings. One never knows when we may be in need of a harvest of kindness and goodwill. I truly believe a person's true character is revealed by what he does when no one is watching or when no demands are being made. Our hearts are truly open books, and we write the story--word after word, chapter after chapter.

Cornmeal Muffins

Bake at 400 degrees.

1 cup cornmeal
1 cup all-purpose flour
3 teaspoons baking powder
1/2 teaspoon salt
1/2 cup butter
1/2 cup granulated sugar
2 eggs
1 cup whole milk

1. In a mixing bowl combine the cornmeal, flour, baking powder, and salt. Set aside.

2. In a separate bowl cream together the butter and sugar. Add the eggs and milk to the creamed mixture; stir with a spoon until blended.

3. Add the flour mixture and stir only until blended.

4. Pour the batter into greased muffin tins.

5. Bake in the oven for 20 minutes or until lightly browned.

Yield: 8 to 12 muffins.

ð   ð   ð

At our home, the bags of flour and cornmeal that we used for the family's cooking needs were stored in a large wooden chest in the farm workers' quarters, which were located on the second floor in the dairy and near the farmhouse. That chest was built by a well-known carpenter, Walter Day, of Wolfsville, Maryland. It was divided in two sections and had a large hinged lid, which we would lift to open until it rested against the wall. Both halves of the chest measured a three-foot cube.

Upon Dad's return home from the mill with the cloth bags of freshly ground flour and cornmeal, he placed them in the chest for safe, dry keeping--flour on one side, cornmeal on the other. From there Mom filled the containers she stored in the kitchen pantry, now handy and ready to use.

We are so spoiled with "convenience" today. In fact, the idea of a microwave oven would have been either too good to believe or a real joke back in the good old days. It is hard for those of us who have lived in a world of electric lights and appliances to imagine what it was like to live in Mom's early years of marriage and cooking without electricity or indoor plumbing. Can you imagine having to depend on oil lamps to light the night or the water pump or the bucket and cistern method to supply the water? Most often, people rose before dawn with lanterns in hand to get an early start with the chores. They went to bed shortly after sunset, simply because their day had been long, and they no longer had natural sunlight by which to work. Now, many years later, we race ahead into the darkness of the night, never missing a beat as the man-made light shines on.

Corn Pone

Bake at 375 to 400 degrees.

1 cup cornmeal
1/2 cup all-purpose flour
1/2 teaspoon salt
3/4 teaspoon baking soda
1 cup sour milk
*(NOTE: Make sour milk by adding 1 tablespoon of vinegar
to 1 cup whole milk and stir.)*
1 egg
1 tablespoon melted butter
1 tablespoon granulated sugar

1. In a large mixing bowl combine the cornmeal, flour, salt,
and baking soda.

2. Stir in the sour milk, egg, butter, and sugar with a spoon.
Stir only until blended.
(NOTE: Do not beat.)

3. Pour the batter into a greased 9-inch square pan.

4. Bake in the oven for 20 minutes or until a wooden pick
inserted into the middle of the pone comes out clean. Bake
until lightly browned and the crust appears dry.

Serve piping hot, spread generously with butter.

Yield: 6 to 8 servings.

ॐ ॐ ॐ

Corn cakes are fine and dandy. The family piled them three deep on their plate, spread on the butter, and poured on the syrup!

Wintertime in Frederick County brings cold, freezing temperatures. All the family remembers Mom making the fire in the kitchen stove in the wee morning hours, and it was not with eagerness that her feet hit the cold floor after a night's sleep in a cozy warm bed.

Without a central heating system installed in the big old house, the kitchen became quite cold overnight, but we knew heat was on its way when we heard Mom up and moving about. If we were not awakened by the creaking noise of Mom's feet touching each step as she walked downstairs, we were by the time she clanged the cast-iron stove lids a couple of times!

Mom poked the kindling into the fire box of the old kitchen range. Next, she brought some corncobs from the pantry and then poured kerosene on them until they were saturated. Then she poked and pushed to get the cobs placed deep in the kindling. Now, having a barn-burner match in hand, she struck the red tip on the top of the cast-iron stove. With a brilliant blaze on the end of that little match, she torched the prepared fire box. On contact with the kerosene a belching flame flew high, but Mom was quick to get the lid down. Minutes later she added larger pieces of wood, while the fire crackled and roared.

A chunk stove provided heat in the living room during cold weather. In the morning and evening Dad rolled wood into the firebox, trying to ensure that room would be kept cozy and warm. He cut logs from the mountain lot and then hauled them to the farm. Later, he sawed them into big chunks that would burn for hours. Years passed and the chunk stove was replaced with a coal-burning heatrola, and finally with oil heat. Each held a degree of advancement in convenience. I shall never forget on cold nights, before we went to bed, all the family lined up our shoes behind the stove--each one had their spot!

Just think of having to tend the fire in the stoves all day long. While cooking on a cookstove, it was imperative to keep the temperature constant by feeding just the right amount of wood. It was important for Mom to recognize the different types of wood since each kind produces a different degree of heat. When baking, if the fire was too hot, the oven would overheat and burn the baked goods. Only Mom enjoyed bread with a tinge of charred crust on top of the loaf! If it did not heat up to the expected temperature, the food never cooked, but dried and was ruined.

Corn Cakes

1 cup cornmeal
1/3 cup all-purpose flour
1 tablespoon granulated sugar
2 teaspoons baking powder
1/2 teaspoon salt
1 cup whole milk
1 tablespoon melted butter

1. In a large mixing bowl combine the cornmeal, flour, sugar, baking powder, and salt.

2. Pour the milk and melted butter into the dry ingredients and stir with a spoon until blended and smooth.

(NOTE: If too thick to pour, add milk to make the consistency of a pancake batter.)

3. Pour the batter on a hot greased griddle to cook. When the corn cakes are full of bubbles and puffed, turn immediately.
(NOTE: Do not allow the cakes to fall before turning over.)

Serve immediately spread with syrup and butter.

Yield: 12 4-inch cakes.

During the days of cooking on the wood-burning kitchen range, folks with large families to feed cooked pancakes on a big 14-inch cast-iron griddle that was placed on top of the hot woodstove.

Mom used a "greaser" to coat the cast-iron griddle when cooking pancake batter. A greaser was nothing more than a 3- to 4- inch square slab of side meat, *referring to bacon*, or a hunk of fatback saved from the hog's back. She held the greaser in her hand by the pigskin side and briskly rubbed the hot griddle or pan, while the heat melted the solid fat and provided grease. The greaser was good for more than a one-time use, and was stored on an old white saucer that had turned brown from the heat as it sat on the back of the stove or in the pantry, until she needed it the next time she cooked pancakes.

Bacon is referred to as *flitch* or side meat in the country. At home, when the side meat was cured, the pig skin remained on the slab of meat. After the slab is cut into slices of bacon, the rind was carefully trimmed away, saved until a dishful accumulated, then Mom fried the strips until crisp and hard. Dad and us children loved to eat them. Fried bacon rinds satisfy that craving for a smoked, salty treat.

Plain Pancakes

1 1/4 cups all-purpose flour
1 tablespoon granulated sugar
1 teaspoon baking powder
1/2 to 1 teaspoon salt
1 egg
1 1/4 cups sour milk
(NOTE: Make sour milk by adding 1 tablespoon of vinegar to 1 cup whole milk and stir.)

1/2 teaspoon baking soda
2 tablespoons melted butter
1/2 teaspoon vanilla, if desired

1. In a large mixing bowl combine the flour, sugar, baking powder, and salt. Set aside.

2. In a separate mixing bowl beat the egg with a rotary beater or wire whisk until light yellow.

3. In another bowl combine the sour milk and baking soda. Blend in the egg with a spoon.

4. Add the melted butter and vanilla. Stir until well blended.

5. Add the dry ingredients and beat until blended and smooth.

6. Pour the batter on a hot greased griddle to cook. When the pancakes are full of bubbles and puffed, turn immediately.
(NOTE: Do not allow the cakes to fall before turning over.)

Serve immediately with syrup and butter.

Yield: 14 4-inch pancakes.

Many of you know Johnny Cake as a quick bread baked in a square pan. In the pioneer days, it was known as journey cake. Folks on a journey usually carried a bag of cornmeal with them. When they stopped to eat they cooked the cake on a flat stone by the open fire. Another stone was tilted vertically and reflected the heat back to the cake. Today, most of us have not had the experience of baking in this fashion and since we are in such a great rush to get to our destination, we would declare no time to stop and cook if put in that position! We would also be a spectacle, and I am certain forbidden by law to stop at a spot of our choice to build a fire and start cooking.

The Johnny Cakes Mom makes are poured on a flat, hot greased griddle to cook on top of the stove and are similar to pancakes. At breakfast or supper, our family enjoyed any kind of pancake served with pork pudding (pronounced puddin' in the country). Pork pudding is a German dish which is made in a large quantity at the fall butchering.

This old-time recipe has not only been tested by time but by nine hungry children. Matter of fact, I came to believe that, at our pleasure, we tested and tried lots of food!

Johnny Cakes

1 cup all-purpose flour
1 cup cornmeal
2 teaspoons baking powder
1 teaspoon salt
1 1/2 cups whole milk
1 tablespoon melted butter

1. In a large mixing bowl combine the flour, cornmeal, baking powder, and salt. Set aside.

2. In a separate small bowl combine the milk and melted butter. Pour into the dry ingredients and stir until well blended and smooth.

3. Pour the batter on a hot greased griddle to cook. When the Johnny Cakes are full of bubbles and puffed, turn immediately.
(NOTE: Do not allow the cakes to fall before turning over.)

Yield: 12 4-inch cakes.

For country folks, there was always the possibility that they would decide to serve a variety of griddle or pancakes at any meal of the day. The farmer's wife had the ingredients handy and the family enjoyed the warm cakes, especially in the wintertime. The assortment of foods was limited back then and we did not consume a refined diet as we do today. In fact, it may be easier to list the foods that were accessible than those that were not available to enjoy.

Would you believe Mom still uses the cake turner she purchased 82 years ago? The untreated wooden handle is dark with stain from years of use and abuse! Its hard and constant contact on the pans ground the edge of the metal paddle blade until it is as sharp as a knife. But Mom feels no desire or need to replace it with a shiny new one! Just think of the numerous cakes and cookies that turner has scooped up and removed from the pan!

Griddle Cakes

1 cup all-purpose flour
2 teaspoons baking powder
1/2 teaspoon salt
1 egg
3/4 cup whole milk
2 tablespoons melted butter or cooking oil

1. In a bowl combine the flour, baking powder, and salt. Set aside.

2. In a separate mixing bowl beat the egg with a rotary beater or wire whisk until light yellow. Add the milk and beat until blended.

3. Stir in the melted butter or cooking oil.

4. Add the dry ingredients and stir with a spoon only until blended.

5. Pour the batter on a hot greased griddle to cook.

6. When the griddle cakes are full of bubbles and puffed, turn immediately.
(NOTE: Do not allow the cakes to fall before turning over.)

Serve immediately with sausage for breakfast or supper.

Yield: 12 4-inch cakes.

&. &. &.

Who would ever believe these inexpensive ingredients could be mixed together and produce a flannel cake that I consider fit to serve a king! Just like my jeweler and goldsmith friend, Aras, who can take pieces of old broken gold jewelry, melt it, and mold a fine new item that becomes a treasure of great worth, bringing joy to the recipient, so too will this recipe become a treasure to your family.

Recently, on a Sunday evening, Mom served flannel cakes that were just the way I like them--light, fluffy with a lightly browned crust. Please try this recipe. I can guarantee you will not be disappointed!

A good breakfast can and should be the best meal of the day. It gets us off to a good start! Our family remembers coming in from outdoors and being immediately welcomed by the warm, steamy aroma of breakfast foods, rich and robust. The smell of sausage or bacon frying in the cool of the morning could certainly wet one's appetite. It never ceases to amaze me how much one can reminisce with the mention of certain foods.

Some of Mom's most pleasant memories are those of her family seated around the table at daybreak. The warm rising sun appeared on top of the eastern mountain, High Knob, and food never tasted so good as back then! Each new day brought my parents a real sense of gratefulness when they saw everyone well and eating. They knew their family was blessed as God had kept us safe through the night and the opportunities of the day were waiting.

Many memories dwell in the secret recesses of Mom's heart today--some were made in the sunshine, some in the rain. Often the sight of an old dish in the corner cupboard, a scratch on a piece of furniture, a photo, or a clock ticking away the minutes will provoke a wonderful memory. Oh how sweet is the company of those thoughts!

Flannel Cakes

2 cups all-purpose flour
2 teaspoons baking powder
1/2 teaspoon salt
2 eggs
1 3/4 cups whole milk
1 tablespoon melted butter

1. In a large mixing bowl combine the flour, baking powder, and salt. Set aside.

2. In a separate mixing bowl beat the eggs with a rotary beater or wire whisk until light yellow. Add the milk and melted butter. Beat with a spoon until blended.

3. Add the dry ingredients. Stir until well blended and smooth.

4. Pour the batter on a hot greased griddle to cook. When the flannel cakes are full of bubbles and puffed, turn immediately.
(NOTE: Do not allow the cakes to fall before turning over.)

Serve immediately spread with butter and syrup.

Yield: 16 4-inch cakes.

&a   &a   &a

Years ago folks did not look for a variety of ways to cook, as we do nowadays. When the housewife found a recipe that satisfied the need, she was content and used it over and over again.

Today, folks can be found who collect cookbooks only for the enjoyment of reading. They have no intention to use the recipes to cook food! I have not figured out how they can have so much control over their appetite to never touch the pots and pans. Think about this--the dread of failure may be keeping some people prisoner in their kitchen? Never forget that a wasted present opportunity is forever lost.

Waffles

2 cups all-purpose flour
2 teaspoons baking powder
2 teaspoons granulated sugar
1/2 teaspoon salt
3 eggs
1 1/2 cups whole milk
5 tablespoons cooking oil or melted butter
1 1/2 teaspoons vanilla, if desired

1. In a large mixing bowl combine the flour, baking powder, sugar, and salt. Set aside.

2. In a separate mixing bowl beat the eggs with a rotary beater or wire whisk until light yellow. Add the milk, oil or butter, and vanilla. Beat with a spoon.

3. Add the dry ingredients and stir until blended.

4. Pour the batter on a hot greased waffle iron and cook until golden brown.

Serve piping hot with syrup.

Yield: 12 waffle squares.

In the country, Buckwheat Cakes are not only a breakfast dish, but a supper time delight. Buckwheat Cake Starter is a portion of the batter that is reserved before the molasses, butter and baking soda are added. It starts the fermentation when added to the next batch of batter.

I remember that Mom and the older women referred to the bread starter they used as "sots," which is a German *satz* yeast. For them, when the sots grew old and no longer acted as the agent to rise the batter, the ladies paid a visit to their neighbor and borrowed a cupful of active starter from their supply.

Buckwheat Cakes

1 cup all-purpose flour
2 cups buckwheat flour
1 1/2 teaspoons salt
1 envelope of dried yeast
1/2 cup lukewarm water
2 cups cold water
1 tablespoon molasses
1/4 cup melted butter
1 teaspoon baking soda
1/2 cup hot water

1. In a bowl sift together the dry ingredients. Set aside.

2. In a small bowl dissolve the yeast in the lukewarm water. Add the cold water.

3. Add the dissolved yeast to the flour mixture and beat until smooth. Cover in a tight container and place in the refrigerator overnight.

4. In the morning mix together in a separate bowl the molasses, butter, and baking soda in the hot water. Stir the mixture into the batter and beat until smooth.
(NOTE: See Buckwheat Starter below.)

5. Let stand at room temperature for 30 minutes.

6. Pour the batter on a hot greased griddle to cook. When the cakes are full of bubbles and puffed, turn immediately. *(NOTE: Do not allow the cakes to fall before turning over.)*

&a   &a   &a

Buckwheat Cake Starter

(NOTE: Using buckwheat cake starter is a quick method to make another bowl of batter when planning to serve cakes several consecutive days.)

1. Reserve 1 cup of the original batter before adding the molasses, butter, and baking soda.

2. Add 1 cup cold water and place in a covered container in the refrigerator until the night before you plan to use it. Then pour off the water that has accumulated on the top.

3. Blend in the amount of flours and salt required in the original recipe for buckwheat cakes. Add 2 1/2 cups cold water and cover. Let stand overnight (not refrigerated).

4. In the morning, stir in the molasses, butter, baking soda, and hot water as directed in the recipe. Let stand 30 minutes, then begin cooking cakes.

&a   &a   &a

The Great Depression of 1929 and the 1930s had come. These were tough, destroying years, survived most successfully by ambitious folks who would not give up. Others lost their will to go on because of the pressure brought on by the uncontrollable difficult circumstances. For them life became unbearable. At different periods during those days, most folks felt they had more than their share of hardships, and rightfully so. Few people had wealth and those without money had to learn to make do with whatever supplies were available to them. This hardship brought many folks to the realization that life, in itself, is a gift and not a right. Often during this period of time, the food that was placed on the table was not what we wanted to eat but what was available. Most learned contentment is not necessarily getting what we want, but being satisfied with what we have. This lesson was hard to conceive, but once learned it was never forgotten.

The farmer and his wife had one advantage during the days of the Depression--they could grow food to supply their family's needs and preserve some to use at a later time. Most often they shared the abundance with their neighbor as well. Folks were truly concerned with the welfare of others during these difficult years. These acts of kindness shown to one another helped to take some of the worries out of life for the weary worn one! Sure enough, time passed and with faith, the good times and prosperity returned.

Drop Biscuits

Bake at 450 degrees.

2 cups all-purpose flour
1 teaspoon granulated sugar

3 teaspoons baking powder
1/2 to 1 teaspoon salt
1/4 cup solid vegetable shortening, softened
1 cup whole milk

1. In a mixing bowl sift together the flour, sugar, baking powder, and salt.

2. Add the shortening to the flour mixture and cut in with a fork.

3. Add the milk and stir with a spoon only until blended. *(NOTE: Do not beat.)*

4. Drop by spoonfuls on a greased cookie sheet.

5. Bake in the oven for 10 to 12 minutes.

Spread with plenty of butter and serve hot!

Yield: 6 to 8 biscuits.

&a &a &a

No place is more likely to have a wonderful, pleasing aroma from tempting foods cooking than the farm kitchen. It is amazing! Someone is always hungry, and someone is always working there.

Home surely brings the sweetest memories of not only scrumptious food but of my parents, sisters, and brothers. By now you may have gathered I have a deep and strong affection for each member of the family. It is good to remember that the smallest deed we do for one another is better than the greatest intention left undone. As years pass, food will live on and be remembered by family and friends.

Plain Muffins

Bake at 375 degrees.

2 cups all-purpose flour
2 to 3 tablespoons granulated sugar
3 teaspoons baking powder
1/2 teaspoon salt
1 cup whole milk
1 egg
1/4 cup cooking oil
1/2 teaspoon vanilla

1. In a large mixing bowl sift together the flour, sugar, baking powder, and salt.

2. Add the milk, egg, cooking oil, and vanilla to the flour mixture. Stir only until blended with a spoon.
(NOTE: Do not beat.)

3. Pour the batter into greased muffin tins, or line the tins with paper liners and sprinkle tops with brown sugar.

4. Bake in the oven for 20 minutes or until lightly browned.

Serve with your favorite jelly.

Variation: Add raisins, other dried fruits, or nuts.

Yield: 8 to 12 muffins.

ટે   ટે   ટે

There is something about hot biscuits oozing with butter that brings instant gratification to one's appetite in the wintertime. The wonderful aroma of biscuits baking in the oven fills the house and seems to warm the attitude of folks. The Depression taught us to never waste, not even one crumb from a biscuit!

Mom rolled the dough and cut out the biscuits with a water glass dipped in flour. Now and then when she was really in a rush, she cut it in blocks with a sharp knife simply because she did not have time to make fancy ones. Despite the shape, the outcome will be the same--delicious biscuits that hit the spot in the morning, noon, or night.

Rolled Biscuits

Bake at 400 degrees.

2 cups all-purpose flour
3 teaspoons baking powder
1 teaspoon granulated sugar
1 teaspoon salt
1/2 stick butter
3/4 cup whole milk

1. In a large mixing bowl sift together the flour, baking powder, sugar, and salt.

2. Add the butter to the flour mixture and cut in with a fork.

3. Add the milk and stir with a spoon only until blended.

4. Knead the dough about 20 times.

5. Roll the dough on a floured surface to 1/3 inch thick. Cut with your favorite cookie cutter and place on a greased cookie sheet.

6. Bake in the oven for 10 minutes or until lightly browned.

Slice biscuit in half with a sharp knife while hot and spread with butter.

Yield: 6 to 8 biscuits.

                                      ða   ða   ða

Banana Nut Bread is delectable! What can be sweeter or more nutritious than the creamy flesh of a ripe banana? This tropical fruit does not lose its pungent flavor when used in baked products. Use a variety of nuts to enhance the flavor.

Banana Nut Bread

Bake at 350 degrees.

2 cups all-purpose flour
1 teaspoon baking soda
3 tablespoons buttermilk
1/2 teaspoon salt
1/2 cup solid vegetable shortening, softened
1 cup granulated sugar
2 eggs
1 cup mashed very ripe bananas
1/3 cup chopped pecans

1. In a large mixing bowl sift together the flour and salt. Set aside.

2. In a cup stir the baking soda into the buttermilk.

3. In a separate mixing bowl cream together the shortening and sugar with a spoon. Add the eggs and the buttermilk mixture. Beat well.

4. Stir in the mashed bananas and pecans.

5. Add the dry ingredients to the batter and stir until well blended and smooth.

6. Pour the batter into a greased and floured loaf pan.

7. Bake in the oven for 35 to 40 minutes or until a wooden pick inserted into the middle of the loaf comes out clean.

(NOTE: Wrap cooled banana bread tightly in freezer wrap and keep frozen for several weeks.)

ea   ea   ea

COOKIES, CAKES & FROSTINGS

Grandmother Clara Grossnickel's Ginger Cookies are zesty with spices! Use a gingerbread boy or one of your favorite old-fashioned cookie cutters. These cookies should be labeled old-fashioned and are definitely in a class of their own--first place! This recipe does not require eggs.

Mom remembers her mother baking ginger cookies when she was just a little girl. She had three older brothers and cookies did not stay around for any length of time in that kitchen. Many were the times Grandmother Grossnickel popped a pan of cookies into the outdoor bake oven once the bread was done.

A cooled bake oven worked great to dry field corn that was ground into cornmeal or for drying slices of raw apple to make the Schnitz that is used in their Schnitz un Knepp dish. I remember my mother storing her dried Schnitz in a white flour sack. She then hung it on a nail that had been driven into the pantry wall. We children would go into the pantry once in awhile, just poking around, and we would open the string around the top of the bag, take out a few Schnitz and chew on them. None of us were particularly fond of them, but it was something to do!

Grandmother Clara Grossnickel's Ginger Cookies

Bake at 350 degrees.

3 1/2 to 4 cups all-purpose flour
1 tablespoon ground ginger
1/2 teaspoon ground cinnamon
1 cup granulated sugar

1/4 cup lard, softened
(NOTE: Solid vegetable shortening can be substituted for lard.)
1 cup dark molasses
1/2 cup brewed coffee, cooled
2 teaspoons baking soda

1. In a bowl sift together the flour, ginger, and cinnamon. Set aside.

2. In a large mixing bowl cream together the sugar and lard with a spoon.

3. Stir in the molasses.

4. Combine the baking soda with the cooled coffee and stir until blended. Add and stir into the mixture.

5. Add the dry ingredients slowly and mix by hand to make a soft dough.
(NOTE: Add more flour if dough is too sticky to roll.)

6. Roll the dough on a floured surface to 1/2 inch thick and cut with a cookie cutter.

7. Bake on a greased cookie sheet for about 12 minutes.

Store in a tight container.

(NOTE: Regulate the spices to your taste.)

Yield: 2 to 3 dozen cookies.

ン   ン   ン

Mom's Molasses Cookies hit the spot with a host of our family members. It does one's heart good to bite into one of these flavorful cookies! Her molasses cookies are best eaten hot--straight out of the oven, but then, *every* cookie is best served piping hot.

When we were children on the farm, the chairs or bench behind the kitchen table presented the best seats in the house to intently watch as Mom mixed cookie dough. Perched there so high that our feet could not touch the floor, we tasted the very first cookies to come from the oven. Mom never made us wait until later to eat the cookies. I will always remember the big dishpan filled with ingredients and seeing butter smash into the sugar with a big spoon. Her strokes through the dough were powerful and quick. She beat it with what appeared to be all her might. When it became too stiff to mix with a spoon, she used her hands. She had dough so deep in the pan it was up to her wrists. I can imagine the aroma that filled the kitchen back then, right now. It was a heavenly scent of brown sugar, sweet butter, spices, and chocolate!

Mom made lots of cookies--not just a few--and within a few days of baking, we polished off the entire batch. When enough children dip their hands into the cookie jar...well need I say more? Mom took great pleasure baking for us and what a loving Mother we have! That sight around the table of chattering little people eagerly awaiting the warm goodies to be removed from the oven must be one she and us children will never forget! Sometimes I find myself thinking about those days, living at home as a child, and I have to remind myself that it was not yesterday as it seems, but many years ago that we enjoyed playing by our mother's side as she worked and baked in the kitchen. These were happy and precious times, always to be cherished and tucked away deep in my heart.

Mom's Molasses Cookies

Bake at 350 degrees.

7 cups all-purpose flour
3 teaspoons baking soda
1 teaspoon salt
1 teaspoon ground cinnamon
1 teaspoon ground ginger
1 cup hot water
1 cup granulated sugar
1 to 1 1/4 cups dark molasses
1 cup solid vegetable shortening, melted

1. In a large mixing bowl sift together the flour, baking soda, salt, cinnamon, and ginger. Sift a second time. Set aside.

2. Pour the hot water into a separate large mixing bowl.

3. Add the sugar and molasses to the water. Beat with a spoon until blended.

4. Add the melted shortening and stir until blended.

5. Stir in the dry ingredients with a spoon or your hand until well blended. Form the dough in a ball and place in a bowl.

6. Place in the refrigerator to chill overnight or put in the freezer for 30 minutes to 1 hour.

7. Roll the dough about 1/4 inch thick on a floured surface. Cut with a cookie cutter and place on a greased cookie sheet.

8. Bake in the oven for about 12 minutes.

Yield: 4 to 5 dozen cookies.

&a   &a   &a

Surely Mom must have baked dozen after dozen of Icebox Cookies down through the years. At Christmastime she brewed root beer and what a combination this was when served on ice with these cookies, especially when black walnuts have been added. No other cookie recipe is more versatile than this one. They melt in your mouth and burst with flavor.

Christmas Day at our house has been a time to reminisce and unselfishly share the happenings in our families' lives. Everyone helped get the meal on the table and many hands made light work! It has been a time to remember treasured moments so rich in holiday baking. Mom began baking all kinds of cookies early, right after Thanksgiving, and it was necessary to constantly replenish the big containers. The holiday season brought lots of visitors to our house, and what seemed to be a sweet aroma coming from the kitchen almost daily.

Years ago, Christmas Day seemed so far away when the December page was flipped open on the calendar, compliments of the Gladhill Furniture Company. The calendar hung on a nail directly inside the living room door by Dad's rocking chair. Most were made of a heavy-gauge oil painting with scenes of the outdoors, little children or animals. Small calendar pages of light-weight paper were stitched to the bottom with cord or heavy thread, since staples were not used back then. Once the month had passed, that sheet was torn off and placed in the kitchen cabinet drawer, handy to use when writing up a grocery list. During the olden days, more old letters, envelopes and calendar pages were carried to the store scribbled with items needed than on unused clean paper.

There were other styles of calendars. Some years the

edition was made from heavy thick cardboard, beautifully cut in an open lace design around a nice landscape pattern. Many had an old English flair. Those had a tiny little pocket that stood out at the bottom and very small pages of the months were attached at that point. Mom and Dad stuffed a few papers in the pocket for safe keeping--maybe a recipe that she was waiting to try, an address, a receipt for a farm item Dad purchased or a few small combs along with some of Mom's hair pins. Calendars were always hung high on the wall, out of the reach of little children. In fact they were placed so close to the high ceilings in most homes that adults needed to hold their heads back to look up and read them! It was not unusual to see several spread around as wall decorations in the same room. Each year, we were excited to see what new picture would be printed on the calendars. Folks displayed enlarged portraits of family members on the walls in their homes, but few living in the country owned works of art, but maybe these calendars and portraits were art enough!

Mom's Icebox Cookies

Bake at 375 degrees.

1 cup lard
(NOTE: Solid vegetable shortening can be substituted for lard.)
1 cup granulated sugar
1 cup brown sugar
2 eggs
1 teaspoon vanilla
1/2 teaspoon baking soda
1 tablespoon hot water

4 cups all-purpose flour
1 cup walnuts or pecans

1. In a large mixing bowl cream together the lard and both sugars with a spoon.

2. Add the eggs and flavoring. Stir with a spoon.

3. In a separate small bowl dissolve the baking soda in the hot water. Add and beat into the above mixture.

4. Gradually add the flour and stir until a soft dough is formed. Stir in the nuts.

5. Form the dough into a long roll and store overnight in the refrigerator. Cover with a dry cloth or piece of plastic wrap.

6. Slice the dough 1/4 inch thick with a sharp knife and place on a lightly greased cookie sheet.

7. Bake in the oven for about 10 minutes.

Store in a tight container.

Variation: Add 1 to 2 ounces melted and cooled unsweetened chocolate to the dough.

Variation: Add 1/2 cup shredded coconut to the dough.

(NOTE: Cookies may be stored in the freezer in a tight container.)

Yield: 6 dozen cookies.

❧   ❧   ❧

This Sour Cream Sugar Cookie is a heavy dough, but it is not dry. Best results are achieved when the dough is rolled thick. Mom has baked sour cream cookies so often she does not need to refer to the recipe to mix up a batch. She has no idea where it originated. She baked them for us when we were small children, and as adults we still enjoy them. Even when the cookies turn out less than perfect, they hit the spot. I especially like them when plenty of dark plump raisins have been pushed into the soft tops before baking. Mom enjoys the light raisins best, but either one will add to the delicious flavor.

Sour Cream Sugar Cookies

Bake at 350 degrees.

6 cups all-purpose flour
3 teaspoons baking soda
1 1/2 teaspoons salt
3 cups thick dairy sour cream
3 cups brown or granulated white sugar
3 eggs, beaten
1 teaspoon vanilla

1. In a large bowl sift together the flour, baking soda, and salt. Set aside.

2. In a large mixing bowl blend together the sour cream and sugar with a spoon.

3. Add the eggs and vanilla. Beat until well blended.

4. Add the dry ingredients one cup at a time to the mixture and continue beating until fully incorporated in the dough.

5. If dough is too sticky to roll, add up to 1 cup of additional flour and stir until blended.

6. Roll the dough 1/4 inch thick on a floured surface and cut with a cookie cutter. Place on an ungreased cookie sheet.

7. Brush the tops of the cookies lightly with whole milk. Top with raisins and/or granulated sugar.

8. Bake in the oven for about 10 minutes or until lightly browned. Baking time will vary with size of cookie.

Store in a tight container.

Variation: Spread a thin layer of icing on cooled cookie tops.
(NOTE: Recipe found on page 145.)

(NOTE: Cookies may be stored in a tight container in the freezer.)

Yield: 6 to 7 dozen cookies.

     ❧ ❧ ❧

Frosted Cremes are delicious! Years ago, before Mom purchased cookie sheets to use when baking cookies, she turned a large cake pan upside down and baked the cookie dough on the bottom of it. It worked!

Mom learned to improvise when the need came for something she didn't have on hand. The reason was that they simply could not afford to waste a penny on anything frivolous while paying for the farm. The time during the 1930s was hard for them and for countless other folks in our community. Even in this day and age, not every family is blessed with good jobs and a large annual income that will allow them the means to meet their every desire.

The more I learn about the living conditions for my family during the early 1920s to 1950s, the more I recognize their sacrifices to gain success came at a high price. Thinking back, maybe food brought one of their greatest pleasures!

Frosted Cremes

Bake at 325 to 350 degrees.

6 to 7 cups all-purpose flour
1 teaspoon baking soda
1 tablespoon ground ginger
1 cup granulated sugar
1 cup lard or butter, softened
(NOTE: Solid vegetable shortening can be substituted for lard.)
1 cup molasses (medium, not dark)
1 cup cold water

1. In a bowl sift the flour, baking soda, and ginger. Set aside.

2. In a large mixing bowl cream together the sugar and lard or butter. Add the molasses and cold water; stir until smooth.

3. Add the flour mixture and stir until a smooth soft dough is formed.

4. Spread about 1/2 inch thick on a lightly greased cookie sheet.

5. Bake in the oven for 20 to 30 minutes, depending on the thickness of the dough. Bake until lightly browned.

6. Allow to cool. Spread with a thin layer of frosting.

(NOTE: Mom uses an old-fashioned variety of icing on Frosted Cremes since it will store better. Use any variety that will form a crust and will not stick to the waxed paper between the layers of cookies. Allow the icing to slightly set before cutting in blocks or diamonds with a sharp knife.)

᨞   ᨞   ᨞

Cookie Icing

3/4 cup powdered sugar
1 tablespoon sweet cream
1/4 teaspoon vanilla
food coloring

Place all the ingredients in a small bowl and beat until smooth. Be sure to use cream or the icing will become brittle when set.

᨞   ᨞   ᨞

Oatmeal raisin cookies are nice to have on hand when hungry children come home from school. They contain lots of healthy oatmeal and rich nutritious raisins.

I can still envision us children arriving home, hopping from the school bus, and the instant our feet hit the kitchen floor you could hear every cupboard door opening and the cookie cans rattling. The search was on for something good to eat. Whichever goodie one of us couldn't find, another child could! Children draw to sweets, and keeping cookies in the jar is a challenge that does not change when a young family is living in the house.

Oatmeal Raisin Cookies

Bake at 375 degrees.

1 to 1 1/2 cups raisins
3/4 cup chopped apricots,
1/2 cup chopped dates
2 1/4 cups sifted all-purpose flour
1 teaspoon salt
1/2 teaspoon baking soda
1 teaspoon ground cinnamon
1/2 teaspoon ground nutmeg
1/2 teaspoon ground cloves
1 cup solid vegetable shortening, softened
1 1/2 cups brown sugar
1 egg
1 tablespoon plus 1 teaspoon water
2 teaspoons vanilla
2 cups quick or old-fashioned uncooked oatmeal

1. In a bowl cover the raisins and chopped apricots with boiling water. Let stand for 10 minutes, then allow to drain in a colander. Chop the dates and place on top of the soaked fruit. Set aside.

2. In a separate bowl sift together the flour, salt, baking soda, cinnamon, nutmeg, and cloves. Set aside.

3. In a large mixing bowl combine the shortening and sugar with a spoon.

4. Add the egg, water, and vanilla. Stir until blended.

5. Add the dry ingredients slowly and stir until well blended.

6. Add the uncooked oatmeal slowly and stir until well blended.

7. Add the dried fruits and stir until well blended.

8. Drop the dough by teaspoonfuls on an ungreased cookie sheet.

9. Bake in the oven for 10 to 12 minutes.

Store in a tight container.

Variation: Mix and match the combination of any dried fruits and nuts.

Yield: 7 dozen cookies.

ð   ð   ð

Raisin Drop Cookies are thick, soft, and filled with plump raisins. This is a nice rich spicy cookie to serve anytime of the year. Try adding a variety of chopped dried fruits, nuts and spices to the dough.

These cookies dunk well in cold rich milk, hot cocoa, coffee, or tea. Nibble if you like, but don't be talked out of enjoying the dunking style of eating a cookie, especially if you are sipping a cup of coffee. Dunking was acceptable in the days gone by and should not be frowned on today, in Mom's opinion.

Raisin Drop Cookies

Bake at 400 degrees.

3 1/2 cups all-purpose flour
(NOTE: Add additional flour if dough is too thin.)
1 teaspoon ground cloves
1 teaspoon ground cinnamon
1/2 teaspoon ground nutmeg
2 cups granulated sugar
3/4 cup lard
(NOTE: Solid vegetable shortening can be substituted for lard.)
1 teaspoon baking soda
1 teaspoon vinegar
3 eggs
1 cup whole milk
2 cups raisins

1. In a large mixing bowl sift together the flour, cloves, cinnamon, and nutmeg. Set aside.

2. In a separate large mixing bowl cream together the sugar and lard with a spoon.

3. In a bowl dissolve the baking soda in the vinegar. Add to the sugar and lard mixture.

4. Add the eggs and milk. Stir until well blended.

5. Add the flour mixture and stir until well blended. Add and stir in the raisins.

6. Drop dough by spoonfuls on a greased cookie sheet. If the dough is too soft to stay on a mound, add a small amount of flour at a time and stir until well blended and stiff.

7. Bake in the oven for about 10 minutes.

Store in a tight container.

Yield: 4 to 5 dozen cookies.

❧   ❧   ❧

Dried Fruit-Filled Cookies are moist and very good. They are gourmet--certainly worth the time and effort to bake. The dough surrounding the filling is tender and bakes to a light golden brown. They will melt in your mouth.

Some of the older folks refer to fruit filled cookies as moon pies, since they can be made in the shape of a half moon. The finished cookies are pretty when the edge is carefully fluted or mashed neatly with a fork. The fork pricks on the cookie tops can be patterned or you can use a sharp knife to cut a design. You can earn the title "culinary artist" as quick as a wink when you bake these special cookies.

Dried Fruit Filled Cookies

Bake at 350 degrees.

7 cups all-purpose flour
2 teaspoons baking soda
2 teaspoons baking powder
1 teaspoon salt
2 cups granulated sugar
1 cup butter, softened
2 eggs
1 cup whole milk
2 teaspoons vanilla

1. In a large mixing bowl sift together the flour, baking soda, baking powder, and salt. Set aside.

2. In a separate large mixing bowl cream together the sugar and butter.

3. Add the eggs and beat until well blended.

4. Add the milk and flavoring. Beat until smooth and well blended.

5. Add the dry ingredients, one cup at a time, and stir with a spoon. Continue adding and beating until all the flour mixture is fully incorporated into the dough. This dough will be sticky.

6. Roll the dough on a floured surface. Remember the stickier the dough, the more delicate the cookies. Cut with a large round cookie cutter or tin can that measures approximately 4 inches wide. Move dough with a wide metal spatula to a greased cookie sheet.

Filling Ingredients:

2 cups white raisins
1 cup chopped dates
1 cup dried chopped apricots
1 1/2 cups granulated sugar
3 cups water
3 tablespoons all-purpose flour (mix the flour in the cold
    water)

7. In a heavy saucepan combine the above ingredients and place over medium to high heat.

8. Bring mixture to a boil while stirring constantly until thick and syrupy.

9. Place a small amount of the cooled fruit filling on half of the circle of dough, fold over and pinch the edge closed. Stick with a fork several times over the tops of the cookies.

10. Bake until lightly browned. Baking time will vary with size of cookie. Start at 10 minutes and adjust accordingly.

Store cookies layered between waxed paper in a tight container in the refrigerator.

Variation: Add red and green candied cherries for holiday color.

Yield: 4 dozen cookies.

🙐   🙐   🙐

Chocolate Coconut Cookies are rich, almost like candy. They are a chewy delight that you can rustle up with little time or effort. No mess of measuring sugar, flour, and shortening. Simple and rich, these were first popular about 40 years ago.

Chocolate Coconut Cookies

Bake at 350 degrees.

2 14-ounce cans condensed milk
6 ounces unsweetened melted chocolate
2 pounds shredded coconut
1 cup chopped nuts

1. In a large mixing bowl combine the condensed milk and melted chocolate. Stir until well blended.

2. Add the coconut and nuts. Stir until well blended.

3. Drop the dough by teaspoonfuls on a greased cookie sheet.

4. Bake in the oven for about 10 minutes. Watch carefully as cookies will burn easily.

(NOTE: Cookies can be stored between layers of waxed paper in a tight container in the freezer for several months.)

Yield: 3 dozen cookies.

ða ða ða

As children we were always intrigued by what was happening in the kitchen, especially, when we smelled cookies baking. We were always Mom's best critics. We never complained and rated each one excellent.

I particularly remember the can of baking cocoa powder sitting on the shelf in the kitchen cabinet. One whiff of the aroma coming from the chocolate could whip up your sweet tooth in nothing flat! We knew Chocolate Drop Cookies with Filling could satisfy that longing.

A majority of the recipes from years gone by required cocoa powder in place of chocolate. The advantage: powder can be stored on the pantry shelf and is less expensive than chocolate. Recipes require additional sugar and shortening when using cocoa powder.

Chocolate Drop Cookies with Filling

Bake at 375 to 400 degrees.

2 3/4 cups all-purpose flour
1/2 teaspoon baking soda
1/2 teaspoon baking powder
1/2 teaspoon salt
1/2 cup solid vegetable shortening, plus 1 tablespoon
1 1/2 cups granulated sugar
2 eggs
1 cup thick dairy sour cream
6 tablespoons baking cocoa powder
1 teaspoon vanilla flavoring
1/2 teaspoon butter flavoring

1. In a large mixing bowl sift together the flour, baking soda, baking powder, and salt. Set aside.

2. In a separate large mixing bowl cream together the shortening, sugar, and eggs.

3. Add the sour cream, cocoa powder, and flavorings. Stir until well blended.

4. Add a cup of the flour mixture at a time. Continue adding a cup and stirring until flour mixture is fully incorporated into the dough.

5. Place dough in a bowl and refrigerate until cool and stiff.

6. Drop dough by teaspoonfuls on an ungreased cookie sheet.

7. Bake in the oven for about 10 minutes.

8. Cool cookies and sandwich together with white filling.

Filling Ingredients:

2 egg whites
4 tablespoons whole milk
2 teaspoons vanilla
4 cups powdered sugar
1 1/2 cups white solid vegetable shortening, softened

9. In a large mixer bowl beat the egg whites, milk, vanilla, and 2 cups of the powdered sugar.

10. Add the remaining 2 cups of powdered sugar and the shortening. Beat until well blended.

Store between layers of waxed paper in a tight container in the refrigerator.

Variation: Use your favorite icing or marshmallow creme.

Yield: 5 dozen cookies.

≥ ≥ ≥

Do you ever have those times when you have a hankering for a little something sweet, yet you do not want to over indulge in sugar? Here is an nutritious oatmeal cracker recipe with only two-thirds cup of sugar, plus it includes lots of wholesome oatmeal. This cracker is perfect, if you like to dunk them in milk or coffee.

Mom baked oatmeal crackers for her babies. They were just right for them to grab and hold tightly in their hand. A tiny hand will squeeze a soft cookie until it crumbles and is lost, while oatmeal crackers have a firm texture but is not hard.

Oatmeal Crackers

Bake at 375 degrees.

2 cups all-purpose flour
1 teaspoon baking soda
1/4 teaspoon salt
1/2 cup butter, softened
2/3 cup granulated sugar
1 egg
1/2 cup whole milk
2 teaspoons vanilla
3 cups oatmeal

1. In a large mixing bowl sift together the flour, baking soda, and salt. Set aside.

2. In a separate large mixing bowl cream together the butter and sugar.

3. Add the egg, milk, and flavoring. Stir until smooth.

4. Add a cup of the flour mixture to the dough and stir until well blended. Continue adding a cup and stirring until all the flour mixture is fully incorporated into the dough.

5. Add a cup of oatmeal to the dough and stir until well blended. Continue adding a cup and stirring until all the oatmeal is fully incorporated into the dough.

6. Roll the dough thin on a floured surface and cut with a cookie cutter or tin can. If dough is too thick to roll, add additional milk and mix until smooth.

7. Place on a lightly greased cookie sheet.

8. Bake in the oven for 10 minutes or until lightly browned. *(NOTE: Do not over bake.)*

Store in a tight container.

Yield: 3 to 4 dozen cookies.

&a   &a   &a

What an Angel Food Cake this recipe produces! This is Mom's most relied upon cake recipe and our favorite. She must have baked hundreds of these light, spongy cakes. Even today, she still bakes one every few weeks, and each one turns out perfect. No fat, no egg yolks! It is best when baking angel food cake to use all ingredients at room temperature. For a successful cake, use clean utensils, free from grease.

Like many of you, I too, lead a busy life. I need to constantly remind myself that one must be careful not to put off the special things we want to do. Whenever possible, we should remove from our lips the phrase, "I'll do it someday," and go ahead making every effort to do the thing that means the most to us now. Bring some happiness to another's life and to yours at the same time. Once in awhile, an opportunity will knock once, and if no response is made, the moment will be lost forever!

Angel Food Cake

Bake at 350 degrees.

3/4 cup, plus 2 tablespoons granulated sugar
1 tablespoon cornstarch in a measuring cup and fill to the
    one-cup mark with all-purpose flour
2 cups egg whites, at room temperature
(NOTE: About 16 egg whites to equal 2 cups.)
1 1/2 teaspoons cream of tartar
1/4 teaspoon salt
2 teaspoons vanilla
additional 3/4 cup granulated sugar

(NOTE: Room temperature egg whites whip up best. Do not allow so much as a speck of yolk to mix with the whites as it will prevent beating up stiff peaks. Be sure utensils are clean, since grease will produce the same effect.)

1. In a large mixing bowl sift together three times 3/4 cup plus 2 tablespoons of sugar, the cornstarch, and flour. Set aside.

2. In a mixer bowl beat the egg whites, cream of tartar, salt, and vanilla until foamy with an electric mixer on medium speed.

3. Now add the additional 3/4 cup of sugar by tapping on the cup and allowing a little to sift into the egg whites while beating. Beat on high speed until mixture is dry and hold a stiff peak.

4. In three portions--and ever so gently--fold the flour mixture into the egg whites with a spoon.

5. Spoon the batter into an ungreased tube pan. Cut through the batter with a knife to destroy any air bubbles. Place pan on center rack in the oven to bake.

6. Bake in the oven for 35 minutes or until top appears dry and lightly browned. If the top starts to burn before the cake is done in the middle, lay a sheet of aluminum foil across the top rack.
(NOTE: Do not seal the foil around the pan.)

7. Invert the pan for 1 hour and remove cake.

(NOTE: Can be stored for a few weeks in the freezer.)

&a   &a   &a

This Jellyroll Cake recipe bakes a fine yellow sponge cake with a dandy velvety crust. Spread with your favorite jelly or filling. No shortening is required in this recipe.

This cake batter is spread thin in the pan and requires little time to bake. Using jelly as the spread on a flat cake is much quicker than mixing up an icing, and covering a layered cake. Mom always made Jellyroll Cakes when she was pushed for time, which tended to be often! Mom's cooking couldn't be complete without this winning recipe.

Jellyroll Cake

Bake at 375 degrees.

1 tablespoon cornstarch in a measuring cup and fill to the
    one-cup mark with sifted all-purpose flour
1 teaspoon baking powder
1/4 teaspoon salt
3 eggs, at room temperature
1 cup granulated sugar
1/3 cup water
1 to 1 1/2 teaspoons vanilla
jelly, for the filling

1. In a large bowl sift together the cornstarch, flour, baking powder, and salt. Set aside.

2. In a separate large mixing bowl beat the eggs with a rotary beater or wire whisk until thick and light yellow.

3. Add the sugar, sifting in a little at a time, and stir with a spoon until blended.

4. Add the water and vanilla. Beat until smooth and well blended.

5. Gradually pour in the dry ingredients and stir until blended.

6. Pour the batter into a greased and floured jellyroll pan.

7. Bake in the oven for 10 to 15 minutes or until lightly browned.

8. Place the warm cake upside down on a cloth sprinkled with powdered sugar. Cool slightly.

9. Spread the top of the cake with jelly. Using the cloth, roll the cake up. Make sure not to roll the cloth with the cake!

10. After a few minutes, remove the cloth and allow the cake to cool completely.

(NOTE: Best stored in the refrigerator.)

❧   ❧   ❧

Letha's Hot Milk Sponge Cake is a family favorite and the recipe is a priceless gem. Mom topped the cake with a variety of icings, either chocolate, coconut, caramel, or peanut butter. Sometimes she placed sliced bananas on top the cake with or without a layer of white icing underneath.

Mom's cakes were always fresh at our house--and may I add--it never stayed around long enough to come near the chance of getting stale! I remember sneaking a piece of cake before mealtime! And oh how I enjoyed the crusty edge Mom cut from the sponge cake: crunchy, perfect texture, and rich with the fragrance of vanilla.

Letha's Hot Milk Sponge Cake

Bake at 350 to 375 degrees.

2 cups sifted all-purpose flour
2 teaspoons baking powder
1/2 teaspoon salt
4 eggs, at room temperature
1 1/2 teaspoons vanilla
1/2 teaspoon butter or coconut flavoring
2 cups granulated sugar
1 cup whole milk
2 tablespoons butter

1. In a large bowl sift together the flour, baking powder, and salt. Set aside.

2. In a separate mixing bowl beat the eggs with an electric mixer until light yellow.

3. Add the flavorings and continue to beat. Also, add the sugar, a little at a time, while continuing to beat.

4. Fold in the flour mixture with a spoon.
(NOTE: Fold, do not stir.)

5. While preparing the above steps, warm the milk and butter. The milk should be hot enough to form a skim on top but do not allow to boil.

6. Add the hot milk all at once to the batter and stir until well blended.

7. Pour the batter into two greased and floured 9-inch cake pans.

8. Bake in the oven for approximately 30 minutes or until a wooden pick comes out clean when inserted into the middle of cake.

When cake is cooled, spread with icing.

With a young family, Mom and Dad visited with the neighbors. They in turn, visited our home. Wherever my parents lived the neighbors were pleasant and warm. During the visit, the men sat to one side of the living room, and the women and children gathered to the other side or in the kitchen. In the summertime, folks sat on our big porch that wrapped itself around two sides of the house, and seated there on metal lawn chairs and a glider to match they watched as the children played ball in the yard. I will never forget catching fireflies and keeping them captive in a glass jar. Cash was scarce in the valley and with no money available to most of the young farmers and their family, they made their entertainment with friends and food.

It was during these delightful times that the women exchanged recipes. The ladies saved used envelopes and old letters having a clean portion to write ingredients on because no one had money to spend on fancy writing tablets or recipe cards. Oft-times the instructions were discussed and never jotted down. At that time there were no housewives who claimed they could not cook--they knew the duty was expected of them, and so they just did it, someway, somehow.

But because of this carelessness in passing recipes along, soon rightful ownership of a recipe was lost. Farmers' wives were notorious for exchanging one ingredient for another and before you knew what was happening, the recipe was far from the original version--not always improved in one's opinion, but certainly different!

Chocolate Chiffon Cake

Bake at 325 degrees.

1/2 cup baking cocoa powder
3/4 cup boiling water
1 3/4 cups sifted cake flour
1 3/4 cups granulated sugar
1 1/2 teaspoons baking soda
1 teaspoon salt
1/2 cup cooking oil
8 eggs, separated
2 teaspoons vanilla
1/2 teaspoon cream of tartar

1. In a small bowl mix cocoa powder and boiling water. Set aside.

2. In a large mixer bowl sift together the flour, sugar, baking soda, and salt. Make a well in the center of the mixture.

3. Add the cocoa powder mixture, oil, egg yolks, and vanilla. Beat with a spoon until smooth. Set aside.

4. In a separate bowl beat the egg whites and cream of tartar with an electric mixer at high speed until stiff peaks form.

5. Fold the egg whites into the batter. Pour into an ungreased 10-inch tube pan. Cut through the batter with a knife to destroy any air bubbles.

6. Bake at 325 degrees for 55 minutes. Increase temperature to 350 degrees and continue to bake for 10 minutes. Bake until a wooden pick inserted into the cake comes out clean.

7. Invert cake to completely cool and remove from the pan.

No icing required.

25   25   25

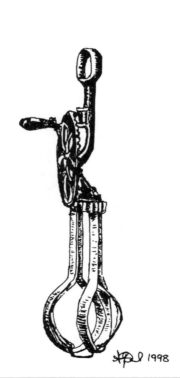

As far as I am concerned, you never go wrong serving this top-notch Vanilla Chiffon Cake to guests. Serve with or without icing. Nearly everyone enjoys a slice of sponge or chiffon cake with fresh fruit or ice cream.

Vanilla Chiffon Cake

Bake at 325 degrees.

2 1/4 cups cake flour
1 1/2 cups granulated sugar
3 teaspoons baking powder
1 teaspoon salt
1/2 cup cooking oil
5 egg yolks, unbeaten
3/4 cup cold water
2 teaspoons vanilla
1/2 teaspoon coconut flavoring
1 cup egg whites
1/2 teaspoon cream of tartar

1. In a small bowl separate the egg yolks from the whites. Set aside.
(NOTE: Usually, 7 to 8 egg whites will equal a cupful.)

2. In a large bowl sift together the flour, sugar, baking powder, and salt.

3. Make a well in the dry ingredients and add the oil, unbeaten egg yolks, water, and flavorings. Beat with a spoon until smooth. Set aside.

4. In a separate large mixer bowl combine the egg whites and cream of tartar. Beat until whites form very stiff peaks.

5. Gradually pour the egg yolk mixture over the beaten egg whites and gently fold with a spoon until blended.

6. Pour the batter into an ungreased tube pan.

7. Bake at 325 degrees for 45 minutes, increase the temperature to 350 degrees for the last 10 minutes.

8. Invert the pan and allow the cake to cool before removing.

No icing required.

≥≈ ≥≈ ≥≈

Adding an envelope of dry whipped topping to a box of cake mix gives the batter the texture of a luscious moist homemade cake and increases the volume. We have no idea where this tasty recipe for Whipped Topping Cake originated or when our family began to use it.

Whipped Topping Cake

Bake at 325 to 350 degrees.

1 package cake mix (any flavor)
1 envelope whipped topping mix (use dry)
4 eggs
1 cup cold tap water

1. Pour all ingredients into a mixer bowl and beat with an electric mixer on high speed for 3 to 5 minutes or until stiff.

2. Pour the batter into two greased and floured 9-inch layer pans and bake for 25 to 30 minutes or until a wooden pick inserted into the middle of the cake comes out clean.

When cake is cooled, spread with your favorite icing.

ᕤ   ᕤ   ᕤ

The farmers' wives always had plenty of milk, cream, butter, eggs, lard, sugar, and flour stored in the kitchen. These are the main ingredients used for "everyday" baking, and with a minute's notice they could whip up a delicate cake.

Regular customers came to our farm to buy fresh eggs and milk. I recall the various times that folks from Washington, D.C., and other nearby cities came with pleasure driving through the valley on weekends. They would stop in and buy the extra produce from the garden. They would ask to purchase eggs, milk, butter, or whatever they thought might be available for them to enjoy. Seldom did Mom refuse the opportunity to make a sale if she could spare the item and not rob the meals on the family's table. The sale meant a little extra cash in her hand for family shopping. Mom was careful, however, never to sell on Sunday. It was the Lord's Day. She and Dad tried their best to keep it holy and a day of rest. It was a time to build faith and find a solution or a way around problems, a time to think forward to victory and look for the best no matter what frustration or hindrance stood before them. They fed on the truth of the Bible and the message delivered in the morning sermon at church. Mom has lived to see the benefits of trusting God to supply the need.

Cold Water Sponge Cake

Bake at 325 degrees.

5 large egg whites
1 teaspoon cream of tartar
1/2 teaspoon salt
5 egg yolks

1/3 cup cold water
1 cup granulated sugar
1 teaspoon vanilla
1/2 teaspoon butter flavoring
1/2 teaspoon coconut flavoring
1 tablespoon cornstarch in a measuring cup and fill to the
    one-cup mark with sifted all-purpose flour

1. In a mixer bowl beat the egg whites with an electric mixer
until foamy.

2. Add the cream of tartar and salt. Continue to beat at high
speed until the egg whites hold a stiff peak. Set aside.

3. In a separate mixer bowl beat the egg yolks, water, and
sugar with an electric mixer at high speed until blended
lightly. Add the flavorings.

4. Sift the cornstarch and flour together and slowly add to
the batter. Beat slowly until well blended.

5. Fold egg yolk and flour mixture into the egg whites.

6. Pour the batter into an ungreased tube pan.

7. Bake for 1 hour or until a wooden pick inserted into the
middle of the cake comes out clean.

8. Invert the pan and allow the cake to cool before
removing.

Serve with or without icing.

❧   ❧   ❧

Most of us take for granted the simple measuring spoon and cup. It was not until the late 1940s that Mom owned either. A teacup, a coffee cup, and the spoons we ate with at the table were what she used for measuring. After all, her friends and family measured ingredients the same way so everyone's recipes worked! The tin cup that was used to take a quick drink of water from the well was not marked with the liquid measurements but the cook also measured with that style of cup. To those early country women, a half of a cup was a half of a cup, no matter if it held eight ounces or not!

In later years, any new tin measuring cup that Mom purchased soon became dented and bent from heavy use. One of the measuring cups that she owns today is split at several spots around the top rim and has to be handled carefully, so as not to snag her hand on the sharp metal edges. Though the handle has been missing, Mom believes it is not worn out yet! She keeps that cup in her sugar can and uses it regularly to measure. It will still hold a cupful and that is all that is necessary. I cannot stop thinking how many times Mom's hand has cradled that old battered measuring cup. Perhaps the memories it brings are the reason she does not part with it.

She also had a metal quart measuring pitcher which was in similar condition to the cup when last seen, but it has been lost for years and nearly forgotten. In those struggling days, nothing was replaced until the item was truly worn out and beyond use. Mom has lived in simplicity all her life, and she sees no need to change her style after 99 years.

Light Yellow Cake

Bake at 350 degrees.

Allow ingredients to reach room temperature before baking this cake.

2 cups plus 2 tablespoons sifted all-purpose flour
1 1/2 cups granulated sugar
3 1/2 teaspoons baking powder
1/2 teaspoon salt
1/2 cup solid vegetable shortening, softened
1 cup whole milk
1 teaspoon vanilla
3 eggs

1. In a large mixer bowl sift together the flour, sugar, baking powder, and salt.

2. Add the shortening, milk, and vanilla. Beat with an electric mixer for a couple of minutes.

3. Add the eggs and beat on high speed for 3 minutes.

4. Pour the batter into a greased and floured 9- by 13-inch cake pan.

5. Bake in the oven for 45 to 50 minutes, or until a wooden pick inserted into the middle of the cake comes out clean.

When cake is cooled, spread with your favorite icing.

≈ ≈ ≈

White cake was baked in the Wiles kitchen and served many a time during the days of World War II. Sugar was rationed and this recipe was a "life saver" because it requires just one cup. Mom guarded her supply with great diligence in order to bake more often for the family. And since this simple recipe requires only the egg whites, the yolks were used to make egg noodles or rivvels.

When the sugar bucket was empty, and Mom could not bake, she went to the bakery in Frederick and bought slightly damaged commercial bakery cookies. The charge for a five-pound box was minimal and affordable. Our family didn't care if the chocolate was spread unevenly, or if one corner was broken off! The cookies satisfied our sweet tooth and it was something that Mom could put in the hand of a little one asking for a sweet treat.

White Cake

Bake at 325 degrees.

2 tablespoons of cornstarch in a measuring cup and fill to the
    two-cup mark with all-purpose flour
2 teaspoons baking powder
1/4 teaspoon salt
4 egg whites
1 cup granulated sugar
1/2 cup butter, softened
2/3 cup whole milk
1 to 1 1/2 teaspoons vanilla

1. In a large bowl sift together the cornstarch, flour, baking powder, and salt. Set aside.

2. In a large mixer bowl beat the egg whites with an electric mixer until stiff and hold a peak. Set aside.

3. In a separate large bowl cream together the sugar and butter.

4. Add the milk and vanilla. Beat until blended.

5. Add the flour mixture. Beat until well blended and smooth.

6. Fold the egg whites into the batter with a spoon.

7. Pour the batter into a greased and floured 9- by 13-inch cake pan.

8. Bake in the oven for 40 to 50 minutes or until a wooden pick inserted into the middle of the cake comes out clean.

When cake is cooled, spread with your favorite white icing and sprinkle with grated fresh coconut.

          ða   ða   ða

Mom made what she referred to as a ribbon cake by beginning with a basic yellow or white cake recipe. She divided the prepared batter into as many portions as she wanted different color ribbons. She added cocoa powder to one, and the remaining dishes of batter were colored with a variety of food coloring. She carefully poured rows of colored batter into a loaf pan that she held tilted to its side in order to stack the batter and to keep it from spreading over the bottom of the pan. The children thought these cakes were wonderful and Mom made them most often for special occasions. Use your imagination when deciding the color of ribbons for this recipe.

The farmhands often complimented Mom, and whoever was helping her in the kitchen that day, on the cakes they served. These days, as soon as Mom finishes a big job in the kitchen she heads for her rocking chair. At her age I would say, it is rest well earned!

Ribbon or Yellow Cake

Bake at 325 to 350 degrees.

3 1/2 cups sifted cake flour
2 cups granulated sugar
4 teaspoons baking powder
1 teaspoon salt
1 cup whole milk
1/2 cup butter, softened
1 teaspoon vanilla
1 teaspoon butter flavoring
2 eggs
baking cocoa powder
food coloring

1. In a large mixer bowl sift together the flour, sugar, baking powder, and salt.

2. Add the milk, butter, and flavorings to the flour mixture. Beat with an electric mixer on medium speed for a couple of minutes.

3. Add the eggs. Beat on high speed for 3 minutes.

4. Divide the batter into separate bowls. Add the cocoa powder to one bowl of batter to reach a chocolate color and mix thoroughly. Add the food coloring to other bowls.

5. Carefully pour rows of colored batter into a greased and floured loaf pan while holding it tilted to one side, preventing the batter from spreading over the bottom of the pan.

6. Bake in the oven for 25 to 30 minutes. Bake until a wooden pick inserted into the middle of the cake comes out clean.

When cake is cooled, spread with your favorite icing.

(NOTE: Use your favorite yellow or white cake recipe to make a ribbon cake.)

ea   ea   ea

Yellow and White Cake has two layers of yellow batter and two layers of white, each layer being very thin. It pleases nearly everyone, especially if you like having icing on each bite of cake! It took a strong arm to beat the batters, but Mom did it many times before she had the luxury of owning an electric mixer. Now we delight in whipping up a cake with "no sweat."

Certain cakes remind Mom of wonderful moments shared through the years with family and friends. Today, she sits in the grand place she calls home and rocks tirelessly in her rocking chair by the window while these vivid memories bring her priceless pleasures to relive.

Mom believes sweet peace belongs to those who are determined to live while sharing and giving to those less fortunate--treating each one who comes in the pathway with respect and love. Mom is grateful for the "good life." Often I stop to wonder how one must feel who has lived for nearly a century. What must her secret thoughts and most sincere wishes be?

Yellow and White Layered Cake

Yellow layer:

Bake at 325 to 350 degrees.

1 1/2 cups sifted cake flour
1 teaspoon baking powder
1/4 cup butter, softened
1 cup granulated sugar
4 egg yolks
1/4 cup whole milk

1/2 teaspoon vanilla
1/2 teaspoon butter flavoring

1. In a large bowl sift together the flour and baking powder. Set aside.

2. In a mixer bowl cream together the butter and sugar with an electric mixer.

3. Add the egg yolks and beat for a couple of minutes on medium speed.

4. Add the flour mixture, milk, and flavorings. Beat for about 3 minutes on high speed.

5. Pour the batter into two greased and floured 9-inch cake pans.

6. Bake in the oven for 15 to 20 minutes or until a wooden pick inserted into the middle of the cake comes out clean.

White layer:

Bake at 325 to 350 degrees.

1 1/2 cups sifted cake flour
1 teaspoon baking powder
4 egg whites
1/4 cup butter, softened
1 cup granulated sugar
1/4 cup whole milk
1/2 teaspoon vanilla
1/2 teaspoon coconut flavoring

7. In a large bowl sift together the flour and baking powder. Set aside.

8. In a large mixer bowl beat the egg whites using an electric mixer until stiff and hold a peak. Set aside.

9. In a separate bowl cream together the sugar and butter with an electric mixer. Add the milk and flavorings. Beat until blended and smooth.

10. Add the flour mixture and beat for about 3 minutes on high speed.

11. Fold the batter into the stiff egg whites with a spoon.

12. Pour the batter into two greased and floured 9-inch cake pans.

13. Bake in the oven for 15 to 20 minutes or until a wooden pick inserted into the middle of the cake comes out clean.

14. Layer the cooled cake, using alternate white and yellow layers. Between each layer, use the icing of your choice.

ò   ò   ò

Through the years, One-Egg Cakes were baked when the hens were not laying eggs at top production, or when Mom was saving the money from selling eggs to buy someone a new pair of shoes, a coat, or some other article of clothing.

Mom enjoyed getting us children all gussied up for church in our best bib and tucker. It was the one time of the week everything matched and we had no patches "showing." Life and its luxuries were not always as we wanted it to be, but the few good things we did have to enjoy were more than precious.

While there were no plastic credit cards to fall back on in tight times during those days, the only credit one talked about when shopping was the little book the general store keeper used to record the debt until the patron settled up when pay day finally rolled around. Using this type of store credit was a last resort to most folks. People held their pride high and used help only when the emergency was severe.

It appears to me these folks had definitely learned to separate their genuine needs from their wants! Folks made every effort to pay off their debt as quickly as possible. They hated to owe anyone anything. Mom and Dad have been blessed and seemed to have enough provisions on the farm to make do until they had the cash to go shopping for a few staples. On many occasions they simply did without, denying they had a need.

One-Egg Cake

Bake at 350 degrees.

2 cups all-purpose flour
1 1/4 cups granulated sugar
2 1/2 teaspoons baking powder
1 teaspoon salt
1/3 cup solid vegetable shortening, softened
1 cup whole milk
1 teaspoon vanilla
1 egg

1. In a large mixer bowl sift together the flour, sugar, baking powder, and salt.

2. Add the shortening plus about half of the milk and vanilla. Beat with an electric mixer on medium speed for about 2 minutes or 300 strokes by hand with a spoon.

3. Add the remaining milk and egg. Beat for 2 additional minutes.

4. Pour the batter into greased and floured 9-inch cake pans. Bake for 15 to 20 minutes or until a wooden pick inserted into the middle of the cake comes out clean.

When cake is cooled, spread with your favorite white or chocolate icing.

Variation: Omit the icing and serve with whipped topping and your favorite fresh fruit.

ᨠ   ᨠ   ᨠ

Grandmother Clara Grossnickel favored molasses cake and passed the recipe along to her daughter, Letha Wiles (my mom). Years ago the country women referred to a recipe as a receipt. Believe me, everyone knew what they were talking about.

All kinds of spices and different types of molasses have always been popular ingredients when baking pies, cakes and cookies. In the country stores during the early 1900s, and for many years after, spices were dipped from the bulk container, which was usually a wooden barrel or keg, into a small brown paper bag and sold by the store proprietor by the ounce. Back then, when the little tüit (paper bag) filled with spice was brought home, they carefully penciled on the side what it contained before placing it on the shelf. They needed to be careful not to get the bags confused with each other, especially if the aroma was not a familiar one. In our area of the country, a paper bag was most often referred to as a sack or tuit. My mother still lets the German word tuit slip from her tongue from time to time. If one said that outside our home today, few, other than an old-timer or two, would know to what one was referring.

Years later, the idea of packaging spices in small bottles with paper labels and little cans with letters printed in brightly colored paints came along, adding to the storekeeper's convenience and the customer's cost. Today the idea of bulk foods has returned to some grocery stores, with self-service and the use of plastic bags as the carry-out container.

These measurements were found in old recipes that Grandmother Grossnickel used: *as much as will lie on a nickel or the end of a knife, 10 cents worth of spice, a pinch, a teacup or coffee cup full, a handful, a lump of lard the size of an egg or walnut, milk enough to make a thin sauce, heaping cup, scant teaspoon and flour enough to make soft or stiff dough.* My opinion of what is a "soft dough" and how thin is "thin sauce," will most likely be a different opinion from yours. And ten cents worth of any spice will be only a trace today, if that!

Clara Leatherman Grossnickel's Molasses Cake

Bake at 325 degrees.

3 cups sifted all-purpose flour
1 1/2 teaspoons ground ginger
2 teaspoons ground cinnamon
1 cup granulated sugar
1/2 cup butter or lard
(NOTE: Solid vegetable shortening can be substituted for lard.)
3 eggs
1 cup sour milk
(NOTE: Make sour milk by adding 1 tablespoon vinegar to 1 cup whole milk and stir.)
1 cup dark molasses
2 teaspoons baking soda

1. In a large bowl sift together the flour, ginger, and cinnamon. Set aside.

2. In a separate large mixing bowl cream together the sugar and butter or lard with a spoon.

3. Add the eggs and beat until smooth with a spoon.

4. Add the sour milk and beat until smooth and well blended.

5. In a small bowl combine the molasses and baking soda. Stir until dissolved. Add to the batter.

6. Add the dry ingredients. Stir until smooth and well blended.

7. Pour the batter into a greased and floured 9-inch square cake pan.

8. Bake in the oven for 40 to 45 minutes or until a wooden pick inserted into the middle of the cake comes out clean.

Serve warm topped with whipped cream.

ஃ   ஃ   ஃ

Mom planned and was accustomed to baking ahead of time, but upside-down cake is best served straight from the oven or while warm. Pineapple and peach are her two favorite fruit toppings. Use only cooked fruit in this recipe, but try adding apricots, raisins or other dried fruits for a nice touch.

An upside-down cake seems better baked in a black cast-iron skillet. Mom especially likes the crispy, brown crust it produces around the edge. I believe most everyone enjoys upside-down cake and that may be due to the fact that they prefer the fruit topping over a cake with a sweet icing.

Upside-Down Cake

Bake at 350 degrees.

Topping Ingredients:

1/3 cup butter, softened
1/2 cup brown sugar
1 16-ounce can of fruit, drained
3/4 cup pecans

1. Melt the butter in a 10-inch cast-iron skillet.

2. Remove skillet from heat and sprinkle brown sugar over the butter.

3. Place the drained fruit and nuts in a pattern on the butter and sugar mixture. Set aside.

Cake Batter Ingredients:

1 cup sifted cake flour
1/2 teaspoon baking powder
1/4 teaspoon salt
2 eggs
2/3 cup granulated sugar
6 tablespoons whole milk
1 teaspoon vanilla or butter flavoring

4. In a large bowl sift together the flour, baking powder, and salt. Set aside.

5. In a separate mixer bowl beat the eggs with an electric mixer on medium speed until light yellow.

6. Add the sugar to the eggs and beat until blended.

7. Add the milk and flavoring. Add the flour mixture and beat for about 3 minutes.

8. Pour the batter slowly into the iron skillet holding the fruit mixture.

9. Bake in the oven for about 45 minutes or until a wooden pick inserted into the middle of the cake comes out clean. Immediately turn upside down on serving plate. Do not remove pan for 3 minutes.

(NOTE: A box yellow cake mix, prepared according to the directions, may be substituted for the batter recipe.)

ੋ   ੋ   ੋ

Mom recalls warning us children not to run or bounce on the floor while she had a cake baking in the oven. She knew from experience that it would fall since the floor boards in the kitchen were old and not solid. To be truthful, we children always heard what she said, but we were never as concerned as she was--we knew if it "flopped" it was our cake anyhow.

When the cake was baked, Mom opened the oven door and pulled the hot pan out, holding it cautiously with feed-bag dishcloths. She spread worn tablecloths over one end of the table and there she turned the cakes out of the pans to cool. At that moment the kitchen had the look and aroma of a bakery with cakes lined up, waiting to be spread with yummy icing. If we saw a dishpan on the table turned upside down, we knew for sure a cake was covered for safe keeping. We often carefully lifted the pan to take a peak, or once in awhile we were brave enough to drag a finger through the icing to get a taste, but we knew not to cut it!

Dad loved Red Devil's Food Cake and Mom remembered to bake it often. Perhaps she knew the way to a man's heart is through his stomach.

Red Devil's Food Cake

Bake at 350 degrees.

1 3/4 cups sifted cake flour
1 1/2 cups granulated sugar
1 teaspoon baking powder
1/2 teaspoon baking soda
1 teaspoon salt
2/3 cup whole milk

1/2 cup solid vegetable shortening, softened
additional 1/3 cup whole milk
2 eggs, unbeaten
2 ounces unsweetened melted chocolate
2 tablespoons red food coloring

1. In a mixer bowl sift together the flour, sugar, baking powder, baking soda, and salt.

2. Add the milk and shortening. Beat with an electric mixer on medium speed for a couple of minutes.

3. Add the additional milk, eggs, melted chocolate, and food coloring. Beat on high speed for 3 minutes.

4. Pour the batter into two greased and floured 8-inch cake pans.

5. Bake in the oven for 30 to 35 minutes or until a wooden pick inserted into the middle of the cake comes out clean.

When cake is cooled, spread with your favorite icing.

(NOTE: Extra food coloring can be added to the cake batter for a richer color.)

&a   &a   &a

When I think of home, what could be sweeter than a whiff of chocolate cake baking in the oven or the smell of fresh mowed hay in the field? Most know the path that leads homeward, and choose to hold it ever near to the core of one's being. These thoughts of home, where love abides, allow a heart to rest in a wonderful state of peace and joy at that remembrance.

Day in and day out, farmers and their families work hard. With so much physical activity, hearty appetites are created and Mom made sure to fill our stomachs with bountiful meals.

On the farm, breakfast was eaten early in the morning, and dinner was the main meal served at noontime. Supper was our evening meal when leftovers were reheated and a few fresh items were cooked to make the meal complete. As strange as it may seem, Mom, as well as most of her children, still serves supper in the evening! Some things never change by one's own desire.

Chocolate Cake

Bake at 350 degrees.

1 7/8 cups sifted cake flour
1 1/2 cups granulated sugar
1 1/4 teaspoons baking powder
1/2 teaspoon baking soda
1 teaspoon salt
5 tablespoons baking cocoa powder
(NOTE: Use additional cocoa powder for a darker color and more flavor.)
2/3 cup solid vegetable shortening, softened

1 cup sour milk
(NOTE: Make sour milk by adding 1 tablespoon vinegar to 1 cup whole milk and stir.)
2 large eggs
2 tablespoons red food coloring

1. In a large mixer bowl sift together the flour, sugar, baking powder, baking soda, salt, and cocoa powder.

2. Add the shortening and sour milk. Beat with an electric mixer on medium speed for a couple of minutes.

3. Add the eggs and food coloring to the above mixture and beat on high speed for 3 minutes.

4. Pour the batter into two floured and greased 8-inch cake pans.

5. Bake in the oven for 30 to 35 minutes or until a wooden pick inserted in the middle of the cake comes out clean.

When cake is cooled, spread with your favorite chocolate icing.

❧ ❧ ❧

Make Chocolate Curls for that special occasion cake. Prepare them when you have plenty of time to devote to the project, freeze and use later. Mom never had time to spend making chocolate curls but I included the instructions because they are a nice addition to the frosting.

Chocolate Curls

6 ounces chocolate chips; either semisweet, milk chocolate, peanut butter, etc.

1. In the top of a double boiler melt the chocolate chips over low heat.

2. Pour melted chocolate on bottom of a cake pan and spread to a 6- by 7-inch patch.

3. Cool chocolate in the refrigerator for 8 to 10 minutes or until firm. Chocolate will not curl if too hard or too soft.

4. Hold a metal wide spatula at an angle and scrape chocolate up, guiding it with your fingers to form a curl.

5. With spatula, transfer to a plate and set in refrigerator until firm.

Use chocolate curls on a cake covered with a smooth layer of icing.

(NOTE: Do not touch curls with your fingers. They will melt.)

ఈ   ఈ   ఈ

No matter what food Mom served, it was tasty! This cake has a caramel flavor due to the required brown sugar in the batter. Growing up in our home, I thought Sunday dinner was by far the best meal of the week. Special pies and cakes were baked for dessert. We looked forward to Sunday, and I still do! No one was in a hurry to finish eating and it was family time. We never wanted to leave the table, and guests were made to feel as if they were family members. The longer we sat chatting, the longer we could prolong the ordeal of washing all the dirty dishes! Then too, Sundays were days of rejoicing in the Lord--we did not live without hope and faith at our house.

Chicken was a favorite meat prepared for Sunday meals, and for certain to be served when the Reverend was invited. We had fried chicken in the late summertime or early fall and in the wintertime we prepared roasted or stewed hens. On Saturday, we killed and dressed the chickens to be served the next day. The meat was put in a deep pan of water and placed on the cold sod cellar floor. We never gave the chore much thought--if we were going to eat chicken, someone was going to have to get the job done! Some things were plain and simple to understand.

When the icebox came along it made safe storage possible for perishable foods. Before having this convenience, the chickens were butchered no more than one day prior to being served. On Sunday morning before leaving for church, Mom prepared food for the noonday meal. All of the members of the household were busy scampering about doing chores. Every item on the menu was made ready to place on the stove to heat as soon as she returned. On those early Sunday mornings she stood over the hot cookstove and fried enough chicken to fill a large roasting pan. Now that was a fresh chicken dinner! After all that, little wonder everyone enjoyed spending Sunday afternoon relaxing on the porch--they surely deserved the time to rest!

Brown Sugar Cake

Bake at 350 degrees.

2 cups sifted cake flour
3 teaspoons baking powder
1 teaspoon salt
1 1/2 cups brown sugar
1/2 cup solid vegetable shortening, softened
1 teaspoon vanilla
1/2 teaspoon butter flavoring
2/3 cup whole milk
additional 1/3 cup whole milk
2 eggs, unbeaten

1. In a mixer bowl sift together the flour, baking powder, and salt.

2. Add the brown sugar, shortening, flavorings, and milk. Beat with an electric mixer on medium speed for a couple of minutes. Add the additional milk and eggs. Beat for about 3 minutes on high speed.

3. Pour the batter into two greased and floured 8-inch cake pans.

4. Bake in the oven for 30 to 35 minutes or until a wooden pick inserted into the middle of the cake comes out clean.

ﻬ   ﻬ   ﻬ

Rich Cherry Cake produces a pretty pink batter with bits of cherry and nut showing. It is a nice special occasion cake.

With no air conditioning in the farmhouse, it became as hot as a giant bake oven in the summertime. We wondered at times if the temperature would ever turn cool again, and how we welcomed the days that brought a cool breeze. We opened the windows in the house, trying to cool down the place. During the mid-summer months, Mom even opened the transom window above the living room door, but most of the time it brought little or no relief. Oh how we dreamed of having an electric fan--a big one that rotated and moved lots of air around the room!

Our only aid to keep us comfortable were hand-held cardboard fans attached to thin wooden handles. The problem being, we had no time to sit down and briskly wave them in front of our face.

When I was a child, Mom kept the fans in the living room in a desk drawer. With them out of sight we children were not tempted to play and break them. Mom perceived what would happen and she knew replacement fans would be hard to come by. We understood whatever was kept in the desk was off limits to us and we dared not explore there. On one side of the fan was a nice colored picture, and the other side had an advertisement written for either Gladhill's or Bittle's Funeral Home. The Brethren Mutual Insurance Company also distributed such fans. If it happened that these fans were misplaced, and if we where sitting in the living room on a hot evening and needed to cool off, we grabbed an old newspaper or paper bag and began flapping it back and forth to get a breeze going around us.

Rich Cherry Cake

Bake at 350 degrees.

2 1/4 cups sifted cake flour
3 teaspoons baking powder
1/2 teaspoon salt
1 1/3 cups granulated sugar
1/2 cup solid vegetable shortening, softened
1/2 cup whole milk
1/4 cup maraschino cherry juice
1/2 teaspoon vanilla
4 large egg whites
20 maraschino cherries, chopped fine
3/4 cup chopped nuts, if desired

1. In a mixer bowl sift together the flour, baking powder, and salt.

2. Add the sugar, shortening, milk, cherry juice, and vanilla. Beat with an electric mixer on medium to high speed for a couple of minutes.

3. Add the unbeaten egg whites and beat with an electric mixer on high speed for 3 minutes.

4. Fold the cherries and nuts into the batter with a spoon.

5. Pour the batter into two greased and floured 8-inch cake pans.

6. Bake in the oven for 30 to 35 minutes or until a wooden pick inserted into the middle of the cake comes out clean.

Variation: Use a basic white icing and for extra flavor substitute cherry juice for part of the liquid required in the icing recipe.

(NOTE: Do not use a boiled variety of icing when adding cherry juice.)

əə   əə   əə

When Mom was busy in the kitchen cooking, we children always knew when she needed to follow the recipe. We knew because if we asked her a question in the middle of her measuring the ingredients, the answer she always gave was "just wait and I'll see," or "maybe." Seldom was it a firm yes or no. She did not want to be held responsible to a promise made while not giving the situation her undivided attention.

As little children we did not understand why she was so intent on accomplishing her chores. Oh how our childhood joy would have been robbed at that time if we had an adult understanding of what she was going through. But on the other hand, our parents would have never wanted us to know when troubles and concerns mounted on them from every side.

Banana Cake

Bake at 350 degrees.

2 egg whites
1/3 cup granulated sugar
2 cups sifted cake flour
1 cup granulated sugar
1 teaspoon baking powder
1 teaspoon baking soda
1 teaspoon salt
1/3 cup cooking oil
1 cup mashed, ripe bananas
1/3 cup buttermilk
1 1/2 teaspoons vanilla
additional 1/3 cup buttermilk
2 egg yolks

1. In a mixer bowl beat the egg whites with an electric mixer on medium speed until foamy. Add 1/3 cup sugar, tapping on the cup to sift a little in at a time, while beating on high speed. Beat until the egg whites are stiff and hold a peak. Set aside.

2. In a separate mixer bowl sift together the flour, 1 cup sugar, baking powder, baking soda, and salt.

3. Add the oil, bananas, 1/3 cup buttermilk, and vanilla to the dry ingredients. Beat with an electric mixer on medium speed for a couple of minutes.

4. Add the additional buttermilk and egg yolks. Beat on high speed for 3 minutes.

5. Gently fold the batter into the stiff egg whites with a spoon.

6. Pour the batter into two greased and floured 8-inch cake pans.

7. Bake in the oven for 30 minutes or until a wooden pick inserted into the middle of cake comes out clean.

When cake is cooled, spread with a white icing.

ൟ   ൟ   ൟ

Not all that we inherit is of monetary value, but useful items, advice, and recipes. Mom was heir to this wonderful soft gingerbread recipe from her Aunt Melissa Harshman. Aunt Melissa is remembered as a kind spoken and gentle lady. She and her sister, Grandmother Clara Grossnickel, lived together for many of their elder years in Ellerton, along Middle Creek in the home Arthur T. Leatherman now owns. Both ladies were widowed. They had grit and courage that was intense and steady as a rock. They were happy, had great faith in God, and both lived a long successful life. Mom is thankful for each memory of her ancestors.

At our house, Mom served gingerbread more frequently when the fall season commenced. The spices are pungent and sweet and get us into the holiday spirit.

Aunt Melissa Harshman's Soft Gingerbread

Bake at 325 degrees.

1 1/2 cups sifted all-purpose flour
1 teaspoon ground ginger
1 egg
5 tablespoons melted lard
(NOTE: Solid vegetable shortening can be substituted for lard.)
1 teaspoon baking soda
1 cup dark molasses
2/3 cup hot water, not boiling
1/2 teaspoon salt

1. In a large bowl sift together the flour and ginger. Set aside.

2. In a separate large mixing bowl beat the egg with a rotary beater or wire whisk until light yellow.

3. Stir in the lard.

4. In a cup combine the baking soda with the molasses and mix well. Then pour into the egg and lard mixture.

5. Add the flour mixture and stir until blended with a spoon.

6. Add the water and salt. Beat until well blended and smooth.

7. Pour the batter into a greased and floured 9-inch square pan.

8. Bake in the oven for 30 to 40 minutes or until a wooden pick inserted into the middle of the cake comes out clean.

Serve warm with whipped cream on top.

ða   ða   ða

Mom knew white cake topped with a rich, dark chocolate frosting was a favorite of Dad's. He enjoyed it served with ice cream or fruit.

Skim Milk White Cake

Bake at 350 degrees.

2 1/4 cups sifted cake flour
1 1/2 cups granulated sugar
4 teaspoons baking powder
1 teaspoon salt
1/2 cup solid vegetable shortening, softened
2/3 cup skim milk
1 teaspoon vanilla
additional 1/3 cup skim milk
4 large egg whites, unbeaten

1. In a large mixer bowl sift together the dry ingredients.

2. Add the shortening, skim milk, and vanilla to the dry ingredients. Beat with an electric mixer on medium speed for a couple of minutes.

3. Add the additional skim milk and unbeaten egg whites. Beat on high speed for about 3 minutes.

4. Pour the batter into two greased and floured 8-inch cake pans.

5. Bake in the oven for 30 to 35 minutes or until a wooden pick inserted into the middle of the cake comes out clean.

When cake is cooled, spread with your favorite icing.

&a &a &a

During the 1996 Christmas season, Mom baked 25 pounds of Letha's Light Fruitcake for sharing with family and friends. Folks who do not relish fruitcake enjoy this recipe since it does not have the usual heavy spices, but does have a high dried fruit and nut content. Mom has used this recipe for many years since she learned it pleases so many folks' appetites. Fruitcake will keep for months when wrapped in a wine-soaked cloth, placed in a tight container and stored in a cool place.

Letha's Light Fruitcake

Bake at 275 degrees.

2 tablespoons light corn syrup
2 tablespoons fresh orange juice
2 tablespoons of sherry cooking wine
1/2 cup margarine, softened
1/2 cup granulated sugar
2 eggs
1 1/2 cups all-purpose flour
6 ounces green candied cherries
6 ounces red candied cherries
6 ounces candied pineapple
8 ounces white raisins
6 ounces dried apricots
1 cup pecans

1. In a small bowl combine the corn syrup, orange juice, and wine. Set aside.

2. In a large mixing bowl cream together the margarine and sugar until fluffy.

3. Add the eggs, one at a time, and beat after each addition.

4. Add, alternating with small amounts, the flour and the liquid mixture.

5. Add the fruit and nuts. Stir until well blended.

6. Pour the batter into a greased tube pan and press down until firmly packed. Bake for 2 to 2 1/2 hours or until lightly browned.

Slice thin and serve with fresh hot coffee.

Variation: Use the following ingredients as a substitute for the fruit and nut content listed in the recipe:

8 ounces white raisins
6 ounces candied cherries
4 ounces candied pineapple
2 ounces mixed candied fruit
2 ounces candied lemon peel
2 ounces candied orange peel
1/2 cup walnuts

(NOTE: Use any combination of dried or candied fruits desired. Use black walnuts, English walnuts, or any combination of nuts.)

ॐ   ॐ   ॐ

On the Middletown farm, black walnut trees stood in the chicken yard, and English walnut trees grew outside the back kitchen door. The trees produced enough nuts to supply the family's baking needs and extra to share.

Hard labor are the words I would use to describe removing the black walnut or hickory nut kernels from their shells. Mom set aside a day when some of us children were at home to help crack nuts--often on a day when the weather was too snowy to be bused to school.

We worked in the wash house, as long as the temperature was not in the single digits. We piled on layer upon layer of clothing. Mom built a blazing, roaring fire in the fireplace and we sat nearby on old chairs, stools, or five-gallon buckets turned upside down, trying to keep warm. We spent hours picking out the nut kernels.

We spread a large cloth over our laps and placed a brick or flatiron on our knees. Then we centered the nut on that hard surface, held it with our fingers, and pounded it with a carpenter's hammer until it broke open. On impact, we had shells flying everywhere. Though that was a successful "crack," every now and then we missed our aim and hit our fingers! At the time, all we could do was jump up and holler. Later, when we ate the goodies that Mom made using these kernels, the pain and hours of work never came to mind!

Letha's Old-Fashioned Dark Fruitcake

Bake at 300 degrees.

1 cup all-purpose flour
1/2 pound mixed fruit
1/2 pound chopped dates
1/2 pound chopped figs
1 pound white raisins
1 cup walnuts
additional 2 cups all-purpose flour
1 teaspoon baking powder
1/2 teaspoon ground cinnamon
1/2 teaspoon ground nutmeg
1/2 teaspoon ground cloves
1 cup granulated sugar
1/4 cup lard
(NOTE: Solid vegetable shortening can be substituted for lard.)
4 eggs
2/3 cup whole milk

1. Place one cup of flour into a bowl. Chop the fruit by hand with a sharp knife into the flour. Add the nuts and stir with a spoon to dust with flour. Set aside.

2. In a separate bowl sift together the additional flour, baking powder, ground cinnamon, nutmeg, and cloves. Set aside.

3. In a large mixing bowl cream together the sugar and lard with a spoon.

4. Add the eggs and milk. Beat until well blended.

5. Add the dry ingredients and stir until well blended.

6. Add the fruit and nuts. Stir until mixed thoroughly in the batter.

7. Pour the batter into a greased and floured tube pan and press down with a spoon.

8. Bake in the oven for 2 hours or until a wooden pick inserted into the middle of the cake comes out clean. Cake should be lightly browned when done.

9. Cool cake completely before removing from the pan.

10. When cake is absolutely cooled, wrap in a wine-soaked cloth and place in a tight container. Store in a cool place.

(NOTE: Slice with a thin sharp knife blade.)

&a   &a   &a

This glaze adds a nice shine to the crust. I remember Mom strewing the hot glaze on top of the cooled cakes and carefully brushing around the sides. She placed pieces of candied fruit on top in a festive pattern.

Fruitcake Glaze

1/2 cup light corn syrup
1/4 cup water

1. In a heavy saucepan combine the syrup and water.

2. Place pan over medium to high heat and bring to a rolling boil. Remove from the heat. Cool slightly.

3. Pour and brush evenly over cold fruitcake before storing.

4. Quickly decorate the top of cake with dried fruit and nuts.

(NOTE: Do not use glaze when wrapping cake in a wine cloth.)

&a   &a   &a

I shall never forget the manner in which Mom or Dad looked straight into the eyes of us children when we got wiry and pulled a shenanigan or two at mealtime. Those scenes are vivid to me and perhaps will never fade from my memory. "Straighten up." That was usually all that had to be said to get our immediate attention and correct the unruly situation. They did not conduct themselves as truant officers but firmly stated with authority what they wanted from us. Little did I know, no one ever so much as thought of panicking at our behavior. My parents were in control! We were testing but not for long because we knew a few manners were expected from us, especially while eating. Mealtime was to be a happy time. The pace of the chattering slowed and a calmness seemed to fall while eating.

During certain seasons of the year when the farm work was not pressing, after Dad had finished eating his meal, he enjoyed pushing his chair away from the table and taking a quick peak at The Frederick Post, the daily newspaper. Content with a full stomach, his head would bend low and commence to nod as sleep overtook him. Soon, his eye glasses would slip down to the end of his nose, and slowly but surely the grip of his hand would relax and the paper would flutter and gently float to the floor. It would be only a short nap while sitting on a straight chair but it was enough to refresh and reenergize.

All was well during these sleepy moments until one of us little ones spotted Dad in the venerable state. We were certain to beckon the other children to come watch. I remember looking at him and wondering what kept him from falling from his seat onto the floor. He was truly asleep and sitting upright! As Dad heard us giggling and sitting around his feet, he often opened his eyes to get a quick peak at what was happening. Then he closed his eyes again, but it took a few moments for the grin to vanish from his face. Oh what I would give to see that tender smile today!

While writing this book, the memories of the past often become very real, and I find myself imaging that I am a little girl living at home again. Those moments, however, are short and are soon overcome with the current cares and duties of life.

Our words are windows to our heart, but a genuine small action of love can linger and warm a soul forever.

Simple Yellow Cake

Bake at 350 degrees.

2 cups sifted cake flour
1 1/3 cups granulated sugar
3 teaspoons baking powder
1 teaspoon salt
2/3 cup whole milk
1/3 cup solid vegetable shortening, softened
1 teaspoon vanilla
1/2 teaspoon butter or coconut flavoring
additional 1/3 cup whole milk
4 egg yolks, unbeaten

1. In a large mixer bowl sift together the flour, sugar, baking powder, and salt.

2. Add the milk, shortening, and flavorings. Beat with an electric mixer for a couple of minutes.

3. Add the additional milk and egg yolks. Beat at high speed with an electric mixer for about 3 minutes.

4. Pour the batter into two greased and floured 8-inch cake pans.

5. Bake in the oven for 30 to 35 minutes or until a wooden pick inserted into the middle of the cake comes out clean.

When cake is cooled, spread with your favorite icing.

ès   ès   ès

Applesauce Cake consists of a heavy and spicy batter with lots of raisins and nuts, if desired. No eggs are required in this recipe. Make this cake in advance of serving--freeze for a month or more before using. It is definitely an old-timer's favorite!

Frequently, modern-day recipes require applesauce in an effort to cut down the fat content. We know folks have been baking this cake for more than a century and not until recently was anyone excited about the nutritional content. Way back then, pleasing one's taste buds was all that mattered to whoever was cooking.

Since Dad was a farmer, he had a stout appetite. And no meal was complete without a piece of cake or pie to finish it off. If there was nothing baked in the house, he never complained but spread himself a thick slice of homemade bread with sweet preserves or molasses.

Applesauce Cake

Bake at 350 degrees.

3 cups sifted all-purpose flour
1 teaspoon ground nutmeg
1 teaspoon ground cloves
2 teaspoons ground cinnamon
2 cups granulated sugar
1/2 cup butter or lard
(*NOTE: Solid vegetable shortening can be substituted for lard.*)
2 cups applesauce
2 teaspoons baking soda
additional 1/2 cup flour

1 pound raisins
1 cup nuts, either English walnuts, or black walnuts

1. In a large bowl sift together the flour, nutmeg, cloves, and cinnamon. Set aside.

2. In a large mixing bowl cream together the sugar and butter or lard with a spoon until smooth.

3. In a separate small bowl combine the applesauce and baking soda until smooth. Then stir in the creamed mixture.

4. Add the dry ingredients and stir until very smooth.

5. In another bowl toss 1 pound of raisins and 1 cup nuts with the additional flour. Add to the batter and stir until blended.

6. Pour the batter into a greased and floured tube pan.

7. Bake in the oven for 45 minutes to 1 hour or until a wooden pick inserted into the cake comes out clean.

8. Cool the cake slightly before removing from the pan.

This cake does not require icing.

&a   &a   &a

We have no idea where the Fresh Apple Cake recipe originated, but adding a combination of dried fruits makes a nice change to the original version. I think apples and raisins are a good combination to use when baking.

It was Mom's habit to serve cake and ice cream when company came, and sharing food or a sweet treat was the natural way of life in our rural area. Mom never cut a small slice of cake, and she always served the ice cream piled high in the dish!

I remember sometimes the conversation with visitors carried a tone of tenderness when a touching event or story was exchanged with dear friends and family. My parents tried to always converse in a kind-spirited fashion, offering comfort whenever possible. One never knows how someone else values those kind encouraging words, as we cannot live successfully without hope and confidence in ourselves.

At times finding someone to listen and knowing that the thoughts and concerns shared will be kept confidential is most important to the hurting one. It is good to love your brother as yourself and to speak accordingly. Mom and Dad's devotion to their family and friends is what their life has been about.

Fresh Apple Cake

Bake at 350 degrees.

4 cups largely diced raw apples, peeled
1 1/2 to 2 cups granulated sugar
3 cups sifted all-purpose flour
2 teaspoons baking soda

1 teaspoon ground cinnamon
1/2 teaspoon ground nutmeg
1/2 teaspoon salt
2 eggs
1 cup cooking oil
1 teaspoon vanilla
1 cup chopped nuts, either English or black walnuts.
1/2 cup raisins
1/2 cup dried apricots
1/4 cup dried or candied pineapple, if desired

1. Wash, peel, core, and dice apples in a separate bowl. Pour the sugar over the apples and allow to set for 1 hour. If syrup does not form on the apples and sugar, cover with 1/4 cup water.

2. In a separate bowl sift together the flour, baking soda, cinnamon, nutmeg, and salt. Set aside.

3. In a large bowl beat the eggs with a rotary beater or wire whisk until light yellow.

4. Add the cooking oil, vanilla, and syrup from the apples to the beaten eggs. Add the dry ingredients and beat until blended.

5. Fold in the apples, nuts, raisins, apricots, and pineapple, if desired. Then stir until blended.

6. Pour the batter into a greased and floured 9- by 13-inch cake pan.

7. Bake in the oven for 1 hour or until a wooden pick inserted into the middle of the cake comes out clean.

ঌ ঌ ঌ

This basic white icing stays soft and spreads evenly on a cooled cake. Some cakes would be very ordinary without the extra touch of a good, rich icing.

Memories come crowding in on Mom when she relates to the days of doing things in the kitchen the old-fashioned way. In the early days of her marriage, she made icing by blending powdered sugar, milk, butter, and flavoring together. And she didn't measure--she just poured ingredients into a bowl and stirred with a spoon until the mixture looked right! Years later, the commercial white shortening came on the market, along with new recipes for soft icings.

Basic White Icing

1 cup white solid vegetable shortening, softened
1 stick butter, softened
1 pound box powdered sugar
1/3 cup evaporated milk
3 tablespoons all-purpose flour
1 teaspoon vanilla
1 teaspoon butter flavoring

1. In a large mixer bowl beat the shortening, butter, and powdered sugar at a very low speed with an electric mixer until creamed together.

2. Add, alternating with small amounts, the evaporated milk and flour.

3. Add the flavorings and beat at high speed until icing is smooth. If icing is too thick to spread easily, add additional evaporated milk and beat well.

Spread icing on a cooled cake.

Variations: add 1/2 cup peanut butter, or 1/2 cup baking cocoa powder, or exchange butter flavoring for coconut flavoring.

ﻚ   ﻚ   ﻚ

White Drizzle Icing

1 cup powdered sugar
2 tablespoons water

Combine the sugar and water; stir until blended. Dip the icing to the cake with a fork and allow to run down the edge. Usually, a fork will work best to drizzle icing.

ﻚ   ﻚ   ﻚ

Melted chocolate candy bars are a quick topping on a sheet cake. Very rich, but that is okay with me since I have always enjoyed good chocolate bars! Be sure to place the bars on a piping hot cake to ensure quick melting and making it easy to spread. Slivered almonds sprinkled on top of the chocolate makes an attractive and tasty addition to the cake. The results of this idea are rich and downright good!

Quick Chocolate Topping

4 to 6 1.5 ounce milk chocolate bars

1. Place chocolate on top of a piping hot sheet cake. Allow time for chocolate to melt and spread evenly over cake with a spatula.

2. Cool cake at room temperature until chocolate is firm and slice.

ès   ès   ès

Was there ever a child born who did not enjoy licking the icing bowl? We children welcomed that sweet taste and Mom intentionally left a dab along the edge of the bowl for us to sample. I so fondly remember the gusto of the vanilla and how the fragrance filled the air in the kitchen when Mom opened the bottle. She sometimes mixed a small amount of vanilla into our milk to make us a special drink.

At the sight of a cake spread neatly with icing, how many times has a toddler just passing by had an uncontrollable urge to taste or somehow managed to stand on the tip of his or her toes and stretch a tiny arm high enough to stick a finger into a cake and grab a bite, when it was thought to be out of reach and absolutely safe? Probably none of us are innocent of that--no, not one!

Lemon Frosting

1 lemon, juice and 1/2 rind grated
2 1/4 cups powdered sugar
1 8-ounce package cream cheese
1/4 teaspoon salt
2 tablespoons evaporated milk

1. In a small saucepan squeeze the juice from the lemon and grate 1/2 of the rind.

2. Mix all the ingredients together and heat while stirring until the mixture forms to a spreading consistency.
(NOTE: Watch carefully--do not melt beyond the spreading consistency.)

&a   &a   &a

When Mom was a child, and also in the early years of her marriage, containers of food that needed to be kept cold were placed in natural spring water. That was their only means of preventing spoilage, before the use of the ice box and modern refrigeration. The icy cold running spring water was piped into a cement trough to control its path. The trough was housed in a small building called a springhouse. Usually, the water flowed from the springhouse back outdoors to a watering trough where the cattle and horses drank. When properly piped, it was clean and safe for human consumption.

They used heavy earthenware crocks that worked as an insulation to retain a cold temperature around the food, even after the pot was carried to the table. Each size crock had a special place in the trough--the large ones were placed at the deep end, the small ones at the shallow end. And if the pot was very small, a brick was placed underneath to keep it elevated above the height of the running water. They covered the crock with a flat lid and placed a brick on top to hold it secure. If they used a jug that did not have a cork available, a clean piece of cloth was wrapped around a corn cob and stuck down into the hole. Often the women placed these earthenware jugs filled with water in the trough. Remember, there was no ice to make cold water to drink.

Housed out in the springhouse was an old wooden churn that Mom used to make butter from the fresh cream. The soft butter was poured into a wooden butter bowl, and salt was worked in while any remaining fluid was worked out. Then it was pressed into a wooden print with a removable bottom. The print Mom used indented the shape of two sheaths of wheat on top of the pound. She cut the pound into two pieces and placed them on covered glass butter dishes, with each half showing its wheat sheath print on top.

Years ago, the cellar floors in homes were dirt or sod. Often water veins or small springs erupted from the dirt floor and caused a small stream to flow right under the house. The housewife took advantage of the situation and carried the containers of food she wanted to keep cool down into the basement and placed them in the flow of water. Or they sat the dishes on the cold ground floor to keep cool. Not a convenient way of doing things, to say the least.

But then, the day of the icebox arrived and folks were overjoyed with the new invention. Once refrigeration was made available for the kitchen, real "honest to goodness" convenience had come!

White Icing

1 egg white
1/4 cup white solid vegetable shortening, softened
1/4 cup butter
1/2 teaspoon butter flavoring
1/2 teaspoon vanilla flavoring
2 cups sifted powdered sugar

1. In a large mixer bowl cream together the egg white, shortening, butter, and flavorings with an electric mixer.

2. Gradually add the sugar and beat until fluffy and light.

Spread icing on a cooled cake.

(NOTE: Icing stays soft and snowy white.)

❧   ❧   ❧

Broiled Coconut Icing makes a crusty, toasted coconut topping that is rich, but not too sweet. I find it ideal to use on a yellow cake. Sprinkle slivered almonds on top on the coconut mixture. This gives a special occasion appearance.

Broiled Coconut Icing

1/2 cup butter, softened
1 cup brown sugar
6 tablespoons evaporated milk
1/2 teaspoon vanilla
2 cups shredded coconut
3/4 cup nuts, if desired

1. In a mixing bowl cream together the butter and brown sugar with a spoon.

2. Stir in the evaporated milk and vanilla. Add the coconut and nuts. Stir by hand until blended.

3. Spread mixture on top of a warm sheet cake with a spatula.

4. Place cake in the oven, 3 inches from top of oven broiler. Broil until icing bubbles and is lightly browned.

(NOTE: Watch carefully--the coconut burns very easily.)

ꝫ   ꝫ   ꝫ

This is the perfect icing for dipping tops or the ends of cookies. When busy, it is a time saving to dunk the cookie into the icing instead of spreading it on with a knife. Rectangular shapes are pretty dipped on one end, then covered with sprinkles or chopped nuts.

Dipping Icing

1 cup granulated sugar
1/2 cup butter, softened
1/2 cup whole milk
1 1/4 cups powdered sugar
1/2 teaspoon salt
1 teaspoon vanilla or your choice of flavoring
food coloring, if desired

1. In heavy saucepan combine the granulated sugar, butter, and milk.

2. Place pan over medium heat and bring mixture to a boil while stirring. Boil for 1 minute.

3. Remove pan from the heat and cool the cooked mixture slightly.

4. Add the powdered sugar, salt, flavoring, and food coloring to the cooked mixture and stir until well blended.

5. Dip tops or ends of cooled cookies in icing and place on a rack to dry.

Variation: In place of icing, melt chocolate chips (any flavor) and dip the end of the cookie, then sprinkle with nuts, sprinkles or coconut.

ะ๛   ะ๛   ะ๛

My mother has had an old bone-handled knife tucked in a drawer in her kitchen for 82 years. She reaches for this trusted relic when spreading icing on cakes or when cutting dough.

From age and extreme wear, the handle is deteriorating and about one-half of the bone is chipped away, but the knife is not beyond use or worn out, no matter how it may appear to you. That handle and Mom's hand have been companions far too long to part now, and she sees no need to replace it with a new one. After all, her hand has held that knife through thick and thin. She believes it was purchased in Ellerton, Maryland, at Bittle's or Summer's store, and was given to her by her mother when she and Dad married.

Mom also has a couple of three-prong forks stored in that same drawer. One of them is missing a steel prong. It too will never be discarded; these old utensils have earned a place of honor in the Wiles' family home. It is not necessarily the beautiful items in a home that capture the heart of a child, but ones that he or she has watched a parent work with. No matter the value of that item, it becomes a treasure of great worth in the eyes of the beholder.

My parents scrimped and saved, and when they finally came to the stage in their life where they could afford something extra or something new for themselves, there was no desire or need to have anything more. Life, each other, and family was their wealth and happiness. That alone filled their wants.

Caramel Icing

1 stick butter
1/2 cup brown sugar
1/4 cup evaporated milk
1 teaspoon vanilla
1/2 teaspoon butter flavoring
1 3/4 cups powdered sugar

1. In a heavy saucepan melt the butter over low heat.

2. Add the brown sugar and evaporated milk. Stir until blended.

3. Remove pan from the heat and allow icing to cool.

4. Add the flavorings and powdered sugar and beat with an electric mixer until smooth and thick enough to spread on cake.

Spread icing onto a cooled cake.

Variation: Sprinkle chopped nuts on top of the icing for added richness.

ès   ès   ès

Lemon Topping

3/4 cup granulated sugar
3 tablespoons cornstarch
1/4 teaspoon salt
3/4 cup water
1 1/2 tablespoons butter
1 tablespoon grated lemon rind
1/2 cup fresh strained lemon juice

1. In a heavy saucepan combine the sugar, cornstarch, and salt.

2. Add the water, a little at a time, and stir until well blended.

3. Place pan over medium heat and bring mixture to a boil while stirring constantly.

4. Boil for 1 minute and remove from the heat. Stir in the butter, lemon rind, and juice.

5. Cool topping to almost room temperature before pouring over hot cake or individual slices.

(NOTE: Use with cake or desserts requiring a topping or filling.)

≈ ≈ ≈

Chocolate Drizzle is nice to pour over a white icing or drip alone on a cake top and allow to trickle down the sides. Cupcakes spread with white icing will become festive when drizzled with chocolate, then add bits of colored candies. Colored chocolate, peanut butter, or butterscotch flavored chips will produce a sight that will make an adult want to lick the spoon! Drizzle adds not only a pleasing effect, but a rich chocolate taste.

Chocolate Drizzle

1 6-ounce package semi-sweet chocolate chips
2 tablespoons butter
1 tablespoon whole milk
2 tablespoons corn syrup

1. In the top of a double boiler over low heat, combine the chocolate chips, butter, milk, and corn syrup. Stir until chocolate chips are melted and mixture is smooth.

2. Pour the mixture on top of cake, allowing to drip and run down the sides. The chocolate will turn firm when cooled.

&a   &a   &a

CANDIES

Apple leather is an old-time sweet treat. Since it is made with natural fruit, it is not as refined as candy, therefore is healthier for the children. Little research on nutrition had been done back when Mom was a young girl. By the same token, folks were not as interested because they did not have that information at their fingertips as we do today.

Apple Leather

5 pounds baking apples
6 tablespoons water
1 cup light corn syrup, adjust to sweetness of apples
ground cinnamon, to taste

1. Wash, peel, core and cut the apples in 1/2-inch slices into a heavy kettle. Pour the water over the apples and cover with a lid.

2. Place pan over medium heat and cook until apples are soft. Stir occasionally to prevent scorching.

3. Remove kettle from the heat and transfer the apples to a food mill or food processor. Puree until consistency of smooth applesauce.

4. Add and stir in the corn syrup.

5. Return the kettle of apple mixture to medium heat and cook for 25 to 35 minutes or until it appears thick, stirring frequently.

6. Remove kettle from heat and stir in the cinnamon.

7. Cool slightly. Pour the apple mixture into a jellyroll pan lined with plastic wrap and spread with a spatula until thin and smooth.

8. Preheat an electric oven on the lowest heat, turn off and set pan of leather in for 2 to 3 days. The oven needs to be heated a couple of times a day. If using a gas oven, do not preheat. The leather must be dried until no longer sticky. The underside of the leather will need a few additional hours to dry once removed from the pan and turned over to pull off the plastic wrap.

When thoroughly dried, the leather can be wrapped in plastic wrap and stored in a tight container in a cool, dry place. It will keep for a few months.

(NOTE: Be certain oven is not hot or the plastic wrap will melt and ruin the leather.)

ૐ   ૐ   ૐ

Peanut and Coconut Brittle Candy is a special treat our family savors during the Christmas holidays. The seasons come and go but without fail, Mom makes Peanut and Coconut Brittle each year. She produced about 22 pounds for Christmas 1997. There is a great satisfaction in knowing people enjoy what you take the time to make. This recipe is bound to take one's fancy! Mom feels so blessed to have enjoyed so many Christmas seasons and at the same time, it has truly been a gift from God alone.

Peanut and Coconut Brittle

1 cup granulated sugar
1 cup light corn syrup
1 tablespoon butter
1/2 to 1 teaspoon salt
1 pound raw peanuts
1 teaspoon baking soda
1 cup of broad sliced (1/4 inch wide) dried coconut

1. In a heavy non-stick saucepan combine the sugar, corn syrup, butter, and salt. Place over medium to high heat and stir until the sugar is dissolved. Add the raw peanuts and bring to a boil.

2. Continue to boil the mixture over medium heat, stirring until nuts turn a light brown color.
(NOTE: Do not overcook.)

3. Remove the pan from the heat and quickly stir in the baking soda and dried coconut.

4. Pour the mixture into a greased or buttered foil-lined jellyroll pan. Cool and break into pieces.

Store the brittle in a tight container in a cool, dry place.

Variation: Omit coconut from the recipe.

(NOTE: Broad dried coconut is not available in most grocery stores. It can be found in country stores in Pennsylvania, or speciality stores that carry candy making supplies. Some health food or organic stores also, on occasion, carry this kind of coconut. Flaked and shredded sweetened coconut or fresh coconut will not be successful in this recipe due to the moisture content.)

ਟ‌ਕ   ਟ‌ਕ   ਟ‌ਕ

A variety of candy can emerge from a classic fondant base. You can make additions and replacements, whether it be flavorings, fruits, or nuts, and come up with a concoction just right for your taste. Food coloring plus content can be matched to the holiday or the occasion. The children can help to knead or shape the candy. Getting them involved in cooking is bound to make treasured moments, never to be forgotten, consequently always to be cherished. It seems memories are sometimes jarred by nothing more than the sight of a food-splattered page in a cookbook, a worn cookie tin, or an old and battered utensil.

Fondant

4 1/2 cups powdered sugar, sifted twice
2/3 cup sweetened condensed milk
1 teaspoon vanilla
1/2 teaspoon butter flavoring
1/2 teaspoon coconut flavoring
food coloring to tint
1/2 cup red candied cherries
1/2 cup green candied cherries
1/2 cup candied pineapple
1/2 cup dried coconut
1 cup nuts
1 6-ounce package semi-sweet or milk chocolate chips
(NOTE: Dipping chocolate may be substituted for the chocolate chips.)

1. In a large bowl sift the powdered sugar twice. Set aside.

2. In a mixing bowl combine the condensed milk, flavorings, and food coloring until well blended.

3. Add the sugar to the above mixture and mix until well blended and smooth. Knead until soft and very smooth.

4. Add the fruit and nuts and continue to knead until fruit is distributed evenly.

5. Place in a bowl with a damp cloth over the top and store in the refrigerator over night.

6. Mold the fondant into any shape or size pieces desired.

7. In the top of a double boiler melt the chocolate chips over low heat. Stir until well blended.

8. Pierce the bottom of the pieces of fondant with a toothpick and dip into the chocolate coating. Remove the pick and allow candy to cool on waxed paper.

Store between layers of waxed paper in a tight container.

&a   &a   &a

While we were children growing up, we would not get commercial candy often, so Mom made us taffy. After boiling, she poured it into a greased flat pan to cool until harden. At that point, she cracked the big slab into bite-size pieces with a clean hammer. The jagged edges of the hard candy were sharp. Unfortunately it cut into the tender skin inside our cheeks as we tried to jam in a piece too large to fit our mouths. We winced, but it was worth any pain we suffered.

Be careful not to let taffy scorch or burn while heating. Cook in a heavy pan and watch carefully.

Taffy

2 cups molasses
1 cup granulated sugar
2 tablespoons butter
1 tablespoon vinegar

1. In a heavy saucepan combine all the ingredients. Stir until the sugar is dissolved and bring to a boil over medium heat. If mixture begins to foam while cooking, reduce the heat.

2. Cook until mixture reaches 260 degrees. This is the hard-ball stage. If a thermometer is not available, cook the mixture until a small amount forms a brittle, hard ball when dropped from a spoon into a tin cup filled with cold water.

3. Remove the pan from the heat and pour candy into a buttered pan.

4. When candy is cool enough to handle with buttered hands, pull until it turns to a light color and becomes hard. Cut into bite-size pieces with buttered kitchen shears. Taffy does not require to be pulled but can be allowed to cool in a buttered flat pan and cracked into small pieces.

Variation: Add a cup of chopped nuts to taffy before pouring it into the pan to cool. If pulling taffy, chop nuts very fine.

(NOTE: If taffy gets sugary, return to heavy saucepan with 2 tablespoons corn syrup and 3/4 cup water. Place pan over low heat and cook until syrup and water is dissolved into the taffy. Proceed to Step 4 in this recipe.)

ða   ða   ða

Making potato candy for Christmas is a popular tradition in the western counties of Maryland. Mom does not make potato candy, but we found this old-fashioned recipe that you might wish to try. It's simple, easy, and tasty!

Making candy can provide an opportunity for even the youngest member of the family to participate. Being a Christian family, Christmas Day is a celebration of a blessed event. Even though my parents never entertained celebrities--their guests as well as the occasion--were most important to them. No better or more important meal than Mom's Christmas dinner was ever served in the White House, I believe. It seemed when life was just about to wear you down, a joyous occasion came on the horizon to boost our spirits. Extravagant gifts and beautiful decorations were not afforded, but love and good cheer were always spread in abundance in our home. Special foods that were only served on this special day were cooked and baked. From these, a bountiful table was set. Children and grownups gathered around the table while the adults helped the little ones as they enjoyed taking a close look at what was being served in each dish.

Potato Candy

1/2 cup warm mashed potato
(NOTE: Do not add milk to mashed potato.)
1/2 teaspoon salt
1 teaspoon vanilla
1/2 teaspoon butter flavoring
1 pound sifted powdered sugar
peanut butter, for filling

1. In a mixing bowl combine the mashed potato, salt, vanilla, and flavoring.

2. Gradually add the powdered sugar to the potato mixture. Stir with a spoon until blended.

3. When mixture becomes a stiff dough, knead with your hands until soft and very smooth.

4. Place the dough in a bowl, cover with a damp cloth, and refrigerate overnight or until firm.

5. Roll the dough thin, 1/8 inch thick, on a cloth dusted with powdered sugar.

6. Spread the candy dough with peanut butter (use any peanut butter that will not separate from the oil). Roll like a jellyroll log and slice.

7. Store slices between waxed paper in a tight container in a cool, dry place.

(NOTE: The amount of water retained in the potato effects the amount of sugar needed to make a stiff dough. Additional sugar may be added. Do not use milk or butter when mashing the potato.)

☙   ☙   ☙

Every year Dad planted and grew popcorn in the truck patch. The patch was a plot of ground, about an acre, where sweet corn and pumpkins, besides a variety of melons, were planted during spring and early summer. It was like having an extra garden in a field near the farm buildings.

Most of her life, Mom used a cast-iron skillet for popping corn. When she raised the lid to check what was happening inside the pan, she found those little kernels were literally exploding with tasty fluff!

Once in awhile a snowstorm would arrive, dropping tons of snow. During these stormy periods, Dad would hurry to finish the barn work, then we would all spend as much time as possible gathered in the house where it was warm. We listened to the radio or sat around and snoozed. The children popped corn and if we had a new catalog, well, more shopping was thought about than you can imagine. We were truly wishing! In that time and place, it seemed that the catalogs carried everything we wanted: musical instruments, perfumes, clothing for the family, kitchen stoves, dolls, patent medicines, something for everyone!

Caramel Popcorn

Bake at 250 degrees.

7 quarts popped corn
1 cup butter
2 cups brown sugar
1/2 cup light corn syrup
1 1/2 teaspoons vanilla
1 teaspoon salt
1/2 teaspoon baking soda

1. Pop corn and transfer to a large metal dishpan. Set aside.

2. In a heavy saucepan combine the butter, sugar, and syrup. Boil the mixture for 5 minutes and remove the pan from the heat.

3. Immediately add while stirring briskly the flavoring, salt, and baking soda.

4. Pour syrup over popcorn and stir to spread evenly.

5. Bake at 250 degrees for 1 hour, stirring every 15 minutes with a large spoon.

6. Spread caramel corn in a lightly buttered flat pan to cool.

Store in a tight can in a cool, dry place. It will keep for several weeks.

&a.   &a.   &a.

At our house, popcorn balls were made and enjoyed by nearly everyone. There were always a few who feared dental problems might occur if they indulged in the tacky treat, but with a teeny bit of encouragement, even they yielded to the holiday speciality. All of the children could get their hands in this project. In the country, popcorn was used in the holiday festivities. During the struggling years the older children popped the corn and strung it on thread to use as Christmas tree decorations.

In the county schools, extra activities planned for Christmas were not heard off. The children strictly learned reading, writing, and arithmetic while in class. The fun times were provided in the home and church.

Schools were not organized by the state until right after the Civil War. And then it was years before the Frederick country schools were organized by any other than a small group of men of integrity from the community. They would meet to make plans for building and operating a local school, acting like a board of directors. There were no big blueprints available for the project, only a show of willing men who were interested in the future leaders of their homeland, working with a readiness to get the job done.

Popcorn Balls

4 to 5 quarts popped popcorn
1 cup granulated sugar
1 cup light corn syrup
1/2 cup water
1 teaspoon vanilla, if desired

1. Prepare popcorn and sprinkle lightly with salt. Transfer to a large metal dishpan. Set aside.

2. In a heavy saucepan combine the sugar, corn syrup, and water.

3. Boil the mixture over medium to high heat until it spins a thin thread when dropped from a spoon, or until it forms a hard ball when a small amount of syrup is dropped into a metal cup of cold water. Add the flavoring and stir.
(NOTE: Add a few drops of food coloring to give a hint of color for a special occassion.)

4. Pour the hot syrup over the popcorn and quickly stir with a spoon. With hands buttered well, carefully form into balls.
(NOTE: Be careful when handling this syrup--it is very hot to the hands.)

When balls are cooled, store in a tight container in a cool, dry place. The balls will keep for several weeks.

&a.   &a.   &a.

I found this anonymous saying and it surely strikes home. "What is it to stay young? To stay young is the ability to hold fast to old friends and to make new ones, to open our heart's door quickly to a light knock." How true it is!

Whether young or old, many of us have a sweet tooth. Of course, what a better way to satisfy than with smooth caramels?

Caramels

1 1/3 cups sweetened condensed milk
2 cups brown sugar
3/4 cup light corn syrup
1/2 cup butter
1/2 teaspoon salt
1/2 teaspoon vanilla
1/2 teaspoon butter flavoring
1 cup nuts

1. In a heavy saucepan combine the condensed milk, sugar, corn syrup, butter, and salt.

2. Place pan over medium to high heat and cook ingredients while stirring constantly with a spoon until mixture reaches 246 degrees on a candy thermometer.

3. Remove the pan from the heat and stir in the flavorings and nuts.

4. Pour and spread the mixture into a buttered 9-inch square pan. When cooled, cut into squares.

❧   ❧   ❧

Seafoam Candy

3 cups brown sugar
1/4 to 1/2 teaspoon salt
3/4 cup water
2 egg whites
1 to 1 1/2 teaspoons vanilla
1 cup coarsely chopped pecans

1. In a heavy saucepan over medium to high heat cook the sugar, salt and water to 252 degrees or until it forms a hard ball when a small amount is dropped into a metal cup of cold water. Remove from the heat.

2. While the sugar water is cooking, beat the egg whites until very stiff. Set aside.

3. Pour the hot syrup over the stiffly beaten egg whites. Add the vanilla and nuts. Beat until the mixture holds its shape.

4. Drop the candy onto waxed paper from a spoon. Allow to set until firm.

Store in a tight container in a cool dry place.

&ta; &ta; &ta;

PIES

On days when Mom returned from the pantry with the rolling pin and board in her hands, we knew she was about to bake pies. I recall how carefully she made each family member's favorite flavor of pie every so often, working hard and long to achieve perfectly finished pies.

I look back to see Mom using her fingers and thumb to flute the dough around the edge of the pie. At that same time, as my young eyes watched, I wondered how she could work so quickly and create such perfection! Mom baked lots of pies because she thought they took less time to make than cakes. In the busy seasons, one of the girls usually baked while Mom cooked the meal.

Today when baking, Mom continues to use the walnut rolling pin and board her Uncle Charles H. Gaver made for her before she married in 1916.

Pie Dough

Dough for a two-crust 9-inch pie.

2 cups all-purpose flour
1 teaspoon salt
2/3 cup solid vegetable shortening
4 tablespoons cold or ice water

1. In a mixing bowl combine the flour and salt.

2. Add the shortening and cut into the flour mixture with a fork.

3. Form a well in the flour and shortening mixture with your hand. Pour the water into the well.

4. Slowly and lightly mix the dough with your fingertips until blended.

5. Press the dough into a ball and roll thin with a rolling pin on a floured surface.

(NOTE: When making pie crusts, bake at 450 degrees for about 8 minutes.)

(NOTE: Dough may be made in advance and stored in the refrigerator for a few days before using. Keep leftover dough in the freezer for topping potpie, or bake a pie shell to freeze and fill with custard later.)

Yield: 2 9-inch crusts.

ᨠ   ᨠ   ᨠ

Even today, there is seldom a week that goes by without Mom baking a pie, cake, or cookies. She often bakes for a sick friend or family member, or for folks who have suffered tragedy. Ever since I can remember, she has had compassion for the hurting one.

To my way of thinking, I believe the fact that Mom still sees things to do for others and does not contemplate quitting and giving up; that is what keeps her going at a ripe old age. Those conditions, as well as a hearty, jolly laugh with her friends and family are worth more than any medication available. I trust and praise God each day for Mom's strength and fortitude. She sets a good example for us. It is so true that a reputation is made in a moment, but character is built in a lifetime.

Meringue for Pies

Bake at 350 degrees.

3 egg whites
1/4 teaspoon cream of tartar
6 tablespoons granulated sugar

1. In a large mixer bowl beat egg whites and cream of tartar until foamy with an electric mixer.

2. Continue to beat at medium speed. While egg whites are firm and before they get stiff gradually add the sugar, a little at a time. Increase the speed to high and continue to beat until stiff.

3. Spread the meringue on top of the custard pie and to the very edge of the shell to prevent shrinking and seeping.

4. Bake in the oven for about 10 minutes or until meringue is lightly browned.

Variation: Top raw meringue with coconut.
(NOTE: Watch carefully--coconut will burn easily.)

(NOTE: Do not use commercial instant pudding pie filling when topping pie with meringue. The filling cannot tolerate the heat required to bake the meringue.)

Yield: Meringue to cover one 9-inch pie.

It would seem that custard pies did not keep long without refrigeration. On second thought, custard pies would not have kept long, with or without refrigeration at our house! Someone could always eat an extra slice of pie. The consistency of this custard pie is firm when cooled and allows a nice slice to be cut without falling apart.

Years ago in the countryside, Mr. Albert Phebus, a produce peddler, traveled from door to door in his green Chevrolet pickup truck. He came to the farm about once a week and Mom bought watermelons and cantaloupes from him. Sometimes she purchased a whole hand of bananas, and when she did, we knew for sure that we could expect banana cornstarch custard pie.

Vanilla Cornstarch Custard Pie

Bake at 350 degrees.

1/4 cup granulated sugar
2 tablespoons cornstarch
1/4 teaspoon salt
1 egg, beaten
2 cups whole milk
1 tablespoon butter
2 teaspoons vanilla

1. Prepare dough for one pie. Roll thin on a floured surface. Bake 2 pie shells. Freeze a baked shell to use later.

2. In a heavy saucepan combine the sugar, cornstarch, and salt. Set aside.

3. In a separate bowl beat the egg with a rotary beater or wire whisk until light yellow. Add to the sugar mixture.

4. Add the milk and stir until blended.

5. Place pan over low to medium heat and boil for 1 minute while stirring constantly to avoid scorching.

6. Remove pan from the heat. Add the butter and vanilla. Stir until blended.

7. Pour custard into a baked pie shell. Cool and top with a meringue.

8. Bake in the oven for about 10 minutes or until meringue is lightly browned.

Cool before serving.

Variation: Banana Cornstarch Custard Pie--line baked shell with sliced bananas and fill with custard.

Variation: Coconut Cornstarch Custard Pie--add 1 cup coconut to cooked custard.

Variation: Chocolate Cornstarch Custard Pie--add about 3 to 4 tablespoons of baking cocoa powder to the custard before cooking.

Yield: 1 9-inch pie.

❧   ❧   ❧

When Grandmother Grossnickel pushed wood into the outdoor bake oven and fired it up, she planned to have all the baked goods she was going to bake that day prepared and ready for the oven.

As a tiny girl, my mom along with her mother regularly made Devil Billies on baking day. A Devil Billy is nothing more than pie crust that they rolled thin, spread with butter, then sprinkled with ground cinnamon and granulated sugar. Next, they rolled it into a jellyroll log, transferred it to a large fresh cabbage leaf, carefully placed it on the hot floor of the bake oven, not using a rack or pan.

Grandmother and my mother baked bread in this oven as well. In the following excerpt from my book, *So Many Mornings*, Mom describes how she (Letha Wiles) baked bread with her mother (Clara Grossnickel) back at the beginning of the 1900s:

My mother baked bread in an outdoor bake oven. These ovens were built from brick or stone and joined with mortar. For convenience, they were usually situated close to the kitchen entrance with a woodpile nearby. At our house, the oven was outside the back door directly under the old pear tree that stood near the dinner bell. Cooling shelves were erected at its sides. A roof extended out over them; it was intended for some protection from the rain and snow. We baked bread no matter what the weather, hot or cold.

Early in the morning, Mother went out the back door with her 'barn burner' matches in hand. She was going to start a wood fire in the bake oven. She pushed plenty of dry wood in to ensure an intense heat. Once the flame was blazing, back into the kitchen she came to prepare the dough. She mixed the ingredients in a big wooden dough tray. The tray was rectangular, being about eight or ten inches deep. She baked rolls as well as loaves.

After the wood burned and the coals died down, she dragged them with a rake from the oven allowing them to drop onto the ground. Then she brought a bucket of water, a long wooden broomstick and a big cloth. She wrapped the cloth around the stick, dipped it into the bucket of water, and swabbed the inside of the red-hot oven where the fire had been minutes earlier. This cooled it to the right degree for baking. After the oven was prepared, she stuck her arm inside the opening to test the temperature. Having no thermometer, if it felt right, she put the pans of risen bread dough in, then patiently waited for them to bake. There was no door on this oven so she propped a large stone over the hole.

Mother knew how long to wait before rolling the stone away from the opening. Somehow she pulled those big pans of bread from that hot oven. Then she carefully sat the loaves on the shelves to cool. The bread smelled so good! It was no sooner out of the oven that I wanted a slice to eat. I especially liked her fresh bread when the crust was on the dark side. Oh my, how I did love it! Later in the day, she called me to come help carry it into the kitchen for storing.

Devil Billies are a nice treat for the children, especially when they are in the kitchen while you are baking pies to be served at a later time and you need a treat to tide the little ones over.

Devil Billy

Bake at 425 degrees.

prepared pie dough
butter
granulated sugar
ground cinnamon

1. On a floured surface roll (any amount) pie dough to the thickness used for a pie crust. Spread thick with butter and sprinkle generously with sugar and cinnamon.

2. Roll the dough like a jellyroll log until it is about 3/4 inch in diameter. Place coiled on a greased pie plate.

3. Bake in the oven until lightly browned. Baking time will vary with the size of the Billie.

Cut the Billie and serve hot or cold with hot coffee. Top with whipped cream or ice cream.

ả.   ả.   ả.

Pecan pie is extremely rich, according to Mom's way of thinking. She did not bake pecan pies, but this is a nice tempting recipe our family uses, so you might enjoy as well.

Pecan Pie

Bake at 350 degrees.

3 eggs, beaten
1 cup white corn syrup
1 cup light brown sugar
1/3 cup melted butter
1 1/2 teaspoons vanilla
1/2 teaspoon salt
1 1/4 cups pecans

1. Prepare dough for one pie. Roll thin on a floured surface. Use half to line a pie pan and set aside. With remaining dough, bake a pie shell to freeze and use later.

2. In a mixing bowl beat the eggs with a rotary beater or wire whisk until light yellow.

3. Add the corn syrup, brown sugar, butter, vanilla, and salt. Stir with a spoon until well blended. Mix in the pecans; they will rise to the top of the baked pie.

4. Line a 9-inch pie pan with dough and pour in the mixture.

5. Bake in the oven for 45 to 50 minutes.

Serve plain, with whipped cream or ice cream.

Yield: 1 9-inch pie.

&ea; &ea; &ea;

Mom worked with this mincemeat recipe for years, adding this ingredient as well as taking that ingredient away from the mixture, until she attained the taste she desired. Suggestions were snatched from recipes she read in the daily newspaper or farm magazines, but she always found herself returning to this basic recipe. It is a favorite pie with many of her friends here in the Middletown Valley. She is not making any first prize claims, mind you, but you can arrive at a conclusion after tasting this for yourself.

Oftentimes cooks prepare mincemeat pie for the fall holiday menus. I would consider it a festive dessert. It is a rich, heavy pie and most folks will plunge into having a slice even after a big meal is enjoyed. This mincemeat recipe is given with the intent of making a supply to store and use at a later time.

Letha's Mincemeat Pie Filling

5 pounds lean ground beef
5 pounds sausage, loose
10 pounds tart apples, chopped fine
8 pounds light raisins
3 pounds granulated sugar
1 pint dark molasses
1 tablespoon salt
4 tablespoons ground cinnamon
1 tablespoon ground cloves
3 quarts of sherry wine or cider
(NOTE: When using cider, loosen the lid on the jug and let sit in a cool place for 4 to 5 weeks prior to making mincemeat. If using wine, Mom prefers one-half water and one-half wine.)

1. In a large kettle combine the beef and sausage in enough water to nearly cover. Cook over medium heat only until the meat changes color. Allow meat to drain in a colander.

2. Combine the meat, apples, raisins, sugar, molasses, salt, cinnamon, and cloves. Stir until mixed well.

3. Add the sherry wine or cider and stir until well blended.

4. Cook the mincemeat slowly for 2 hours. Pour boiling mincemeat into sterilized canning jars and seal with lids. Or fill jars, seal, and place in a hot water bath for 30 minutes.

(NOTE: Mincemeat will keep for several years when canned and stored in a cool, dry place.)

(NOTE: Mincemeat for one pie can be frozen in individual containers.)

Yield: 14 quarts.

ᴥ   ᴥ   ᴥ

Letha's Mincemeat Pie

Bake at 400 degrees.

4 cups prepared mincemeat
prepared pie dough
2 tablespoons butter, to spread on bottom crust

1. Prepare dough for a two-crust pie. On a floured surface roll the dough thin to line the pie pan and cover the top.

2. Line the bottom of a 9-inch pie pan with dough. Spread lightly with butter. Pour in the mincemeat.

3. Wet the edge of the dough with water and cover with top crust. Press down on the rim of the pie plate and trim excess dough from the edge. Crimp edge with fingers or a fork. Cut several slits in the top crust with a sharp knife to allow the steam to escape.

4. Bake in the oven for 30 to 35 minutes or until lightly browned.

(NOTE: Pies can be baked days in advance. Store in the refrigerator. Warm uncovered in a low temperature oven before serving. Baked pies can also be frozen, thawed and warmed before serving. Do not microwave.)

Yield: 1 9-inch pie.

ॐ   ॐ   ॐ

Egg custard pies require lots of eggs. Every farmer's wife liked having the hens on the farm, assuring them a fresh supply of eggs to use in cooking. By the same token, the farmer enjoyed his wife preparing plenty of fresh eggs for his breakfast.

Mom kept a flock of Rhode Island Red laying hens on the farm because she liked the large brown eggs they produced. Not only that, she preferred the plush appearance of the red feathered chicken over the white and black speckled feathered Dominecker or the white feathered White Rocks.

Egg Custard Pie

Bake at 400 degrees.

2 2/3 cups scalded whole milk
4 eggs
2/3 cup granulated sugar
1/2 teaspoon salt
2 teaspoons vanilla
ground nutmeg, if desired

1. Prepare dough for one pie. Roll thin on a floured surface. Use half to line a pie pan and set aside. With remaining dough, bake a pie shell to freeze and use later.

2. In a heavy saucepan scald the milk over medium heat. A light skim will form on top of the milk.
(NOTE: Do not allow to boil.)

3. In a mixing bowl beat the eggs with the rotary beater or wire whisk until light yellow. Combine the milk and remaining ingredients with the eggs. Stir until well blended.

4. Pour the mixture into a 9-inch pie pan lined with dough. *(NOTE: Do not use a top crust.)*

5. Bake at 400 degrees, on the lowest rack, for 10 minutes, then lower the temperature to 300 degrees for 15 minutes. Lower the temperature to 250 degrees for the last 5 minutes of baking.
(NOTE: Watch carefully--do not allow custard to boil.)

Yield: 1 9-inch pie.

ءﻪ   ءﻪ   ءﻪ

Egg Custard

Bake at 400 degrees.

1. Follow the recipe for making the Egg Custard Pie on page 183, but do not prepare dough.

2. Bake in glass baking cups placed in a shallow pan filled with about 1 inch of water.

3. Bake at 400 degrees, on the lowest rack, for 10 minutes, then lower the temperature to 300 degrees for 15 minutes. Lower the temperature to 250 degrees for the last 5 minutes of baking.
(NOTE: Watch carefully--do not allow custard to boil.)

ءﻪ   ءﻪ   ءﻪ

Lott's Two-Crust Lemon Pie is a zesty old-fashioned pie. The filling is amazingly smooth and pungent with lemon flavor. When eating this pie you can enjoy the aroma before the fork ever arrives at the mouth. This recipe reminds Mom of days gone by!

Years ago, whenever a neighbor experienced a death in the household, folks prepared food for the bereaved family. This kind gesture unburdened them from preparing food during this time of sorrow. When Grandmother and Grandpap Grossnickel visited and offered their sympathy, she often got up early in the morning and baked pies to take along.

Mom firmly believes no matter what adverse circumstances come--and they do come--we must be ardent and never hindered to the point of giving up. Don't lose your will to press on. In spite of our failings and weaknesses, through all trials and obstacles, God's promise to help us is the same as the day He made it. His word will not change. Once again, these promises are the means of rescue. I find this still true, therefore, I acknowledge the fact along with my mother. Confidence in these promises will bring sweet peace and finally rest! I have heard repeated many times, that *you never lose so much as when you lose your peace*!

Mom's life has been rich in her faith and she not only wishes to pass along recipes to you, but the hope and trust in God. Success with happiness is tied directly to Him, she believes. She trusts the living God, giving the high recommendation that He is the key to live a long and healthy life. Mom would not pretend, but she would be quick to tell you that her feet have walked through too many rivers of problems, and through these experiences she has gained too much through faith to lose sight of her goal now!

Some of us may have a few furrows dug deep into our forehead, because the world is intent on dragging us down, but don't ever give up.

Lott's Two-Crust Lemon Pie

Bake at 400 degrees.

2 small or 1 very large grated lemon
(NOTE: Use juice and rind of the lemon.)
1 egg
1/2 to 3/4 cup granulated sugar
3 tablespoons all-purpose flour
1/2 teaspoon salt
1 cup thick dairy sour cream
5 cups tap water

1. Prepare pie dough for one pie. On a floured surface roll the dough thin to line the pie pan and cover the top of the pie.

2. Wash the lemons throughly and cut into halves. Squeeze the juice from the lemon. Grate the pulp and rind, using all but the ends of the lemon. Set aside.

3. In a separate bowl beat the egg with a rotary beater or wire whisk until light yellow.

4. Pour all the ingredients into a heavy saucepan and stir until blended. Boil and stir the mixture until slightly thickened. Cool to almost room temperature.

5. Line a 9-inch pie pan with dough. Pour in the lemon mixture.

6. Wet the edge of the dough with water and cover with the top crust. Press down on the rim of the pie plate and trim excess dough from the edge. Crimp edge with fingers or a fork. Cut several slits in top crust with a sharp knife to allow the steam to escape.

7. Bake in the oven for 20 to 30 minutes or until lightly browned.

Yield: 1 9-inch pie.

ð ð ð

It can truthfully be said, no pie is more flavorful than pumpkin pie. Spices such as cinnamon, ginger, nutmeg and cloves that are baked in the pie will create a wonderful aroma in the kitchen. Of course, the flavor will delight your taste buds. This old-fashioned pumpkin pie is substantial, in addition to being more hardy than some of the delicate chiffon types of custard that we make today.

Pumpkins mature in the fall of the year when the weather commences to turn cold. Mom prefers the goose neck pale yellow-skinned variety and she preserves a supply to use at a later time by either canning or freezing. Of course, if pumpkins are in season or out of season, the pie will be welcomed on your table. What a treat!

Pumpkin Pie

Bake at 325 degrees.

2 cups cooked pumpkin
3/4 cup granulated sugar
2 tablespoons cornstarch
1/2 teaspoon salt
1/2 to 1 teaspoon ground ginger
1/4 teaspoon ground nutmeg
1 teaspoon ground cinnamon
3 eggs
1/2 cup whole milk
1 large can evaporated milk

1. Prepare dough for one pie. On a floured surface roll the dough thin and line two pie pans. Set aside.

(NOTE: When using fresh pumpkin, wash and peel away the outside skin. Remove the seeds and chop the flesh into 2-inch blocks. Cook until tender in a heavy saucepan with about 1/2 inch water in the bottom of a 5-quart Dutch oven. When tender, beat with a mixer or food processor until smooth.)

2. In a large mixing bowl combine the pumpkin, sugar, cornstarch, salt, ginger, nutmeg, and cinnamon. Stir with a spoon until well blended. Set aside.

3. In a separate bowl slightly beat the eggs with a rotary beater or wire whisk. Add the whole milk and evaporated milk. Stir in the pumpkin mixture and blend well.

4. Pour pumpkin filling into two 9-inch pie pans lined with dough.

5. Bake at 325 degrees for 50 minutes. Reduce the heat to 300 degrees and bake for 20 additional minutes. Bake until the pumpkin filling in the middle of the pie is well set. *(NOTE: Do not allow filling to boil.)*

Serve with a dollop of whipped cream placed on top.

Yield: 2 9-inch pies.

&a   &a   &a

Grape lovers will know they are going first-class when indulging a bite of fresh grape pie that is served as a seasonal treat.

In years gone by, most often every farm had a concord grape harbor growing somewhere nearby the house. When an abundance of grapes were produced, Mom made grape pies. Grapes are popular to use when making jelly and jams. In the days preceding freezers, foods in season were either eaten promptly or canned for later use. Mom canned grapes in excess of what we could use when picked fresh from the vine.

In the good old days in the summertime, Mom hated to push wood into the firebox of the old black iron cook stove in order to get the oven hot for baking. Within minutes, the whole house became stifling, and unfortunately, it stayed hot for most of the day. Working in the heat in an enclosed area can sap your energy in no time flat. It seemed that only when it was morning, and time to arise from the bed, that the cool of the night had made the house somewhat comfortable.

Grape Pie

Bake at 425 degrees.

5 to 6 cups concord grapes
1 1/3 cups granulated sugar
4 tablespoons all-purpose flour
1/2 teaspoon salt
2 teaspoons of fresh squeezed lemon juice
4 tablespoons butter, to spread on bottom crust and dot on
    top of fruit

1. Prepare dough for one pie. On a floured surface roll the dough thin to line the pie pan and cover the top of the pie. Set aside.

2. Wash and remove skins from the concord grapes. Reserve the skins. Place the pulp of the grapes in a heavy saucepan and bring to a rolling boil over medium to high heat. Stir often to prevent scorching.
(NOTE: Do not add water.)

3. Transfer the hot grapes to a fine colander or strainer and press through to remove the seeds.

4. In a large bowl combine the sugar, flour, and salt. Add the lemon juice, grape pulp, and reserved skins. Stir until well blended.

5. Line a 9-inch pie pan with dough. Spread lightly with butter. Pour in the grape mixture and dot top with butter.

6. Wet the edge of the dough with water and cover with the top crust. Press down on the rim of the pie plate and trim excess dough from the edge. Crimp edge with fingers or a fork. Cut several slits in the top crust with a sharp knife to allow steam to escape.

7. Bake in the oven for 35 minutes or until lightly browned.

Yield: 1 9-inch pie.

 za.   za.   za.

Nothing will make a better pie than fresh berries--so, happy berry picking! Mom never thinks of picking huckleberries, a type of glossy black wild blueberry, without recalling the days in her early years of marriage, and going deep into the mountain around the Middlepoint area of Maryland by horse and spring wagon to pick berries in the wild patches. Most any wild berry, like elderberries or fox grapes, were not left to go to waste.

The most productive huckleberry patches were found in areas of the mountain where fires had at sometime in the past erupted with flames. The large trees usually survived the flames, and with enough vegetation destroyed, sunshine could lead in to the soil to encourage and sprout up new berry bushes. On an acreage where timber or logs have been cut from the woods, with only the tree stumps remaining, thick berry bushes most often can be found.

The body took a beating in the woods as the thorns pricked the tender layer of skin on the arms and legs. Of course, garments were also snagged or torn on the thorny bushes. Long ankle-length dresses were in style for the ladies, and unfortunately they were expected to wear them whatever the occasion. Short hem lines or women dressed in slacks were thought indecent in Mom's little world. These women could easily get their clothing hung up on a thorny bush and yank out a swatch of fabric ever so quickly.

To reach the large berry patches, sometimes it was necessary to wade through areas where the brushes and thick deep underbrush had grown. Mom feared snakes might be hiding in these wilderness areas, and she hated with a passion the thought of a reptile being near her. All this, however, is the price one paid for fresh berries back in the good old days. The hard truth: life was a risky business in more ways than in the huckleberry patch! Even today, with the mention of huckleberries, Mom will quickly reminisce about her adventures in the berry patches! My oldest brother will tell you a few stories as well.

Wild Huckleberry Pie

Bake at 425 degrees.

2 teaspoons lemon juice and fill cup with water to 1/2 mark
(NOTE: Or use juice from canned berries.)
1/2 cup granulated sugar
(NOTE: Adjust sugar when using canned berries.)
2 tablespoons cornstarch or all-purpose flour
2 3/4 cups fresh huckleberries
4 tablespoons butter, to spread on bottom crust and dot on
   top fruit

1. Prepare dough for one pie. On a floured surface roll the dough thin to line the pie pan and cover the top of the pie. Set aside.

2. In a small saucepan mix together the juice, sugar, and cornstarch or flour until blended. Add the berries to the mixture and cook over medium heat until steaming hot.

3. Line a 9-inch pie pan with dough. Spread lightly with butter. Pour in the berry mixture and dot top with butter.

4. Wet the edge of the dough with water and cover with the top crust. Press down on the rim of the pie plate and trim excess dough from the edge. Crimp edge with fingers or a fork. Cut several slits in the top crust with a sharp knife to allow steam to escape.

5. Bake in the oven for 35 minutes or until lightly browned.

Yield: 1 9-inch pie.

❧   ❧   ❧

While plums are not popular for making a fruit pie, they do produce a tasty one! Most varieties of plums can never be sweetened beyond their sour twinge no matter how much sugar is added. In Mom's young days, pies were not removed from the table or returned to the pie safe if a slice had been taken from the plate. If the men came into the house and at the same time saw an opened pie, they grabbed a knife, cut a slice, picked it up in their hands to devour as they hurried back to the barn or field.

I remember the farmers' wives kept an old-fashioned glass spoon holder on the table. A holder was shaped like a wide vase, had two small handles on the sides, and some were pretty fancy. On some tables the spoon holder could be a canning jar or a small pitcher, which worked just as well. Spoons were not placed by each place setting on the table because the housewife did not care to wash one thing unnecessarily. So the holder on the table kept spoons handy for those who needed one. Jelly jars, butter dish, sugar bowl, vinegar cruet, tooth pick holder, syrup jar, plus a large salt and pepper shaker set remained after the table was cleared of food and dirty dishes. Mom spread a cloth over all the containers to keep them out of sight.

Without the modern-day kitchens there were no rows of cabinets for storing frequently used items. No electric dishwasher either! The wives and mothers in the family had so much to do, they had no concern about how the kitchen table appeared between meals so long as things were neat and tidy. At that point in time, high style and lavish home furnishings were not the norm or what one expected to find in the country kitchen.

Folks learned to improvise and use whatever was on hand to make do--their prized possession was most often something meager and made with their imagination and ingenuity. They knew the true meaning of "makeshift." The decorating theme in the homes in those early days was cleanliness and accessibility: making things handy whenever possible. Maybe fresh cut flowers graced the table in the summertime. Often they were carelessly stuck in an old jar, perhaps one with a crack around the top edge that had been discarded because it could no longer keep a seal.

While the family was living at home on the farm, we learned to save steps whenever possible. Another time saver practiced in our home was that after we finished the main course, we filled our dinner plates with dessert to avoid soiling an extra dish. The children took turns washing high stacks of dishes for the large family, and consequently we become wise quickly. Not using so many dishes made less work, and these were my thoughts when it was my turn in the dishpan of hot lye-soap water. Immediately, upon notice of whose turn was at hand, everyone's consideration was more earnestly appreciated! There was no commercial liquid dish soap to whisk away the grease, while providing a gentleness to your hands. I can still see that cake of lye soap on a saucer by the kitchen sink.

Plum Pie

Bake at 400 degrees.

1 quart canned pitted plums and the juice
1 tablespoon instant clear jell or cornstarch
1/4 teaspoon salt
1 to 2 tablespoons butter, to spread on bottom crust

1. Prepare dough for one pie. On a floured surface roll the dough to line the pie pan and cover the top of the pie. Set aside.

2. Remove the pits and quarter the plums. Place in a heavy saucepan. Combine all the ingredients except the butter and heat over medium to high heat until plums are hot.
(NOTE: When using fresh plums, add 1/2 cup of water and cook until thoroughly heated.)

3. Line a 9-inch pie pan with dough. Spread lightly with butter. Pour in the plum mixture.

4. Wet the edge of the dough with water and cover with top crust. Press down on the rim of the pie plate and trim excess dough from the edge. Crimp edge with fingers or a fork. Cut slits in top crust with a sharp knife to allow the steam to escape.

5. Bake in the oven for 25 to 35 minutes or until lightly browned.

Serve a slice with a glass of cold milk.

Yield: 1 9-inch pie.

~ ~ ~

Of all desserts, pies may be the first choice to many folks, and this is especially true in our family. It is a perfect dessert to serve with any menu, at a casual picnic, or at a fine dining occasion. Mom seldom, if ever, measured ingredients to make pie dough; she simply knew from the feel and look of the mixture when to stop pouring and mixing. Though cookbooks were not a necessity when she was cooking, I am sure there was a rare moment when a slip of an ingredient would have caused Mom to wonder what had gone wrong! Frequently, modern-day cooks long to achieve Mom's level of confidence when cooking, but at the same time most will agree that this talent comes with many years of experience.

Fresh Fruit or Berry Pie
(Blackberry, Blueberry, Raspberry, Cherry, or Peach)

Bake at 425 degrees.

4 cups fresh fruit
1 to 1 1/2 cups granulated sugar, adjust to tartness of fruit
1/3 to 1/2 cup all-purpose flour
1/2 teaspoon salt
4 tablespoons butter, to spread on bottom crust and dot on
    top of fruit

1. Prepare dough for one pie. On a floured surface roll the dough thin to line the pie pan and cover the top of the pie. Set aside.

2. In a small bowl combine the sugar, flour, and salt. Toss the mixture over the fruit. Cook over medium heat in a heavy saucepan until fruit is hot.
(NOTE: Do not allow to boil.)

3. Line a 9-inch pie pan with dough. Spread lightly with butter. Pour in the fruit mixture and dot top with butter.

4. Wet the edge of the dough with water and cover with the top crust or lattice work strips. Press down on the rim of the pie plate and trim excess dough from the edge. Crimp edge with fingers or a fork. When using a solid top crust, cut several slits with a sharp knife to allow steam to escape.

(NOTE: For interwoven lattice top, weave 1/2-inch strips of dough crisscross on top of pie.)

5. Bake in the oven for 35 to 45 minutes or until lightly browned.

Yield: 1 9-inch pie.

Back in the early 1900s to 1930s, it was not uncommon to serve pie to the farm family after they had eaten a hearty breakfast. A farmer's home-cooked breakfast usually consisted of eggs, meat, potatoes, gravy, bread or biscuits, canned fruit, with milk in addition to coffee...and then pie!

Commonly, such chores as preparing the farmland for planting, demanded the men to walk, following behind the horse, not riding a modern-day tractor as practiced today. The farmer's day was long and exhausting. The average American worker may have earned about twelve dollars a week during the early 1900s, but farmhands never reached this level of wages. Without a doubt, whatever they did collect for their week's work was definitely earned by the sweat of their brow!

Canned Fruit or Berry Pie

Bake at 425 degrees.

3 1/2 cups canned fruit, drained
1/2 cup reserved fruit juice
3/4 cup granulated sugar, adjust to tartness of fruit
4 tablespoons instant clear jell or cornstarch
1/2 teaspoon salt
4 tablespoons butter, to spread on bottom crust and dot on
    top of fruit

1. Prepare dough for one pie. On a floured surface roll the dough thin to line the pie pan and cover the top of the pie. Set aside.

2. Drain the fruit and reserve 1/2 cup of juice.

3. In a small bowl combine the sugar, jell or cornstarch, and salt. Toss over the fruit. Add the reserved juice. Place pan over medium to high heat and stir until fruit boils. Boil for 1 minute.
(NOTE: Food coloring can be added to enhance the color of the filling.)

4. Line a 9-inch pie pan with dough. Spread lightly with butter. Pour in the fruit mixture and dot top with butter.

5. Wet the edge of the dough with water and cover with the top crust. Press down on the rim of the pie plate and trim excess dough from the edge. Crimp edge with fingers or a fork. Cut several slits in the top crust with a sharp knife to allow the steam to escape.

6. Bake in the oven for 35 to 45 minutes or until lightly browned.

Serve fruit pie hot or cold, with or without ice cream.

Yield: 1 9-inch pie.

ð ð ð

No pie is more American than apple pie. It is a favorite to millions! Many housewives, Mom included, stored the freshly baked pies in a pie safe. The safe did not provide very safe keeping as it was nothing more than a wooden cabinet with tin pierced panels in the doors. Most safes had dimensions of 42x40x16 inches and stood on legs about twelve inches from the floor. A tiny butterfly closure turned on a mounted screw to provide a latch for holding the double doors closed.

One never knew which child's appetite would draw them to the pie safe to test the pies! If Mom was planning to save pies to use later for something special, she always made an extra one for the children to eat beforehand, then she warned us not to cut any of the other pies she had prepared. It is torture for a child to smell the aroma of pie baking, and be expected not to taste until the next day. It is torture for us older folks as well, but we should have better control!

Farmers' Apple Pie

Bake at 400 degrees.

6 to 7 cups sliced raw apples
1/2 cup granulated sugar
1 tablespoon instant clear jell or cornstarch
1/2 teaspoon ground nutmeg or cinnamon
1/4 teaspoon salt
4 tablespoons butter, to spread on bottom crust and dot on
    top of apples

1. Prepare dough for one pie. On a floured surface roll the dough thin to line the pie pan and cover the top of the pie. Set aside.

2. Wash, peel, core, and slice apples into a heavy saucepan. Set aside.

3. In a small bowl combine the dry ingredients and toss over apples.

4. Place the pan over medium heat and cook until apples are heated.

5. Line a 9-inch pie pan with dough. Spread lightly with butter. Pour in the apple mixture and dot with butter.

6. Wet the edge of the dough with water and cover with top crust. Press down on the rim of the pie plate and trim excess dough from the edge. Crimp edge with fingers or a fork. Cut several slits in the top crust with a sharp knife to allow the steam to escape.

7. Bake in the oven for 25 minutes or until lightly browned.

Serve topped with vanilla ice cream.

Yield: 1 9-inch pie.

≈ ≈ ≈

Raisin pie is rich, in addition to being sweet. It could be considered a special occasion dessert to share with company. No better feeling will ever come to us than after we have shared. In short, I believe sharing is love! When we try our best to live unselfishly, the result will be that each of us will have something to offer a friend, no matter how modest it may be. We should be willing to give a hand when folks are down. Life can and will be certain to get sweeter as the days go by when we have lived, not merely for ourselves, but for our fellow man. There is great satisfaction in giving unconditional love. Our senses get dulled when our mind is set on self only. We should be careful not to get caught in this risky trap.

It is terribly dangerous to become so self-sufficient we lose track of what needy creatures we truly are. Unfortunately, too many of us have tunnel vision. All we see is the hard times we have gone through. At the same time, we fall short on the desire and determination to encourage the one losing all hope in similar situations as we have endured. Encouragement costs so little to give. It means so much to the weary one.

Raisin Pie

Bake at 425 degrees.

2 cups boiling water
1/2 cup granulated sugar
1/2 teaspoon salt
2 tablespoons all-purpose flour or cornstarch
2 cups raisins
1 to 2 tablespoons butter, to spread on bottom crust

1. Prepare pie dough for one pie. On a floured surface roll the dough thin to line the pie pan and cover the top of the pie.

2. In a heavy saucepan combine boiling water, sugar, salt, and flour or cornstarch. Stir with a spoon until dissolved. Add the raisins.

3. Place pan over medium heat and cook while stirring for about 5 minutes or until mixture is thick like a gravy.

4. Line a 9-inch pie pan with dough. Spread lightly with butter. Pour in the raisin filling.

5. Wet the edge of the dough with water and cover with top crust. Press down on the rim of the pie plate and trim excess dough from the edge. Crimp edge with fingers or a fork. Cut several slits in the top crust with a sharp knife to allow the steam to escape.

6. Bake in the oven for 30 to 35 minutes or until lightly browned.

Serve with hot coffee.

Yield: 1 9-inch pie.

ᘓ   ᘓ   ᘓ

When youngsters, as we drifted off to sleep at night we anticipated the new day in the morning would soon arrive. All the children had assigned jobs around the house and barn. We were never too young to help out. All of us took turns doing chores before and after school. Believe me, if we rotated we never lost track of whose turn was coming up.

Mom kept a clean, tidy house and each of us did our part to help. With so many activities going on in the kitchen, things became topsy turvy during the day, but before we went to bed everything was put back in its place. The floors were cleaned, and every pan was washed and returned to the cupboards. She created order out of chaos and the end of each night brought a clean start for the next day. Even the little ones were put to bed fresh and clean!

At the end of the day when bedtime came, and we resisted a bath, Mom was quick to say, "What if you should become ill tonight? You don't want to be caught dirty when the doctor comes to visit." She was right--once in awhile one of us children did get sick and J. Elmer Harp, the town's doctor, would make a house call in the wee morning hours, often on what seemed to be one of the coldest, stormiest nights of the year.

Green Tomato Pie

Bake at 425 degrees.

4 cups chopped green tomatoes
2 teaspoons lemon juice
1 cup granulated sugar
1/2 cup brown sugar

2 tablespoons all-purpose flour
1 teaspoon ground cinnamon
1/2 teaspoon ground cloves
4 tablespoons butter, to spread on bottom crust and dot
    on top of fruit

1. Prepare pie dough for one pie. On a floured surface roll the dough thin to line the pie pan and cover the top of the pie.

2. Drop whole tomatoes in boiling water and allow to sit a minute or two. Lift from the water and remove the skin.

3. In a bowl, slice or chop the tomatoes and drizzle with lemon juice. Set aside.

4. In a separate small bowl mix together the sugars, flour, cinnamon, and cloves until blended. Pour over the tomatoes and toss lightly until covered.

5. Line a 9-inch pie pan with dough. Spread lightly with butter. Pour in the tomato mixture and dot the top with butter.

6. Wet the edge of the dough and cover with top crust. Press down on the rim of the pie plate and trim excess dough from the edge. Crimp edge with fingers or a fork. Cut slits in top crust with a sharp knife to allow the steam to escape.

7. Bake in the oven for about 30 minutes or until lightly browned.

Yield: 1 9-inch pie.

&a   &a   &a

DESSERTS

Mom made both strawberry and peach shortcake for the family. In fact, any fresh berry is good served on this shortcake shell.

Have any of you ever spent hours kneeling on the straw spread between the rows of strawberry plants, picking berries for a large family? Doesn't it seem to take forever to fill a gallon bucket? It's an endless job--and thankless too--until the finished product is sampled. Then, thanks for the time spent in the strawberry patch comes rolling in!

Strawberry Shortcake
(Fresh Fruit)

Bake at 400 to 425 degrees.

2 cups all-purpose flour
3 teaspoons baking powder
1 tablespoon granulated sugar
1 teaspoon salt
1/2 stick butter, softened
3/4 cup whole milk
4 to 5 cups strawberries or other fresh fruit

1. In a large mixing bowl combine the dry ingredients and cut the butter in with a fork.

2. Make a well in the mixture and slowly add the milk. Stir lightly with a fork, making a dough.

3. Knead the dough about 20 times.

4. Roll the dough on a floured surface to 1/4 inch thick.

5. Place in a greased pie plate, like making a regular pie crust. Trim excess dough from the edge of the plate. Flute the edge. Prick over the bottom and around the sides of the dough with a fork.

6. Bake in the oven for 20 to 25 minutes or until lightly browned.
(NOTE: Watch carefully--baking time will vary depending on thickness of the dough.)

7. Fill the slightly cooled crust with fresh strawberries or fresh fruit and serve with milk or ice cream.
(NOTE: Sprinkle tart fruit with sugar before pouring into the crust.)

Yield: 1 9-inch crust.

         🙟   🙟   🙟

Cottage Pudding is a type of shortcake with fruit baked in the dough. Additional fruit is often served along side in the same dish. Mom served it with fresh or canned fruit. Serve piping hot with a pitcher of rich milk on the table, handy for pouring over individual servings.

Cottage Pudding
(Peach or Berry)

Bake at 325 to 350 degrees.

2 1/2 cups all-purpose flour
4 teaspoons baking powder
1/2 teaspoon salt
2/3 cup granulated sugar
1/4 cup butter, softened
1 egg
1 teaspoon vanilla
1 cup whole milk
1/2 to 3/4 cup fresh peaches or berries, if desired

1. In a bowl sift together the flour, baking powder, and salt. Set aside.

2. In a separate large mixing bowl cream the sugar and butter until smooth. Set aside.

3. In a small bowl beat the egg until light yellow and add the vanilla. Pour into the sugar and butter mixture. Beat until fluffy.

4. Add the dry ingredients alternately with the milk. Add the peaches or berries and stir only until mixed.

5. Bake in the oven in a greased and floured 8-inch square cake pan for about 25 to 30 minutes.
(NOTE: Additional baking time may be necessary if fruit has been added to the batter.)

Yield: 8 servings.

       æ   æ   æ

Table Dainties are a marvelous treat! Truly delicate and dainty. I assure you it is the best sweet quick bread recipe you will ever taste.

Today our lifestyles are different from our parents. But we children have instilled in us that desire to provide an abundant table for our family and friends. Mom served big bowls of food family style, and we will never forget mealtime, likewise the love served with it. Mom often mentioned that she thought of those children who are put to bed hungry and cry themselves to sleep night after night.

Table Dainties

Bake at 400 degrees.

2 cups sifted all-purpose flour
3 teaspoons baking powder
1 tablespoon granulated sugar
1 teaspoon salt
3/4 stick butter, softened
3/4 cup whole milk

1. In a large mixing bowl sift together the dry ingredients and cut the butter in with a fork.

2. Add the milk. Stir with a fork to make a soft dough.

3. Knead the dough about 20 times.

4. Roll the dough on a floured surface to about 1/4 inch thick.

Topping Ingredients:

1 egg
3/4 to 1 cup brown sugar
1 to 2 cups flaked coconut

5. In a small bowl gradually add the sugar to the egg and mix together with a spoon until smooth. Spread half of the topping mixture on the dough.
(NOTE: The amount of sugar needed will vary with the size of the egg. The egg mixture must be thin enough to spread easily on top of the rolled dough. Additional topping may be desired.)

6. Roll the dough like a jellyroll log and cut into 1-inch slices. Carefully place slices in a greased 9- by 13-inch cake pan, about 1 inch apart. Pour the remainder of the topping over the dough.

7. Sprinkle top with coconut.

8. Bake in the oven for 15 to 20 minutes or until a wooden pick inserted into the middle of dainties comes out clean. Topping will be crispy. Baking time will vary with size of the rolls.

(NOTE: If coconut begins to burn, lay a piece of aluminum foil over the top rack, close to the top of the pan. Do not cover tightly.)

Yield: 1 dozen squares.

æ   æ   æ

As time permitted, Mom baked cherry rolls since they are a favorite dessert with the Wiles' household. These are just plain good--no other words are needed to explain their taste and appeal!

This dessert is bright and colorful, can be made to suit the sweet tooth, or kept tart for the one preferring less sugar content. Mom preferred using cherries when making the rolls, but other fruits can be used.

Cherry Rolls

Bake at 400 degrees.

2 cups all-purpose flour
3 teaspoons baking powder
1 tablespoon granulated sugar
1 teaspoon salt
1/2 stick butter, softened
3/4 cup whole milk
3/4 cup additional butter, for spreading on dough
1 can cherry pie filling
2 cups canned sour cherries, drained and pitted

1. In a large mixing bowl combine the dry ingredients and cut the butter in with a fork.

2. Add the milk. Stir with a fork to form a soft dough. Knead the dough about 20 times.

3. Roll the dough on a floured surface to 1/4 inch thick and spread thick with butter.

4. In a bowl combine the cherry pie filling and the well drained canned sour cherries.
(NOTE: Use all canned pie filling, if desired. Spread the cherries thick or thin as desired on top of the buttered dough.)

5. Roll the dough like a jellyroll log. Dampen the edge of the dough with water and pinch closed. Cut into 1-inch slices with a sharp knife. Place the slices flat in a greased 9- by 13-inch cake pan. Keep about 1/2 to 1 inch apart and fill that space with additional cherries.

6. Bake in the oven for 20 to 25 minutes or until lightly browned.

Variation: Use your choice of fruit pie filling.

Yield: 1 dozen squares.

৯৯ ৯৯ ৯৯

Stewed apples can be served with a meal or as a light dessert at the end of the meal. The York Imperial apple is perfect for making stewed apples with raisins. Some of Mom's favorite varieties are Early June Transparent, Early Rambo, Grimes Golden, Yellow Delicious, MacIntosh, York Imperials, Smith's Cider, Pound, Paradise, and Stayman.

Letha's Stewed Apples with Raisins

8 York Imperial apples
1 1/2 cups granulated sugar
1/4 teaspoon salt
2 2- to 3-inch cinnamon sticks
8 to 10 whole cloves
1 cup raisins
1 cup water

1. Wash, peel, and core the raw apples. Cut each halve in 2 to 3 pieces and place in a bowl. Set aside.

2. In a large kettle combine the remaining ingredients and cook until sugar is melted.

3. Add the pieces of apple and continue to cook over medium heat until tender.

Garnish with a sprinkle of ground cinnamon or a few cinnamon candies on top of individual servings. Serve hot or cold.

Yield: 4 to 6 servings.

❧   ❧   ❧

For years, Mom and Dad traveled over the Smithsburg mountain to purchase fruit from the Raymond and William Gardenour orchards. During the 1940s and 1950s, often the radiator in Dad's old Chevy overheated, causing the water to boil, then spill out. I remember arriving at the packing house and rolling into the parking space with the steam escaping fast and furious from under the hood. I can still remember Dad going up the steps that led to the floor of the packing house that was filled with baskets overloaded with flavorful ripe fruit. "Good measure" was their policy. The air was filled with the sweet bold scent. Dad inquired of Mr. Gardenour if he had a bucket handy for him to use to get some water. He explained his dilemma and when the radiator had cooled, he filled the tank up to its top. Meanwhile, Mom was deciding which baskets of fruit she wanted to purchase. When planning a day of canning, we never came home with a basket, but six to eight bushels at a time.

Heading home, by the time we made it over the mountain the car overheated and was steaming hot again. Now we stopped at Lee Delauter's store, in Middlepoint. Once more Dad asked for a bucket of water to fill the auto's radiator tank. Both Lee and his wife, Pauline, greeted us with big smiles!

Some 50 to 60 years later, the doors of the Delauter's business remain open with the three sons and their families passing out the same honest-to-goodness kindness. There, you can still find help when in trouble--the only difference now is a new generation! My hope is that the legacy of their business will be carried on by still another generation.

Apple Roll

Bake at 375 degrees.

3 to 4 cups sliced raw apples
2 cups all-purpose flour
3 teaspoons baking powder
2 tablespoons granulated sugar
1 teaspoon salt
1/2 stick butter
3/4 cup whole milk
2 tablespoons butter, to spread on top of dough
sugar and cinnamon, to sprinkle on top of apples

1. Wash, peel, core, and slice apples. Set aside.

2. In a large mixing bowl combine the dry ingredients and cut the butter in with a fork.

3. Add the milk. Stir with a fork until a soft dough forms.

4. Knead the dough about 20 times.

5. Roll the dough on a floured surface to 1/3 inch thick. Spread lightly with butter.

6. Spread a thin layer of sliced apples over the prepared and rolled dough. Sprinkle with sugar and cinnamon to your taste. Roll the dough like a jellyroll log and place in a buttered 9- by 13-inch cake pan.

Syrup Ingredients:

1 cup water
2 tablespoons butter
1 1/4 cups granulated sugar
1 1/2 tablespoons all-purpose flour

7. In a heavy saucepan bring the water and butter to a boil.

8. In a separate small bowl combine the flour and sugar to prevent lumping. Add to the boiling water. Boil for about 6 minutes or until slightly thickened.

9. Pour half of the syrup over and around the roll. Place pan in the oven. After 10 minutes, pour remaining syrup on top of the roll and continue baking until lightly browned.

10. Bake in the oven for 30 to 45 minutes.

Variation: Cut the roll into 1-inch slices and place flat in a 9- by 13-inch cake pan. Extra apples may be dropped around the roll or the slices and baked in the syrup.

Yield: 8 servings.

&a. &a. &a.

Apple dumplings are nothing more than little apple pies. Their flavor is out of this world and when covered with milk or vanilla ice cream you have a real treat. Mom baked them in her old black Girard Novelty wood-burning kitchen range. She was as happy as the day is long when she and Dad purchased a new white Home Comfort range. It was a beauty, and Mom was in paradise right in her own kitchen! White enamel over cast iron was high-class. Besides that, it was simply bigger and better. She could not, however, part with her old Girard Novelty, so she moved it into the farm worker's quarters. Mom fired it up and used it when canning in the summertime, allowing the farmhouse kitchen to remain somewhat cool.

Apple Dumplings

Bake at 425 degrees.

6 to 8 apples
granulated sugar
ground cinnamon
butter
pie dough
(NOTE: Recipe found on page 170.)

1. Prepare pie dough for one pie.

2. Peel, halve, and core 6 to 8 apples.

3. Roll the dough thin on a floured surface and cut into squares large enough to wrap a whole apple.

4. Holding a square of dough in your hand, place half an apple on top with center cavity facing up. Fill with sugar and cinnamon. Dot with butter.

5. Place another apple half on top and completely surround with dough. Place in a buttered flat pan.

(NOTE: Bake in the oven with or without syrup in bottom of pan.)

Syrup Ingredients:

1 cup granulated sugar
2 cups water
4 tablespoons butter
1/4 to 1/2 teaspoon ground cinnamon

6. In a heavy saucepan combine all the ingredients. Place pan over medium to high heat and boil for 3 to 4 minutes.

7. Pour the syrup around the dumplings that have been placed in a buttered flat pan.

8. Bake in the oven for 30 to 40 minutes or until lightly browned. Baking time will vary with size of dumpling.

Serve with fresh milk or vanilla ice cream.

Yield: 6 to 8 servings.

&a &a &a

For most of Mom's adult life, she has canned bushels of peaches each year. She likes Hale Haven, Belle of Georgia, Shippers Red, Sun High, Red Haven and Summer Crist peaches. Canned food in the cellar brought a degree of comfort to Mom, almost as comforting as having money in the bank. She knew she could always prepare a complete meal without ever leaving the farm, no matter the size of the crowd that appeared at the table. Each year she canned vegetables, meats, and fruits but those days of preparation came with a high price of hard labor plus the time involved.

In August 1997, Mom, when in her late nineties, decided she needed to can peaches. She peeled one bushel of Sun High peaches while her oldest daughter preceded with the canning process. What a great privilege to be blessed with health and mind to continue enjoying the canning season in her golden years of life. Mom has dozens of jars of fruits and vegetables lined on the shelves in the basement of her home waiting to be enjoyed during the winter months. Once a provider, always a provider, it seems to me.

One way she used canned fruit was in her fruit cobblers. In my opinion, no dessert is more versatile or mouthwatering than a fruit cobbler. Use your favorite fruit, fresh or canned, along with your imagination to create an original dish. Add a few candied cherries for color. Raisins and other tidbits of dried fruit create interest and appeal. Top the finished cobbler with ice cream or whipped topping. If you are one for pouring milk over this type dish, pour and enjoy...or simply eat it plain! One might consider baking fruit cobbler more often when it proves to be simple to make and such a delightful dessert.

Canned or Fresh Fruit Cobbler

Bake at 375 degrees.

Fruit Mixture Ingredients:

1/2 cup granulated sugar
1 tablespoon cornstarch
2 1/2 cups canned fruit or berries and juice
(NOTE: For fresh fruit, use 3 1/2 cups fruit and 1 cup water or fruit juice.)

1. In a heavy saucepan combine the sugar and cornstarch. Stir fruit and juice into the mixture.

2. Place the pan over medium heat and bring mixture to a boil while stirring constantly.
(NOTE: When using fresh fruit, boil for 5 minutes.)

3. Pour the mixture into a 1 1/2-quart baking dish and dot with butter. Sprinkle with cinnamon and sugar, if desired.

Dough Ingredients:

1 cup all-purpose flour
1 tablespoon granulated sugar
1 1/2 tablespoons baking powder
1/2 teaspoon salt
3 tablespoons solid vegetable shortening
1/2 cup whole milk
1 teaspoon vanilla

4. In a mixing bowl sift together the dry ingredients. Cut in the shortening with a fork.

5. Stir the milk and vanilla into the mixture to form a dough. *(NOTE: Do not beat.)*

6. Drop the dough from a spoon on top of the hot fruit.

7. Bake in the oven for 20 to 25 minutes or until lightly browned.

Best served hot.

Yield: 8 to 10 servings.

ﺑ   ﺑ   ﺑ

Rice with Sweet Cream

2 cups cooked white rice
1/2 cup sweet cream
1 teaspoon butter
granulated sugar, to taste
salt, to taste

In a heavy saucepan combine all the ingredients. Place the pan over medium heat and cook until a gravy forms on the rice.
(NOTE: Do not allow to boil.)

Serve with your favorite fruit.

Yield: 4 servings.

ﺑ   ﺑ   ﺑ

Think of preparing a messy meal, then think of cleaning the kitchen without running water! In the early days of Mom's married life there were no modern conveniences, such as indoor plumbing in the farmhouse. So it was a must that the water pails be kept filled, wood must be carried to the stove, and a hot fire must be built to heat the water. Everyone had a job. No one was overlooked. Filling the woodbox was left for the children to do after the school day was over.

Self-cleaning ovens and hot water heaters are among the expected conveniences in our homes today and certainly not considered a brand new invention. God forgive us for being so ungrateful and thoughtless by taking for granted the inventions of this day and age.

Rice Pudding

Bake at 350 degrees.

2 eggs
1/2 cup granulated sugar
1/2 teaspoon salt
ground cinnamon or nutmeg, if desired
2 teaspoons vanilla
2 cups whole milk
2 cups cooked rice
1/2 cup raisins

1. In a large mixing bowl blend together the eggs, sugar, salt, cinnamon or nutmeg, and vanilla. Set aside.

2. In a heavy saucepan heat the milk over low heat until a skim forms over top. Combine with the egg and sugar mixture.

3. Add the cooked rice and raisins and stir until blended.

4. Pour the mixture into a baking dish sprayed with cooking oil. Sprinkle top with cinnamon or nutmeg, if desired.

5. To bake, place the dish in about 1 inch of water in a shallow baking pan. Bake in the oven for about 1 hour or until a knife inserted into the middle of the custard comes out clean.

Variation: Add a variety of dried fruits to the rice pudding.

Yield: 6 servings.

əa   əa   əa

We could depend on Mom whipping up bread pudding when the bread lasted long enough to get stale! No one complained. When the dish appeared on the table, we all enjoyed having it. Most of Mom's friends loved her bread pudding and they would come to expect certain dishes when enjoying a meal in our home. Mom considers bread pudding a side dish and served it with meals to the farmhands during the busy season. Manual workers deserve to be rewarded with good food, and plenty of it!

It seems good food and good friends go together. Each time Mom loses a dear friend, a little empty space is felt in a corner of her heart, but she thanks God for new friends who fill those voids. Most can never be duplicated, nor would she try if that were possible. Old friendships are beautiful, and one is always saddened by that loss.

Bread Pudding

Bake at 350 degrees.

2 cups whole milk
3 large eggs, slightly beaten
1/2 cup granulated sugar
1/4 cup melted butter
1/2 teaspoon salt
1 teaspoon ground cinnamon and nutmeg
1 teaspoon vanilla
3 to 4 cups broken white bread pieces
3/4 cup raisins, if desired

1. In a mixing bowl blend together the milk, eggs, sugar, butter, salt, cinnamon, nutmeg, and vanilla.

2. Place the broken bread pieces in a greased baking dish and sprinkle with raisins, if desired. Pour the milk mixture over the bread pieces.

3. Place the dish in about 1 inch of water in a shallow pan and bake for about 1 hour or until lightly browned on top.

ð   ð   ð

Applesauce

4 quarts quartered apples
2 cups water
granulated sugar, if desired

1. Wash, peel, core, and quarter the apples. Transfer to a large heavy kettle and add the water.

2. Place pan over medium heat and cook until apples are tender and falling apart. Run through a colander, food mill or beat until smooth with an electric mixer.

3. Before serving applesauce, add sugar, if desired.

Variation: Add a little vanilla to the applesauce just before serving, or sprinkle top with a sugar and cinnamon mixture.

ð   ð   ð

Nothing new seems to happen to the cream puff recipe. It has remained about the same down through the years. The puffs can be filled with chicken or ham salad and served as little tea sandwiches. A variety of flavored cornstarch custards can be used for the filling: coconut, vanilla, or chocolate. Years ago cornstarch custard was also known as Blue Munge. The only difference in the two recipes is the omission of butter in Blue Munge.

Mom made cream puffs often while living on the Middletown farm. She had a flock of a hundred or so laying hens, plus she raised young chickens each year. When the pullets or young hens begin to lay, the eggs are small and the huckster or peddler had a hard time selling them to his cliental. To avoid this problem, he did not buy them. Mom used as many of the tiny eggs as possible in cooking and baking. For one regular size egg, she would use two or three little ones.

Mom usually bought more little chicks than she needed to grow into laying hens. Once they weighed a few pounds, she slaughtered and fried the excess chickens for the family's meals. Or sometimes a deal was made with the huckster to sell the extra roosters. The huckster traveled from farm to farm as he bought or sold the farmer's poultry, eggs, and other fresh produce. He made a weekly run through the countryside with horse and wagon. Then, once the gasoline engine became popular, the truck became his mode for transportation.

When the last huckster who made weekly runs to the farm purchased chickens, he pulled his truck to the gate that entered the chicken yard from the main road. Then he carried the wooden coop, as well as a pair of hanging scales into the hen house. He hung the scales on a nail driven into the ceiling rafter for that purpose. The huckster and Mom caught the roosters, held them by their legs until they had as many as they could comfortably hold in their hands. Next, they slipped a rope around a group of chicken's legs and hung them, head down, from the scale. The huckster waited patiently until the chickens settled down and stopped moving about--the movement caused the hand on the scales to bounce crazily. Once stabilized he read the weight and recorded the numbers with a tiny pencil in a little carbon and original receipt book. Price per pound was determined and agreed upon earlier, and once the chickens were in the coop the currency was exchanged between the two of them. That closed the deal so the huckster was on his way to the next farm, and Mom carried on with her daily routine, but with a few extra dollars now waiting to meet some pressing need.

Cream Puffs

Bake at 400 degrees.

2 cups water
1 cup butter
2 cups sifted all-purpose flour
8 eggs

1. In a heavy saucepan combine the water and butter. Bring to a full boil over high heat.

2. Reduce the heat and add all of the flour at once. Stir with a spoon rapidly until dough leaves the sides of the pan and forms a ball.

3. Remove the pan from heat.

4. With a spoon, beat in the eggs, one at a time. Beat, after adding each egg, until the dough is very smooth.
(NOTE: Do not beat eggs before adding to the mixture.)

5. Drop the dough from a spoon on an ungreased cookie sheet.

6. Bake in the oven for 45 to 50 minutes. Baking time will vary with the size of the puff. When puffs are done they will appear dry and lightly browned.

7. When puffs are cooled cut a slit in the top with a sharp knife. Fill with your favorite custard or pudding.

(NOTE: Empty puffs may be stored in the freezer in a tight container.)

Yield: 8 to 10 large puffs.

ꝫ ꝫ ꝫ

Before the days of refrigeration, most foods were prepared and eaten on the same day or stored in a running stream of cold spring water in the springhouse. But then the invention of an icebox came along. It was the convenience country housewives longed and hoped for. Finally, Mom had an icebox, only because Dr. J. Elmer Harp was kind enough to ask if she would like to have one that was being replaced at the Lamar Nursing Home in Middletown. She was delighted to have the second-hand luxury. The icebox was a white enamel cabinet with shelves for holding the food and a compartment to store a 50-pound block of ice. The ice provided and maintained a cool temperature as long as it remained frozen. When melted, the water drained into a pan, and unfortunately, the temperature would rise. There was enough space in the box to store milk, butter, a few containers of food, and that was about it. Actually, we had very little food on hand that needed to be kept cold. With a large family, plus the hired hands, we consumed the food prepared for the day.

Sweet & Sour Spiced Apples

7 York Imperial apples
1 1/3 cups granulated sugar
1/3 cup water
2/3 cup vinegar
2 cinnamon sticks, 2 to 3 inches
12 whole cloves
1/2 teaspoon all-spice

1. Wash, peel, and core the raw apples. Cut each halve in 2 to 3 pieces. Set aside.

2. In a heavy kettle combine the remaining ingredients and boil for 20 minutes over medium heat to make a syrup. Stir frequently to prevent scorching.

3. Add the apples to the syrup and cook until tender, but not mushy.

Serve spiced apples hot or cold along with the main course.

Variation: Add red, green, or yellow food coloring to the syrup to enhance the color, if desired.

Yield: 4 to 6 servings.

ða   ða   ða

Most folks of all ages enjoy baked apples served with the main course or as dessert. When added to a pork meal, they break down the richness and fat.

It was time to do the last-minute touches on the meal when Mom heard the machinery come clinking and rattling from the fields and down Route 17 which runs through the middle of the farmland. When my parents farmed with horses, their metal shoes clattered and banged as they made each step on the old cement road. The horses were hitched to the machinery with heavy chains that jangled--the steel wheels thundered and screeched as they turned over flint stones that lay in their path. The men could never sneak up on Mom because she heard the horses coming long before she saw anyone.

With a large crowd to cook for, Mom planned what she would prepare for a meal ahead of time. She baked or cooked early in the morning and kept the items warm in the warming closet. A warming closet is part of the wood-burning range, but is nothing more than a long shelf with a hinged door. It was attached to the back of the stove, but at the same time, it hung partly over the cooking surface. The closet stayed warm by the rising heat from the stove top.

Baked Apples

Bake at 350 degrees.

apples
butter
granulated sugar
ground cinnamon

1. Wash, peel, cut apples in half, and core. Place the apple's cavity facing up in a buttered baking dish. Sprinkle with sugar, cinnamon, and dot each half with butter.

2. Bake in the oven for about 20 minutes or until tender. *(NOTE: Baking time and sugar required will vary with different apple varieties.)*

Variations: At the end of baking time, turn heat off, remove the dish from the oven, top apples with marshmallows, return dish to oven and toast lightly.

     ð   ð   ð

This is an old-fashioned homemade ice cream recipe that Mom used before the idea of adding commercial pudding mixes came along. Thick sweet cream can be substituted for the whole milk when added richness is desired.

Mom added whichever fruit was in season to the ice cream mixture. She likes peach and strawberry flavors. She used an old steel food grinder to grind the fruit or when it was extremely ripe, she mashed it with her old-fashioned potato stumper.

Everyone who was old enough to turn the crank on the freezer got a turn whether we wanted one or not! We had a very slim chance of escaping this chore, especially if we intended to partake in the ice cream. When the ice cream was frozen firm, Mom dipped it out of the canister into pans that had tight covers and stored it in our deep freezer. But before owning this convenience, she threw an old hand-hooked rug or heavy quilt over the top of the old wooden ice cream freezer to prolong melting while she waited a few hours to serve. We could not wait too long before indulging--no one wanted to risk the ice cream melting after we worked so hard to get it frozen!

What a refreshing treat ice cream was on a hot summer's day! Mom and Dad could not afford commercial ice cream for a large family, but saw to it that we did not go without this special treat. Back at the turn of the nineteenth century, when Mom was a youngster, her dad treated her to ice cream at the confectionary shop. A dish of ice cream cost five to ten cents, and you could purchase a decent pair of shoes for $1.50. I could conjure up a lot of opportunities to buy shoes if they only cost $1.50 today!

Homemade Ice Cream

4 large eggs
2 1/2 cups granulated sugar
6 cups whole milk
4 cups light sweet cream
1/2 teaspoon salt
2 tablespoons vanilla
2 cups chopped or mashed fresh fruit

1. In a large bowl beat the eggs with a rotary beater or wire whisk until light yellow and fluffy. Add the sugar gradually and stir until well blended.

2. Add the remaining ingredients and stir until well blended.

3. Pour the ice cream mixture into the canister. Position the dasher, cover, and place the assembled canister inside the freezer tub. Pack the tub with alternate layers of crushed ice and salt, using 1 pound of coarse salt to about 8 pounds of ice.

(NOTE: When using today's modern ice cream freezer, process according to the freezer's instructions.)

Yield: 3 1/2 quarts of ice cream.

❧   ❧   ❧

Not always, but sometimes Mom used a "cooked base" when making ice cream. It is amusing how much we would have enjoyed a helping of today's slick, solid store-bought ice cream back then, when the only kind we could afford was homemade. Today making ice cream remains a special event, but the big difference is that modern ice cream makers utilize an electric motor, in place of a lot of elbow grease. Only yesterday, it was considered a chore and by no means, fun! Today, it is a wonderful memory. How the times do change!

Cooked-Base Ice Cream

4 eggs
2 tablespoons cornstarch
2 tablespoons all-purpose flour
1/2 to 1 cup rich sweet cream
1 gallon of whole milk
4 cups granulated sugar
1/2 teaspoon salt
1 to 2 teaspoons vanilla

1. In a bowl beat the eggs with a rotary beater or wire whisk until light yellow and fluffy. Add the cornstarch, flour, and sweet cream with the beaten eggs. Mix until smooth. Set aside.

2. In a saucepan heat the milk, sugar, and salt.

3. Add the egg mixture and bring to a boil while stirring constantly. When thickened, remove from the heat and add the vanilla. Let the mixture stand until cool and pour into the canister of the ice cream freezer.

4. Position the dasher, cover, and place the assembled canister inside the freezer tub. Pack the tub with alternate layers of crushed ice and salt, using 1 pound of coarse salt to about 8 pounds of ice.

Serve garnished with fruits, nuts, and sauces.

(NOTE: When using today's modern ice cream freezer, process according to the freezer's instructions.)

Yield: 1 gallon of ice cream.

෨ ෨ ෨

Hot Fudge Sauce

1 6-ounce package semi-sweet chocolate chips
1 cup small marshmallows
1/4 cup thick sweet cream

Melt all ingredients over low heat in a double boiler. Use immediately or store in the refrigerator in a tight container. Reheat in a double boiler when ready to use.

Drizzle over ice cream and enjoy!

෨ ෨ ෨

SALADS & DRESSINGS

In the country, most farm families planted and harvested an abundance of potatoes. What would a farm family do without potatoes at a hot cooked meal? Or what would a picnic be without potato salad? Every day Mom and her children peeled potatoes piled high in a dishpan and thought nothing of it. They were grown on the farm, they were plentiful, and they were served regularly in every style imagined.

Potato or Macaroni Salad

6 medium potatoes, cooked and diced
(NOTE: To make macaroni salad omit the potatoes and use 4 cups cooked elbow macaroni.)
4 hard-boiled eggs, diced
1 to 1 1/2 cups mayonnaise
1/2 cup diced raw celery
1/2 cup diced raw carrots
1 small diced raw onion
1 teaspoon wet mustard or mustard seed
1/2 teaspoon celery seed
salt and pepper, to taste

1. In a large mixing bowl combine the diced potatoes and eggs. Set aside.

2. In a separate bowl combine the remaining ingredients. Pour the mayonnaise mixture over the potatoes and eggs. Stir lightly until evenly coated.

Store in a tight container in the refrigerator.

Yield: 8 servings.

ð€   ð€   ð€

Cottage Cheese Salad is one of Mom's favorites. Anytime you use cottage cheese when preparing food, you are adding a nutritious and wholesome ingredient.

Cottage Cheese Salad

1 10-ounce box thawed whipped topping
1 6-ounce box of small curd-cottage cheese
1 small box orange gelatin
1 can crushed pineapple, drained
1 small can mandrin oranges, drained
1/4 cup coconut
1 cup pecans

1. In a mixer bowl blend the whipped topping and cottage cheese on low speed with an electric mixer.

2. Add dry gelatin to the above mixture and stir until blended. Fold in crushed pineapple, oranges, coconut, and pecans.

3. Pour mixture into a greased mold or glass serving dish. Cover with plastic wrap. Return to the refrigerator and allow to set for a few hours before serving.

Yield: 8 servings.

      ða   ða   ða

Homemade mayonnaise is rich and smooth, as you would expect. It gives potato salad a nice change in taste from commercial dressings. How often Mom stood in the kitchen with her pots and spoons on the table, ready to prepare a dish only to find an ingredient she needed was not in the cupboard. It did not stop her from going on with her cooking. It was no big deal! She could not do anything about the situation, so she improvised and made do with what she had. Most often she would not have had the time to spare to go to the store anyway, and the lack of money was a drawback as well. But, whatever dish Mom made, the result was always tasty.

Homemade Mayonnaise

1 egg
1 tablespoon all-purpose flour
2 tablespoons granulated sugar
1/2 cup whipping cream
1/2 cup vinegar
1/2 cup water
1 teaspoon mustard
1/2 teaspoon salt

1. In a small bowl beat the egg with a rotary beater or wire whisk until light yellow. Set aside.

2. In a heavy saucepan combine the flour, sugar, cream, vinegar, water, mustard, and salt. Add to the beaten egg and stir until well blended.

3. Cook the mixture over medium to high heat until it boils and thickens to the consistency of a thick gravy. Remove from the heat and cool.

Use immediately or store in a tight container in the refrigerator.

&a&a &a&a &a&a

Tired of using commercial dressing day after day? Try this recipe for making an occasional replacement dressing. It is creamy and smooth with a delightful flavor.

Cooked Salad Dressing

1/2 cup all-purpose flour
1/2 cup granulated sugar
1 1/2 to 2 teaspoons salt
1 1/2 teaspoons wet mustard
1/4 teaspoon paprika
1 cup water
1/2 to 3/4 cup vinegar
4 egg yolks, slightly beaten
1 tablespoon butter

1. In a heavy saucepan combine the flour, sugar, salt, mustard, and paprika. Add the water and vinegar. Stir until well blended.

2. Cook over low heat until thick and boil for 1 minute. Remove from heat and cool slightly.

3. Add the slightly beaten egg yolks and butter to the mixture. Beat with a spoon until smooth. Cool.

Use immediately or store in a tight container in the refrigerator.

❧   ❧   ❧

Sunday mornings at the Grossnickle's Church of the Brethren, when the summertime and balmy weather set in, the doors were opened to provide a fresh breeze. Being located in the country with mountains and woods nearby, an unannounced visitor occasionally crept in without warning.

Quentin Grossnickle recalls that it was somewhere around the 1950s when he, along with his wife and family of small children, were all seated on a pew and at peace with the world, so to say. The preacher was delivering the morning message and all ears and eyes were attuned to his voice and his stature there on the pulpit.

Nearly everyone was giving their full attention. Suddenly, Quentin felt a soft pat and a hand on his shoulder. He turned just enough to lend an ear to another faithful member of the congregation who was seated directly behind him. In a calm but yet urgent voice, Carrie Leatherman whispered, "There is a copperhead coming up under the bench. Get him." Quentin did not hesitate to follow her instructions and to take a look at the floor. Low and behold there it was. He moved his hand, quietly as possible, to pick up a hymnal. As the book for his weapon and with an eye on his target he proceeded to smash and hold down the snake just at the back of his head and with as strong a grip as possible. No one screamed. No one knew what was going on from the other side of the room, but slowly the minutes ticked away as Quentin held the old serpent there on the floor under the pages of hymns until he died. It was about 18 to 20 inches long and certainly not welcome to slither among the congregation. Today we sit in our air-conditioned buildings with the finest padded pews, but the folks of not so many years ago can tell us many stories that should bring appreciation to our hearts for the good life.

Cucumber Salad

2 large raw cucumbers
2 medium raw onions
1/2 cup vinegar
1 tablespoon granulated sugar
salt and pepper, to taste

1. Wash, peel, and slice thin the fresh cucumbers and onions. Place in a glass bowl with enough salt water to cover. Soak for 10 minutes.

2. Allow the water to drain from the vegetables and squeeze out the excess water with your hands. Return vegetables to the glass dish.
(NOTE: Do not be concerned that vegetables are slightly smashed.)

3. In a separate bowl combine the vinegar, sugar, pepper and salt, to taste. Stir until blended.

4. Pour dressing over the vegetables and allow to sit 1 hour before serving.

Yield: 4 servings.

❧   ❧   ❧

Lemon Vegetable Salad is cool, crunchy, and refreshing. It is nice to serve when a heavy meal is planned.

Lemon Vegetable Salad

1 small package lemon gelatin
1 cup boiling water
8 ounces cream cheese, softened
1 medium container thawed whipped topping
3/4 cup shredded carrots
1 1/4 cups crushed pineapple, drained
3/4 cup chopped fine celery
1 cup chopped fine pecans
1/2 cup coconut

1. In a mixing bowl combine the gelatin and boiling water.

2. Add the softened cream cheese and stir until dissolved. Place the mixture in the refrigerator and when almost set, beat with an electric mixer until smooth.

3. Add the whipped topping, carrots, pineapple, celery, pecans, and coconut. Stir until blended.

4. Pour mixture into a greased mold or glass serving dish. Cover with plastic wrap. Return to the refrigerator and allow to set for a few hours before serving.

Yield: 6 servings.

&a   &a   &a

Cucumber and onion salad is especially for onion lovers. Using a mild onion will cut the pungent taste and will not harm the recipe.

As a young woman, Mom was not privileged to go to the hardware or supply store in the early spring and buy onion bulbs to plant in the garden to produce that year's crop. Instead, during the previous year, she let some fall onions stand out in the soil with the intent of letting them go to seed. The seeds form in a round ball at the tip of the onion top. Before the frost arrived, Mom cut the tops of the matured onion off at the ground and gathered them by the handful. She tied them into small bundles using an old strip of cloth. Then she found a cool, dry place to hang them upside down to dry. When the big blossom tops were dry she rubbed them between her hands and allowed the little black seeds to fall from their hulls into an old shallow pan. Again, the seeds were placed in a dry, cool room and allowed time for all the moisture to evaporate before storing in a small paper bag.

Mom recalls when she married and moved to the farm, finding in the corner of the back porch a bundle of dried onion tops tied with the strings from an old apron. It was hanging on a hook driven into the ceiling. Here were onion seeds waiting for her! Early in the spring of the year, these little seeds were planted in the freshly tilled soil and when it produced a tiny bulb on the root, the onion and its top were pulled up and allowed to dry. Now this little onion was sheltered over the winter and come the following spring, it was planted in the garden. And so the cycle continued from year to year. People saved wherever possible and however involved the procedure, which proved the saying, "we have more time than money."

Cucumber and Onion Salad

4 1/2 cups sliced fresh cucumbers
1 to 2 large sliced raw onions
1 cup thick dairy sour cream
2 tablespoons vinegar
1 tablespoon granulated sugar
1 1/2 teaspoons salt

1. Wash, peel, and slice thin the fresh cucumbers and onions. Set aside.

2. In a small bowl combine the remaining ingredients and stir until blended. Pour over cucumbers and onions.

Serve immediately.

Yield: 4 servings.

ᐥ   ᐥ   ᐥ

Garden leaf lettuce makes a cold refreshing dish, and the cool crispness is pleasing to one's taste in the hot weather. After a summer shower the green lettuce was brighter than at any other time or any other plant, and it stood brighter than the white picket fence that ran along the garden's edge. Mom had a beautiful garden from early spring and even through the fall when the turnip, kale and endive seeds sprouted fresh greens through the ground.

The hotbed was nothing more than a bottomless concrete box about three feet wide and deep, six feet long, covered with glass window frames, and buried along the paved path that ran through the center of the garden to the chicken house. In the spring of the year before sowing the seeds, Dad dumped a few wheelbarrow loads of manure from the horse stalls into the box to cover the bottom of the bed, then he threw some rich topsoil from the garden on top. The warm spring sun provided heat and light for the seeds, and the hot bed was ready to be planted with tomato, pepper, and cabbage seeds. As we peaked through the glass on a cold day, we could see the sprouts poking through the dark soil, and that gave us the assurance that warm weather was certain to arrive. Mom strewed in lettuce seeds in the bed, after the other plants were removed.

Dad and the farmhands not only came to the house to eat a meal, but it was a time to get out from under the hot sun, cool down, and rest for a few minutes. The men looked forward to the surprise of what foods had been prepared for them as they sat down to the table to eat. After the meal, when the dishes where cleared away from the table, either one of us children or Mom would fold up the corners of the feed bag tablecloth and roll it into a ball and capture the crumbs. No matter the weather, we opened the back door and let the cloth fall open to shake in the wind. Every crumb that made its way outside was one less we had to sweep up from the floor!

Fresh Garden Leaf Lettuce Salad

2 quarts chopped fresh leaf lettuce
1 cup sweet cream
1/4 cup vinegar
1/3 cup granulated sugar
salt, to taste
pepper, if desired

1. Wash and remove any discolored leaves from leaf lettuce. Allow to drain in a colander. Set aside.

2. In a separate bowl combine the remaining ingredients and stir until well blended. Pour the dressing over the lettuce and serve.

Serve with boiled or home-fried potatoes, and don't forget the buttered bread!

Yield: 6 to 8 servings.

&a   &a   &a

This fruit salad is nice to serve to a large group of people, so Mom always prepared it for butchering day and Christmas dinner. These special meals at our house were sumptuous.

Mom did not enjoy butchering day at home. The job was pure drudgery and offered very little pleasure when all of the responsibilities for getting the work done were on her and Dad's shoulders. She had two sittings of people at the big table. The women ate after all the men and children were fed.

Just about the time the farmer's wife thought she could take a break from cooking for the butchering and holidays, here came the harvesters and haymakers. On a farm something is either happening--or about to happen--all the time! One never knew for sure what the day would hold.

Butchering Day Fruit Salad

peaches, chopped
pears, chopped
pineapple, chopped
seeded cherries
oranges, chopped
seedless grapes
bananas, sliced

1. In a large bowl or dishpan combine equal portions of the fruits, whether canned or fresh, except bananas.

2. When ready to serve, add sliced bananas only to the portion that is going to be used.

(NOTE: Bananas will turn dark after refrigeration, other fruits will keep fresh for days.)

ða   ða   ða

SOUPS

Noodle lovers will enjoy this recipe. Egg rivvels are a flour and egg mixture which is lightly rubbed together with your finger tips to form crumbs or rivvels. They are a form of German noodle and are dropped into boiling broth to cook. You may use either the whole egg recipe or the egg yolk recipe when preparing rivvel soup. Rivvels add body and are excellent added to bean or rice soup.

Whole Egg Rivvel
(for soup)

1 egg
1 cup all-purpose flour

Break the egg in a small bowl. Work the flour lightly through egg with the tips of your fingers.
(NOTE: Do not beat the egg. Handle gently, rubbing so as to make a rivvel and not a ball.)

(NOTE: Rivvels cannot be made until ready to drop into the boiling broth.)

èa   èa   èa

Egg Yolk Rivvel
(for soup)

1 egg yolk
3/4 cup all-purpose flour

Break the egg yolk in a small bowl. Work the flour lightly through egg with the tips of your fingers.

èa   èa   èa

Lunch is often a hurried meal as we try to crunch as many hours of work in a day as possible, so serve a quick soup to save time. On early winter evenings when the day gets cold and dark as night, soup makes a nice suppertime meal.

Beef or Chicken Rivvel Soup

prepared egg rivvels
(NOTE: Recipes found on page 260.)
8 cups of rich broth, beef or chicken
salt and pepper, to taste
parsley, if desired

1. In a large kettle bring seasoned broth to a boil.

2. Make either variety of egg rivvels.

3. Drop the rivvels slowly into the boiling broth while stirring constantly. Cook for 5 minutes. Remove from heat and serve.

Variation: Add small pieces of meat to the soup for added nourishment. Add parsley and seasoning of your choice. Add bits of finely chopped cooked onion, carrot, or celery.

Yield: 4 to 6 servings.

&a   &a   &a

Milk rivvel soup is hearty and sticks to your ribs on a cold winter's day. Thinking back, Mom remembers her first electric stove, refrigerator, freezer, toaster, and mixer. She can also retrace far too well memories of standing by the wood-burning kitchen range while cooking. How she longed for a cool breeze to kiss her cheeks after the heat had reddened them. She recalls how she equally welcomed that same heat when the freezing winter wind blew in every tiny crack around the doors or windows.

Mom's hands have prepared more meals than she can imagine--often made in haste and when her tired and worn body cried for rest. She was a busy farmer's wife and a young mother. She is the one who lovingly fed us children when our hands were too small to hold the spoon. On a hot summer's day--time and time again--she stood in a stifling kitchen by a red-hot range cooking food, sweat dripping from her brow, with a crying baby on one arm and a toddler pulling on her apron, begging to be rocked for his or her nap. With such duties, I am sure she daydreamed at least once in awhile, of some kind of relief or escape. She was only human, but she did not let any hardship become a stumbling block. Instead she turned the experience into a stepping stone while looking forward to better days ahead.

Milk Rivvel Soup

prepared egg rivvels
(NOTE: Recipes found on page 260.)
8 cups of whole milk
2 to 4 tablespoons butter
salt and pepper, to taste

1. In a large heavy kettle combine all ingredients except the rivvels and bring to a boil.

2. Make a batch of either variety of egg rivvels.

3. Drop the rivvels slowly into the milk mixture while stirring constantly and continue to heat only until the milk returns to a boil. Remove from heat immediately.

Variation: Add parsley and seasoning of your choice. Add bits of finely chopped and cooked onion, carrot, or celery.

Yield: 4 to 6 servings.

❧   ❧   ❧

I remember on Sunday afternoons, when we did not have company, everyone was quiet following the noon meal. We children played around and looked for anything we could find to get into. I recall, Mom used one of the eleven rooms in the old farmhouse for what she called a *trash room*. There was nothing in there but items she was not using, but wanted to store and keep. We thought it was the grandest, cleverest idea to go play in that room. In fact, we could find all kinds of mischief to get into! Most of the time, I am sure we thought only for a few seconds about what we were going to do, and then got right into it. We rearranged everything in that room by the time we were ready to walk out.

An old-fashioned stereoscope and slide cards were placed here and there in boxes that were sitting around in the room. A stereoscope is an instrument with two glass lens. A stand is attached to insert and hold a photo postal card. You look through the glass at a photo of duplicate scenes, one for each eye. The photo is taken at slightly different angles and are viewed side by side, thus the two photographs are seen as a dimensional picture. The cards were professionally made and purchased according to the subject of your interest. The photos were not of folks we knew, and we could not identify the scenes. Imagine being desperate for entertainment, getting out the stereoscope, and looking at the same couple of dozen pictures you have seen one time after another. The photos were not color or black and white, but a shade of light cocoa. I remember one photo in particular. It was of a handsome man dressed in nickers and a beautiful lady sitting on a sofa in a parlor room. Imagine the enjoyment one might get from repeatedly viewing that scene!

Utensils used in Letha's kitchen since 1916. Pie board and rolling pin were made by her Uncle Charles H. Gaver. Photo by Philip H. Georg.

Letha, the Wiles homestead in the background, 1997.

Letha making biscuits, 1997.   Photo by Doris Grossnickle.

Letha with a pan of her apple dumplings, 1998.

Handmade Stottlemyer highchair purchased in 1917.
Dad's straw hat and Mom's sunbonnet.
Photo by Philip H. Georg.

Letha cooking, 1998. Photo by Philip H. Georg.

Letha by the squash patch, 1997.

Letha's old earthenware bowl.   Photo by Leslie Everheart.

Bean & Egg Rivvel Soup

12 cups ham broth
2 to 3 cups cooked navy beans
1 medium raw onion, diced fine
1 cup chopped cooked ham
2 teaspoons butter
salt and pepper, to taste
prepared egg rivvels
(NOTE: Recipes found on pages 260.)

1. In a large kettle combine all ingredients except the rivvels. Bring to a boil.

2. Make either variety of rivvels.

3. Drop the rivvels slowly into the broth while stirring constantly and continue to heat until a boil returns. Cook for about 5 minutes.

Yield: 6 to 8 servings.

ᏏᏏ ᏏᏏ ᏏᏏ

Mom has owned a long handle steel meat fork ever since she and Dad started housekeeping, nearly a century ago. It is made from a metal so strong that it would be a challenge to bend by hand. It is still in use in Mom's kitchen, and seldom has a large piece of meat been cooked and lifted from the pan of broth with any fork other than this trusty old relic! It is another one of Mom's best companions in the kitchen.

Beef or Chicken Noodle Soup

prepared Homemade Egg Noodles
(NOTE: Recipe found on page 267.)
8 cups beef or chicken broth
1 teaspoon dried parsley or chopped fresh parsley
salt and pepper, to taste

1. In a large kettle bring the seasoned broth to a boil. Slowly add the noodles.

2. Cook for about 5 minutes, stirring occasionally.

Variation: Add chopped beef or chicken.

(NOTE: Noodle recipe will make more noodles than needed for 8 cups of soup. Any extra supply of noodles can be thoroughly dried and stored in a tight container in the refrigerator for using at a later time. Noodles must be throughly dried before storing, to prevent molding.)

Yield: 6 to 8 servings.

≈ ≈ ≈

Homemade Egg Noodles

3 egg yolks
1 whole egg
3 tablespoons cold water
1 teaspoon salt
2 cups all-purpose flour

1. In a mixing bowl stir together the egg yolks and whole egg. Add the cold water and salt. Stir until blended with a fork.

2. Add the flour and work with your finger tips to form a dough. Divide into 3 portions and roll into thin sheets on a floured cloth.

3. Allow the dough to dry on the counter top for several hours.
(NOTE: Additional drying time may be needed. Dough should be dry to touch.)

4. Dust sheets of dough lightly with flour. Stack and roll like a jellyroll log. Cut into 1/4-inch strips when dry with a sharp knife.
(NOTE: Be sure the noodles are thoroughly dried before storing, to prevent molding.)

ᏱᏱ ᏱᏱ ᏱᏱ

Six-Egg Yolk Noodles are delicate and full of flavor. Effort is required to prepare the dough, roll, dry and then cut into thin strips, but you will find that your time has been well spent once you taste these noodles.

Six-Egg Yolk Noodles

6 egg yolks
6 tablespoons water
2 1/2 to 3 cups all-purpose flour
1/2 teaspoon salt

1. In a mixing bowl beat the egg yolks and water with a fork until well blended.

2. Stir in the flour and salt to make a stiff but pliable dough. Divide into four portions and roll into thin sheets on a floured cloth.

3. Allow the dough to dry on the counter top for several hours.
(NOTE: Additional drying time may be needed. Dough should be dry to touch.)

4. Dust sheets of dough lightly with flour. Stack and roll like a jellyroll log. Cut into 1/4-inch strips when dry with a sharp knife.
(NOTE: Be sure the noodles are thoroughly dried before storing, to prevent molding.)

ð ð ð

Home-Grown Onion Soup is best made with strong onions from the garden. Some varieties purchased in the grocery stores are too mild for success with this recipe. I can guarantee you on a winter's night, as soon as the snow began to fall or on a cold rainy night when we were chilled to the bones, Dad would suggest Mom make onion soup for supper. The aroma from the onions would fill the house and lingered well into the night. Despite the good taste, this certainly is not a soup to be served when extravagance is called for--it is *everyday* style.

Home-Grown Onion Soup

4 medium home-grown raw onions, diced
2 cups diced raw potatoes
8 cups water
2 beef bouillon cubes
2 tablespoons butter
salt and pepper, to taste
5 slices of buttered bread

1. In a large kettle combine all the ingredients, except the bread, and cook until tender.

2. While the soup is cooking, cut the buttered bread into cubes and place in a shallow pan. Bake at 375 degrees until lightly browned.

3. When potatoes are tender, pour the bread cubes into the soup mixture. This thickens the broth and the soup is ready to serve.

Yield: 4 to 6 servings.

ैं ैं ैं

Fresh whole milk with rich sweet cream was a necessity in Mom's kitchen and especially when she planned to make creamy potato soup. On the farm she always had plenty of potatoes and milk. Mom could milk a cow in nothing flat!

Creamy Potato Soup

3 to 4 cups peeled, cubed potatoes
2 teaspoons dried onion
1/2 cup diced raw celery or sprinkle with celery seed
2 cups water
4 tablespoons butter
1 to 2 teaspoons dried parsley
1 teaspoon salt
pepper, to taste
1 to 2 eggs
2 tablespoons all-purpose flour
additional 1/4 cup water
3 cups whole milk, or use evaporated milk, or sweet cream
    for richness

1. In a heavy kettle cover the potatoes, onion, and diced raw celery, or seeds with water. Cook until tender.
(NOTE: Do not drain the water from potatoes.)

2. Add the butter, parsley, salt, and pepper. Do not remove pan from the stove but reduce the heat to prevent mixture from boiling.

3. In a small bowl combine the eggs, flour, and the additional 1/4 cup of water. Beat until smooth. Slowly pour into the hot soup while stirring constantly. Continue to cook until thickened.
(NOTE: Do not allow to boil.)

4. Add the milk and continue to cook the soup slowly until thickened.

Variation: Serve in individual bowls topped with shredded cheddar or American cheese.

Yield: 4 to 6 servings.

ʑ ʑ ʑ

Eating a large bowl of vegetable soup makes you feel warm and satisfied. Even today at 99 years of age, Mom still makes gallons of this soup to share with her family and friends, both young and old.

Mom canned soup mixture and always had it on hand for a quick meal. She liked to see plenty of jars sitting on the shelves in the cellar, filled with food from her garden. Mom's big garden meant we would be living well during the winter months, until the next harvest.

Mom and all the children worked in the garden when we picked bushels of green beans. It seemed you were never too young to work at gathering vegetables or pulling weeds! Picking beans was a much harder job than setting in the shade snapping them! We begged Mom to let us pull the stalks up at the first picking, making it easier on our backs, but she refused since she hoped for more beans to appear or the small ones to mature with time.

I remember sometimes we went to the garden early in the morning to work. Other times we would wait until the cool of the evening set in to begin toiling. When the sun finally dropped behind the mountain, we children sighed with relief because we knew soon we could no longer see to pull beans! Mom was not so happy as she had planned to finish the job that same day. She was not one to put off until tomorrow what she could do today. She knew the new day in the morning would bring plenty of work with it.

Letha's Vegetable Soup

This recipe requires a large kettle.

1 1/2 to 2 pounds of lean ground beef
3 cups shredded raw cabbage
1 cup chopped raw carrots
1 cup chopped raw celery
1 teaspoon dried onion flakes (or use fresh onion)
2 teaspoons salt
pepper, to taste
2 cups of fresh or frozen peas
2 cups chopped cooked green beans
2 15-ounce cans of white soup beans
4 cups cooked tomatoes
4 cups cooked sweet corn
1 tablespoon chicken granulated bouillon
all-seasoned salt, to taste
pepper, to taste

1. In a very large kettle cook the beef in enough cold water to cover. Stir while cooking to keep meat from lumping. Strain through a colander, reserving the broth. Set meat aside.

2. Add the cabbage, carrots, celery, onion, all-seasoned salt, and pepper to the broth. Cook until vegetables are tender. If you do not have enough broth to cover the vegetables, add water.

3. In a separate saucepan cook the fresh or frozen peas until tender in a small amount of water.
(NOTE: Do not drain.)

4. At this time combine all the ingredients in one large kettle. If additional broth is needed, add water and granulated bouillon. Chicken or beef broth may be added.

5. Freeze soup in containers to suit your family's needs. Or return soup to heat and boil for 5 minutes. Fill sterilized canning jars and seal. Place jars in a hot water bath and cook for 1 hour. Store in a cool dry place.

(NOTE: Mom also adds frozen mixed vegetables to soup for variety.)

Yield: 5 to 6 quarts of soup.

ã   ã   ã

Coffee soup is good when you need a pick me up or when the cold weather has penetrated your bones and you come into the house looking for a quick bite to eat. In days gone by, often the pot of brewed coffee was already sitting on the back of the cookstove when it was decided to have a cup of hot coffee soup. Grandmother Grossnickel made this simple soup. Simplicity was the way of life when Mom was a little girl.

Coffee Soup

1 cup black perked coffee
sweet cream, to taste
granulated sugar, to taste
1 slice of white bread

1. Perk fresh black coffee. Pour into an individual serving bowl. Add sweet cream and sugar, to taste.

2. Break white bread in small pieces and drop into the bowl of coffee.

Coffee soup must be served hot to ensure a rich coffee flavor.

ੴ ੴ ੴ

My mother and Grandmother Grossnickel made cracker soup for anyone around the house who was ill and not feeling well. It just seemed to settle well when we could not tolerate regular food. As a child, I remember Mom holding us on her lap and cradling us in her arms when we were sick. Sometimes in the dark of the night she would get up and carry us to her rocking chair to rock. We sometimes noticed her eyes would close in and out of catnaps. When the weather was real cold and stormy outside, the house had a bit of a chill inside as well, since there was no modern insulation. She covered us with a blanket or an old coat and soon with the warmth of her body next to ours, we were comfy and warm as toast.

Grandmother Grossnickel's Cracker Soup

1 cup boiling water
1 teaspoon butter
1/2 teaspoon granulated sugar
salt and pepper, to taste
saltine crackers
sprinkle with ground nutmeg
sprinkle with ground cinnamon

1. Boil a cup of water. Add the butter, sugar, salt and pepper, to taste.

2. Break saltine crackers into the boiling water. Sprinkle with nutmeg and cinnamon, to taste.

ès ès ès

"Soup and sandwich" go together like ice cream and cake. This was the perfect meal on wash days. It was not until the mid-1960s that Mom had an automatic washer and dryer. Nor did she have an electric or gas hot water heater. Early in the morning she went down to the wash house, started a fire in the fireplace, and filled the black cast-iron butchering kettles with water. While she impatiently waited for the water to heat, she filled the wooden wash tubs with cold rinse water. Now, she pulled the hinged arm holding the kettle from the fire, and carefully, she poured the boiling water into the washer's tub and over the bar of lye soap. She started the agitator in the tub to help dissolve the soap. Finally, she was ready to run the clothes through the washing process. Doing the laundry was some ordeal.

In the winter months Mom was nearly frozen, and in the summertime she was nearly smothered as she hung the clothes out in the yard on the metal clothesline that was attached from the dinner bell pole, to the smokehouse, to the wash house, on to the corner of the old dairy, and back to the dinner bell pole. Even after hanging, the clothes had to be taken from the line and back into the house to be ironed with a heavy black flatiron that she heated on top of the cookstove. These irons did not heat to a consistent temperature: sometimes they were burning hot and the fabric scorched, and other times they were cool and the wrinkles would not budge. Mom padded a board and placed it between the slats of chair backs to use as an ironing board.

When wash days were rainy or snowy, I remember Mom hung the wet garments on a clothes horse, referring to a wooden rack she sat up inside the house and near the kitchen stove. On those bad weather days she kept a ripping hot fire going in the cookstove and it did not take long until the clothes were completely dry and ready for wearing again.

She never heard of an electric dryer when she was a young woman. There was no electricity available in the country in the early 1900s when she was a little girl, and our family did not have use of the convenience until 1932. If the weather was freezing, Mom often hung the clothes to dry on the lines she had strung across the attic, only to be disappointed. If it was really cold outdoors, the wet garments would not dry. Up there it was just too cold. Drying them indoors did not make a pretty sight in the kitchen but it was the price paid for dry garb to wear.

Tomato Soup

4 cups tomato juice, from fresh tomatoes
salt and pepper, to taste
1 teaspoon baking soda
4 cups whole milk
1 tablespoon butter, if desired

1. In a heavy kettle heat the seasoned tomato juice to a boil. Add the baking soda and stir.
(NOTE: To make tomato juice, bring 4 to 5 cups of chopped raw tomatoes to a boil over medium heat. Strain through a colander to remove the skin and seeds.)

2. Heat the milk in a separate saucepan. Add butter, if desired. When both tomatoes and milk are hot, combine.
(NOTE: Do not allow soup to boil after milk has been added.)

Break crackers or toasted bread on individual servings.

≈   ≈   ≈

Rice soup is simple and easy to prepare. It was often served in our home if Mom had cooked more rice for the previous meal than was needed.

Rice Soup

4 cups cooked rice
(NOTE: Do not use minute rice.)
8 cups beef or chicken broth
1 teaspoon dried parsley or chopped fresh parsley
salt and pepper, to taste
prepared rivvels
(Rivvel recipe found on page 260.)

1. In a large kettle bring the seasoned broth to a boil.

2. Prepare the rivvels and slowly add to the boiling broth. Cook for about 5 minutes.

3. Add the cooked rice and stir to distribute.

4. Add the meat and continue to cook until it is hot through.

Yield: 6 to 8 servings.

&a   &a   &a

MAIN DISHES

Both the Grossnickel and Wiles side of our family are of German descent. For as long as Mom can remember, while living at home with her family, the delightful old-fashioned German dish of Schnitz un Knepp has been served. Once you acquire the taste, nothing will take its place.

Schnitz un Knepp

12 cups ham broth
4 cups apple Schnitz

(NOTE: The Schnitz, or dried apples, can be purchased in grocery stores but you can make them. Wash the apples, cut into halves, remove the core and cut into 1/2-inch wide slices. Do not peel the apples. Spread the slices over a drying rack and place in a warm oven. Warm the oven and then turn off the heat. Repeat warming the oven several times a day. If you are going to store the apples, allow time for all moisture to evaporate. This will avoid molding and spoilage.)

1. Soak 4 cups of dried apple Schnitz in enough water to cover for a few hours. Set aside.

2. Pour 12 cups of ham broth into a large heavy flat kettle with a tight lid. Taste the ham broth, and add water if too salty.

3. Drain the dried apple Schnitz and add to the ham broth. Boil slowly for about 1 hour.

Dumpling Ingredients:

3 eggs
1 cup whole milk
1 tablespoon solid vegetable shortening, melted
2 cups all-purpose flour
1/4 cup granulated sugar
2 teaspoons baking powder
1/4 teaspoon salt

4. In a mixing bowl beat the eggs with a rotary beater or wire whisk until light yellow. Add the milk and shortening. Stir with a spoon until blended.

5. Combine the flour, sugar, baking powder, and salt. Add to the egg mixture. Stir until blended.

6. Drop the batter by spoonful into the boiling broth and apples, trying to keep dumplings from touching.

7. Cover and cook for about 20 minutes.
(NOTE: Do not lift the lid while cooking--dumplings will fall.)

Serve immediately, as the dumplings will fall if allowed to sit.

Yield: 8 servings.

❧　❧　❧

Letha's Slippery Cooked Potpie is a German dish that will stay with you long after you have enjoyed the meal.

When Slippery Cooked Potpie was on the day's menu, my dad was a happy man. While still seated at the table, he often leaned his straight chair on its two back legs and commented how much he enjoyed the potpie. He was most content with life on the farm and truly grateful for a home, a good wife, a healthy family, and good food. Farm life added true value in his heart and his reward was the inner satisfaction of having done his job well. He enjoyed the blessings of the day in a world of continuous rude awakenings, much the same as we experience today.

Letha's Slippery Cooked Potpie

1 chicken, 3- to 4-pounds
chicken bouillon cubes
parsley
salt and pepper, to taste
4 medium potatoes, peeled and cut into chunks

1. In a large heavy kettle cook the chicken until tender in enough water and salt to make 3 1/2 quarts of broth.

2. Remove the meat from the bones and cut in large pieces. Set aside.

3. Strain the broth and return to the kettle. For additional flavor, add chicken bouillon cubes. Season the broth with parsley, pepper, and additional salt if needed.

4. Add potatoes to the broth and cook until almost done.

Dough Ingredients:

2 cups all-purpose flour
1/2 teaspoon salt
1/2 cup solid vegetable shortening
1/4 cup cold water

(NOTE: The dough must be used as soon as it is prepared. It cannot be dried like a soup noodle and stored to use later.)

5. In a mixing bowl combine the flour and salt. Cut the shortening into the flour with a fork.

6. Add the cold water slowly while stirring with your finger tips to make a light dough.

7. Form dough into a ball. Roll thin on a floured surface. Cut into 1 1/2-inch squares with a sharp knife.

8. When potatoes are almost done and while the broth is boiling, carefully drop in the dough, a piece at a time, trying to keep squares separated.

9. Cook until potatoes are done and dough is tender.

10. Add the chicken and allow to heat.

Serve piping hot.

Variation: Use Egg Potpie Dough recipe found on page 286.

෨ ෨ ෨

Egg Potpie Dough

2 eggs
2 cups flour
3 tablespoons cream

1. In a large bowl break the eggs and slightly beat. Add the flour and work together while slowly adding the cream.

2. Form the soft dough in a ball. Roll thin on a floured surface. Cut into 1 1/2-inch squares with a sharp knife.

(NOTE: The dough must be used as soon as it is prepared. It cannot be dried like a soup noodle and stored to use later.)

ð   ð   ð

Anyone who neared the farmhouse kitchen door usually knew when Mom was cooking. They could hear the pans and dishes rattling as she hustled around getting the meal prepared in record time. She hated the men having to wait for her to get the meal on the table. That seldom happened! Somehow, she was always up and at it before the rooster crowed in the morning.

Back then, while getting a meal prepared, Mom used the kitchen table as a work space since she did not have a modern kitchen with counter tops until the early sixties. Since we were not the "well to do," the table was covered with bright colored print oilcloth. When we were ready to sit down to eat a meal, another feed bag tablecloth was placed on top.

When we had lots of people to seat for the meal, we ate in the sun parlor at the long oak table. After we finished eating, and as soon as the dishes were washed we made place settings back on that table to be ready for the next meal. Mom spread a large cloth over the clean dishes for protection. The old kitchen in the farmhouse was plain and simple but it was the place you could find comfort, as Mom was usually there. And not only that, you could always find something prepared to eat and stashed away in a safe place there.

Baked Potpie begins with a dish of raw vegetables and is covered with a pie dough crust that bakes into a brown and crispy layer of pastry hiding the steaming vegetables. Delicious! A potpie can be conveniently baked in the oven while you are busy with other chores. It is handy for those hurry up and eat days. Extra seasoning can be added for fuller flavor. Potpie is another farmer's meat and potato dish.

Baked Potpie

Bake at 350 degrees.

1 to 2 cups cooked and coarsely chopped chicken or beef
1 cup shredded raw cabbage
1 cup diced raw celery
1 cup sliced raw carrots
1/2 cup diced raw onions
4 medium raw potatoes, diced fine
1 cup raw peas
parsley, if desired

1. Prepare the vegetables and meat. Mix together and pour into a large greased flat baking dish. Set aside.

Gravy Ingredients:

2 to 3 cups broth, seasoned
4 tablespoons cold water
1 tablespoon all-purpose flour
1 tablespoon cornstarch

2. In a heavy saucepan bring the broth to a boil.

3. While the broth is heating, combine the cold water, flour and cornstarch in a separate cup. Stir until a smooth paste is formed.

4. Reduce the heat under the pan of broth. While stirring pour in the thin flour paste. Cook slowly, stirring frequently, until gravy thickens. About 8 minutes.

5. Pour the hot gravy over the meat and vegetables.

Dough Ingredients:

1 cup all-purpose flour
1/2 teaspoon salt
1/3 cup solid vegetable shortening
2 tablespoons cold or ice water

6. In a mixing bowl combine the flour and salt. Add the shortening and cut in with a fork.

7. Form a well in the flour mixture with your hand and fill with the water. Slowly and lightly mix the dough with your finger tips until blended.

8. Press the dough into a ball and roll on a floured surface. Cut into 2-inch squares and place on top of raw potpie.

9. Bake in the oven for about 1 hour or until potatoes are tender.
(NOTE: If dough turns brown before potpie is done, lay a sheet of aluminum foil loosely over the top to prevent burning. Do not seal the aluminum foil.)

(NOTE: To save time make the dough in advance and store in the refrigerator for a few days before using.)

Yield: 8 to 10 servings.

❧   ❧   ❧

Egg Noodle Casserole, along with a salad, makes a complete meal. It is a hearty, filling dish. This type of dish is great for serving when the volume of work around home is pushing in on you.

Today one never thinks of needing to make egg noodles from scratch. We add the item to our grocery list, we purchase it, thus having noodles on the pantry shelf ready and waiting for us to use. Well, it wasn't that easy for Mom. If today's cook needed to preserve food, bake the bread, carry the water, carry the wood into the house for the cook stove, and hitch the horse to the buggy or walk to the local general store for staples, we would certainly have a change of lifestyle, to say the least, but that was life for the farm woman when Mom was young.

Egg Noodle Casserole

Bake at 350 degrees.

2 cups chopped cooked chicken
2 chopped hard-boiled eggs
1 cup diced raw celery
1 cup whole milk
1 small can mushrooms, drained
1 can cream of mushroom soup
1 can cream of chicken soup
1 10-ounce bag of soup egg noodles
all-seasoned salt
reserved chicken broth
1/2 pound grated cheddar or American cheese
1 cup crushed butter-rich crackers

1. Cook the chicken in salt water until tender. Remove the meat from the bones and chop coarsely. Reserve the broth.

2. In a mixing bowl combine the cooked chicken, eggs, celery, milk, and mushrooms. Add the soups. Set aside.

3. In a saucepan of boiling water cook a 10-ounce bag of egg noodles until almost tender.

4. Pour cooked noodles into a colander and rinse under cold running water. Allow to drain.

5. Mix noodles and the above soup mixture together. Sprinkle with all-seasoned salt and add enough reserved chicken broth to make the consistency of a creamy casserole.

6. Pour into a large flat baking dish and transfer to the oven.

7. About 10 minutes before removing from the oven, sprinkle top of casserole with grated cheese and crumbled crackers. Dot with butter, if desired.
(NOTE: Use a buttery cracker.)

8. Bake in the oven for 30 to 40 minutes or until bubbly and hot.

Yield: 8 servings.

&a   &a   &a

This is my favorite baked bean recipes and I know of no other bean dish that is tastier. It is superb! Mom adds saltine crackers to this baked bean dish and I think it improves the taste and texture.

During the Great Depression and World Wars I and II, most families ate lots of cooked dried beans, due to the ration on certain items and lack of money to purchase choice foods. That brought us no harm since we all know that beans were a good source of protein and fiber.

Our family suffered due to conditions caused by the nation's economy. Spirits were dampened by the rations as well. Tears must have dimmed my parent's eyes from time to time due to stress alone. I say this, and then I think of all the families living who have lost loved ones to these conflicts. Suddenly, I am reminded a loss other than death, is of no importance no matter how bad the situation. I have often thought, is it any wonder most of us have a consuming hatred for war and a constant longing for world-wide peace?

Letha's Baked Beans

Bake at 300 to 325 degrees.

3 cups cooked white navy beans
1/4 pound bacon, chopped and fried
1 small onion diced fine, or use dried onion flakes
1/3 cup molasses
1/3 cup brown sugar
1 teaspoon mustard
2 cups of canned tomatoes
(NOTE: Cook chopped raw tomatoes to equal 2 cups.)
saltine crackers

1. In a heavy saucepan cook the beans until tender. Set aside.
(NOTE: Canned beans can be used.)

2. In a small skillet fry the bacon and onion. Set aside.
(NOTE: If bacon produces an excess of fat, you may want to drain and discard.)

3. In a large mixing bowl combine the molasses, brown sugar, mustard, and tomatoes. Add to the beans and bacon. Stir until combined.

4. Pour the mixture into a large baking dish.

5. Break a few saltine crackers over the top and push down into the bean mixture with a spoon.

6. Bake in the oven for 30 to 45 minutes or until bubbly.

Variation: This recipe can be modified by using a variety of beans and seasoning.

Yield: 4 to 6 servings.

≥≥ ≥≥ ≥≥

Mom's chicken dressing or stuffing is a favorite dish with our family. Seldom, if ever, has a roast chicken or turkey dinner been served at home without bread dressing. Mom thinks it fits like a hand in a glove with baked poultry meals. The butter required in this recipe adds richness, but can be reduced if you are watching the fat content in your diet.

Most often, Mom would set aside a few days for butchering poultry on the farm. The whole day was spent killing, plucking, and cleaning chicken. Then at the end of the day, we packaged the meat for freezing. I can remember what a grueling day's work that was!

Chicken Bread Dressing

Bake at 375 degrees.

1 1/2 sticks butter
1 cup raw celery, diced fine
4 quarts broken white bread
1 teaspoon salt
pepper, to taste
1 teaspoon dried onion flakes (or sauted fresh onion)
dried or fresh parsley, to taste
1 1/2 to 2 cups hot broth

1. In a small skillet melt the butter and saute the celery until tender. Set aside.

2. In a large pan combine the broken bread pieces, salt, pepper, onion, and parsley. Pour the butter mixture over the bread and toss lightly.

3. Place in a large buttered flat baking dish and pour the hot broth evenly over the top.
(NOTE: Do not pour broth on prepared dressing until ready to place in the oven.)

4. Bake in the oven for 20 to 25 minutes or until top is lightly browned.

Serve bread dressing with any type of poultry meal you enjoy along with a cranberry sauce of your choice.

Yield: 8 servings.

ℓℓℓ

In Middletown, at the L. Z. Derr store, a huge round cake of cheese, covered and molded with a black waxed cloth, sat on the shelf in the aisle behind the counter that held the old manual cash register. I recall well this old register and how it clinked and clattered as the storekeeper pushed the keys to ring up the bill. When we asked to purchase cheese, Osmond or Miss Oneida would pick up the large sharp knife and cut off a slice, place it on parchment paper on the scales, look at us, and ask, "Is it alright if its a bit over a pound"? No problem. The cheese had a good taste and we could use it.

No cheese today can come near to the taste of that one. To say the least it was superior to any other. The reason some of today's dishes do not taste the same as those of yesterday, is because we cannot purchase the identical ingredient that we used back then. Some products are improved; others we long for and remember with fondness.

L. Z. Derr store has been out of business for years now but not forgotten by the town's people! They were honest folks who served our town well for so long.

Baked Macaroni

Bake at 350 degrees.

1/2 pound of uncooked elbow macaroni
1/2 to 3/4 pound of American or cheddar cheese
2 tablespoons butter
all-seasoned salt
pepper, to taste
2 cups whole milk
butter, to dot top of macaroni

1. In a heavy saucepan cook the macaroni in salt water until tender. Rinse and allow to drain in a colander.

2. Spray a baking dish with cooking oil and pour in a layer of macaroni, cover with a layer of American or cheddar cheese, dot with butter, and sprinkle with pepper and all-seasoned salt. Continue making layers.

3. From the edge of the dish pour milk over the mixture.

4. Bake in the oven for about 30 minutes or until it bubbles.

Variation: Add crumbled fried bacon over top of baked macaroni. Return to the oven for a minute or two.

Yield: 6 servings.

&a. &a. &a.

Letha's macaroni is a quick and simple recipe and children love it. Certainly, many of Mom's recipes have little ones in mind, since they were always around. Mom is now a great, great grandmother.

Letha's Macaroni

3/4 cup uncooked elbow macaroni
3 cups water
1 tablespoon butter
3/4 cup whole milk
1 cup American cheese
all-seasoned salt, to taste

1. In a saucepan cook macaroni and butter in water until tender. Most of the water will evaporate from the macaroni while cooking.
(NOTE: Do not drain the small amount of water that remains on the macaroni.)

2. Reduce the heat and add the milk to the cooked macaroni. Add small pieces of American cheese to the simmering noodles and season with all-seasoned salt. The cheese will thicken the milk to a creamy sauce.

Serve hot.

Yield: 4 to 6 servings.

                                             ॐ   ॐ   ॐ

Mom seldom disposed of left-over food. Somehow, she figured ways to serve it at the next meal with a different twist. In other words she *doctored it up*, making the family think it was something special. She made a variety of macaroni dishes that were quick to prepare when she needed a little something extra to put with a meal.

When cooked macaroni was left over after serving the meal, Mom saved it, coated it with egg, and fried it in a little butter for supper. She also cooked fresh macaroni for the purpose of making this dish.

Fried Macaroni with Egg

2 cups cooked elbow macaroni
1 egg
1 tablespoon of cream
salt and pepper, to taste
butter, for frying

1. In a bowl beat the egg with a rotary beater or wire whisk until light yellow and stir in the cream. Stir in the cooked macaroni and sprinkle with salt and pepper.

2. In a skillet heat a few tablespoons of butter and pour in the egg covered macaroni. Fry over low heat until egg clings to the macaroni with a texture of a moist scrambled egg.
(NOTE: Do not overcook or dish will be dry.)

Variation: Add cheese, chopped ham, or chopped raw peppers. Add all-seasoned salt. Season with parsley or chopped onion.

№ № №

Letha's old-fashioned spaghetti sauce is not like the ordinary manufactured spaghetti sauce we think of today. This type of sauce made from home-canned tomatoes is thin, juicy, and delicious, almost abandoned by the new modern sauces we find in jars on the shelves in the grocery stores.

One can appreciate the countless hours Mom has spent over the years in servitude just to feed us. Growing up we did not have prepared sauces, but Mom took the time to prepare a dish that we thought was just as good, if not better.

Our family may have been considered poor in money, but we were never underprivileged. Love was served in abundance in a home where we trusted and respected our parents and each other.

Letha's Old-Fashioned Spaghetti

2 pounds lean ground beef
2 medium onions, diced fine
6 tablespoons butter
4 cups home-canned crushed tomatoes or juice
(NOTE: Fresh cooked tomatoes may be substituted for canned.)
1 pound spaghetti
1 cup grated cheese

1. In a skillet brown the ground beef. Allow to drain in a colander. Set aside.

2. In the same skillet brown the chopped onion in butter. Add the tomatoes, beef, and onion. Set aside over low heat.

3. In a heavy kettle cook the spaghetti in salt water until tender. Pour into a colander and rinse with cold water. Allow to drain.

4. Return spaghetti to the heavy kettle and add the tomato mixture. Simmer until steaming hot. Stir frequently to prevent scorching.

5. Pour into serving bowl and sprinkle with shredded cheese.

Yield: 8 servings.

ə̃a   ə̃a   ə̃a

By the time you eat a serving or two of Chicken and Dumplings, you know what "stick to your ribs" means! Mom stewed old hens for making this dish. When she went to the chicken house to catch chickens, she used a long wire chicken hook to snag the bird by the leg. The hook was made from a long, heavy gauge wire about the thickness of a lead pencil and about four feet long. One end turned into a hook and on the other end was a small wooden handle. Mom could stand her distance while she pulled the hook around the chicken's leg without it knowing what was about to happen. She drew the fluttering bird back to her and grabbed it with her hand. Carefully, she dropped it into a wooden coop and the capture was complete.

Catching one chicken upset the whole flock and when the chickens became aware of what was happening, they squawked as they darted under and over one another. They ran to huddle and then stacked thick in a corner of the chicken house. In a matter of seconds she could create a noisy, wing-flapping time in the henhouse! Given a few minutes, they gained their composure enabling Mom to catch the next one.

Chicken and Dumplings

1 frying chicken or stewing hen
5 cups chicken broth
salt, to taste
dumplings

1. In a heavy kettle cook the chicken in salt water until tender. Remove the meat from the bone and tear in strips. Set aside.

2. Strain the broth and return to the kettle. Bring to a boil and add the chicken.

Dumpling Ingredients:

1 1/2 cups all-purpose flour
2 teaspoons baking powder
1 teaspoon salt
3 tablespoons solid vegetable shortening
3/4 cup whole milk

3. While broth is heating to a boil, prepare the dumplings.

4. In a mixing bowl sift together the flour, baking powder, and salt.

5. Cut the shortening into the mixture with a fork.

6. Add the milk slowly and stir until blended.
(NOTE: Do not beat.)

7. Drop the dough by spoonfuls into the kettle of boiling broth, being careful to keep them separated.

8. Cook uncovered for 10 minutes. Cover with a tight lid and cook for 10 more minutes.

Variation: Add parsley or onion.

Yield: 8 to 10 servings.

ᕤ   ᕤ   ᕤ

There is absolutely nothing fancy about cornmeal mush. In fact, you either like it, or you don't! Each December, when the darkest time of the year arrived, or when the winter months dragged, and the cook ran out of ideas of what to prepare for the evening meal, she could always make a pot of mush. Mom intentionally prepared more than needed for one meal, then she cooled the leftover and come morning, she sliced it, and fried it for breakfast. Not exactly a meal of splendor, but when Mom served mush, she knew without a shadow of a doubt that she had filled our empty tummies.

Cornmeal Mush

2 quarts water
2 cups yellow cornmeal
1/2 cup all-purpose flour
1 teaspoon salt

1. In a heavy kettle, bring the first quart of water to a boil.

2. In a large mixing bowl combine the cornmeal, flour, and salt with the second quart of cold water. Add the mixture into the boiling water and stir.

3. Reduce to medium heat and cook the cornmeal mixture slowly until thick like the consistency of a heavy cake batter. Stir constantly to prevent lumping.

4. Fill individual bowls and pour excess into a loaf pan. *(NOTE: Use later for fried mush.)*

Serve hot with butter on top. Cover with rich milk.

&a &a &a

I can clearly see that these old traditional dishes, such as fried mush, are often forgotten only because today's generation needs a quick and easy method of cooking. Mom enjoys eating fresh fried mush between slices of toast spread thick with molasses.

Fried Cornmeal Mush

prepared cornmeal mush
(NOTE: Recipe found on page 304.)
shortening, for frying

1. Prepare mush and pour into a greased loaf pan. Cool.

2. When mush is firm, slice 1/2 to 3/4 inch thick and dredge through flour. Place the slices in a skillet of hot shortening and fry until crispy and brown.
(NOTE: Do not cover pan with a lid.)

Serve hot with syrup, jelly, or as Mom prefers, molasses.

(NOTE: Cornmeal mush can be stored in a tight container in the refrigerator and fried a few days later.)

&a. &a. &a.

A fritter is a small, simple cake of fried batter. Use your imagination and choose different fruits and vegetables to add flavor and texture to this recipe.

Mom has a large tanish-yellow earthenware bowl with fine dark blue stripes around the top rim which she has used for years and years. It is not in perfect condition, as it has seen a full life. This bowl is an oldie and holds a prominent spot on the shelf in Mom's work kitchen in the basement. I could say, it is like a dependable friend to her! It has held more cake batter than one can ever imagine. Just think, nine children in the kitchen scampering about over the years, and the bowl remains in one piece! That is a miracle in itself.

At home, sitting in the kitchen cabinets, there is also a small pink earthenware bowl with two little yellow flowers embossed on the side. It has a distinct crack from the top rim down into the bottom of the bowl, but Mom doesn't notice or even care. She has eaten her cereal from that bowl for so many years she would not think of parting with it. And the reason for this is that it not only holds her cereal, but ceaseless, precious memories as well. You see, there was another bowl, identical except it is yellow--that one was Dad's.

While in her golden years, with her hair turned to silver white, and without the love of her life, that bowl somehow holds a special comfort while having breakfast alone. It seems in times such as these that it helps to recall each happy moment of the past. I have thought about this. We must be wise to save anything that would provoke a recollection of a treasured moment from the past, a memory that adds comfort or laughter to our lives. This reminds me of a saying: *Time endears and cannot fade memories love has made.*

Golden Brown Fritters

1 cup all-purpose flour
1 teaspoon baking powder
1 teaspoon salt
2 eggs
1/2 cup whole milk
1 tablespoon melted butter
1 teaspoon vanilla
1 cup apples or peaches, sliced thin
cooking oil, for frying

1. In a bowl combine the dry ingredients. Set aside.

2. In a separate bowl beat the eggs with a rotary beater or wire whisk until light yellow. Add the milk, melted butter, and vanilla. Stir with a spoon until blended.

3. Add the dry ingredients and stir until smooth. Add the fruit and stir.

4. In a deep skillet heat cooking oil over medium to high heat. When hot, drop the batter by spoonfuls into the oil and fry until golden brown, but do not cover with a lid.

5. Remove fritters from the oil and allow to drain on paper towels and serve topped with syrup, or powdered sugar.

Variation: Use cooked rice or corn in place of fruit.

Yield: 10 fritters.

&a &a &a

VEGETABLES & PICKLES

I often wonder now, as Mom worked in the soil in the garden back then, if perhaps the sun did shine warmer on her tired back than she could bare, since she often worked in the cool evening hours until dark as she hoed around all of the plants and pulled up weeds. Having such a long day, she never had a free minute of time for herself. For a farmer's wife, however, there was no other way. The future depended on how much every one was willing to give of their time and energy towards making success happen. Sometimes Mom and Dad must have thought the toils of life were beyond their endurance. I believe they agreed with the statement of *one today being worth two tomorrows*.

The children worked in the garden and in the house, along with helping to take care of the babies. We were so worn out by evening that the night brought happy sleep. Meanwhile, no one had the opportunity or pleasure of being bored!

Candied Sweet Potatoes were a favorite on the farm. After growing the sweet potatoes, we use this tried and true recipe.

Candied Sweet Potatoes

5 to 6 medium raw sweet potatoes
1 1/2 cups granulated sugar
1/2 teaspoon salt
1 stick butter
1 cup water or enough to cover the bottom of the kettle
(NOTE: Do not cover potatoes with water.)

1. Peel fresh raw sweet potatoes, cut into halves or quarters, to make one layer over the bottom of a 5-quart non-stick Dutch oven.

2. Pour the sugar, butter, and salt evenly over the raw potatoes.

3. Add a cup of water or enough to cover the bottom of the kettle. Cover pan with a tight lid.

4. Place pan over medium to high heat and cook until the syrup is thick. Move the pan around over the stove burner, with a shaking action, every few minutes to prevent potatoes from sticking. If a spoon is used to move the potatoes, they will break easily.
(NOTE: Watch carefully--potatoes will quickly scorch and burn.)

5. When potatoes are tender and if there is still water in the pan, remove the lid and continue to boil allowing it to evaporate and syrup to form. Again, shake the pan frequently to prevent scorching.

Variation: Cook fresh pineapple with the potatoes.

Yield: 6 to 8 servings.

૨ં&&   ૨ં&&   ૨ં&&

Each fall some of the choice sweet potatoes from the harvest were saved to plant and produce next year's crop. The potatoes that were selected were allowed to air dry for a few weeks in the wash house, then each one was wrapped in newspaper and layered in a heavy cardboard box. Mom stored the box in the house in a cool, dry closet, guarding so they did not freeze.

Come spring, Mom buried the seed sweet potatoes in rich soil in the hot bed or she would use an old discarded dishpan. She sat the pan in the warm kitchen at a spot where the sun shone in the window. Once the green sprouts with tiny tender leaves came out they were transplanted to the garden, but only after the chance of freezing temperatures was over. The soil was piled or shaped into a one-foot high mound in a long row across the plot, and Mom carefully poked a hole in the dirt, plopped the sprout in, poured in some water, and carefully pushed the dirt around it. New sweet potatoes grew from these plants during the summer months, making a crop ready to be harvested come early fall.

Years ago Mom fried sweet potatoes or white potatoes in home-rendered lard. The combination of lard and an old cast-iron skillet produced delicious crispy potatoes--not too healthy by today's standards, but nevertheless it was a taste to savor!

Fried Sweet Potatoes

raw sweet potatoes
granulated sugar, to taste
salt, to taste
shortening, for frying

1. Wash and peel the fresh raw sweet potatoes. Cut slices 1/4 to 1/2 inch wide across the whole potato.

2. Place the slices in a heavy skillet of hot shortening and sprinkle tops with sugar and salt. Fry until tender.
(NOTE: Do not cover with shortening.)

Serve immediately while piping hot.

ᓚ   ᓚ   ᓚ

Whether a simple or elaborate meal is being planned, Oven Method Sweet Potatoes fits the menu.

Oven Method Sweet Potatoes

Bake at 350 degrees.

6 medium raw sweet potatoes
1/4 cup water
1 cup brown sugar
1/4 cup butter
salt, to taste

1. Wash, peel, and cut the sweet potatoes in halves. Place in a flat greased baking dish.

2. Pour the water in the baking dish. Sprinkle tops of sweet potatoes with sugar and dot with butter. Sprinkle with salt.

3. Bake in the oven for about 45 minutes or until potatoes are tender.

Variation: Garnish with marshmallows, either small or large ones. Return the dish to the oven, turn off the heat and allow marshmallows to puff up and toast until the tops are crispy with cracks of softened marshmallow showing.

Yield: 6 to 8 servings.

ઢ ઢ ઢ

Leftover potatoes will become a favorite when prepared following this Eggs Over Potatoes recipe. It is a great dish for the short-order cook.

There were special work days on the farm. Without the aid of modern machinery, the bygone days of thrashing, silo filling, and hay making required numerous men working on the farm. A farmhand expected, and rightfully so, to eat his meals at the farmer's family table. So a busy season at the barn indicated busy days in the kitchen. Feeding crews of famished harvesters, about 14 men at a meal, was not uncommon on the farm.

Mom or one of the children rang the dinner bell to indicate to the men, the meal was ready. Without the noise of the modern tractor motors, the dinging ring was easily heard from out in the fields, far away. The bell was mounted on top of a tall pole that stood out back of the kitchen door. A heavy rope was attached to the clapper and hung down making it easy for the children to reach and pull when they ran out to ring the bell.

At the sound of the bell, the horses laboring in the field pawed their feet on the ground to get the men's attention. The horses knew it was mealtime for them too. A few ears of corn would be tossed into their feed box in the horse stable in the barn, and they knew a fresh drink of cold spring water would be waiting in the barnyard watering trough. The horses had responded to the men's commands all morning, and they had earned a break in the shade, out from under the heat of the hot sun. The loaded wagons of hay, corn, or grain were heavy to pull and worked every muscle.

As the men made their way to the farm house, they too, breathed a sigh of relief when they reached the large maple tree that provided shade for the immediate area around the house and small buildings. The men freshened up for the meal at the water faucet outdoors at the side of the farm workers' quarters, while we children sat on the tall steps, high above and watched. They threw their hats near our feet and most of them gave us a smile and sometimes asked "what are you doing?" Of course, we seldom answered as we were overwhelmed with so many of them around us.

Mom provided wash basins, cakes of soap, and hand-made flour sack towels placed on a nail under the opening at the steps by the water faucet. As the men washed their faces and hands before coming to the table they scrubbed to rid themselves of the chaff and dust from the field. They splashed water around their head and neck trying to cool down. When it came Dad's turn to draw water in the basin, he usually reached up and gave us a little pinch on our leg and a wink of his eye. We enjoyed being perched there on those high steps looking down on everyone.

When all the men had finished "shining up" they walked behind Dad, up the porch steps, to the kitchen and through the door into the farm house. Dad walked to his place at the head of the table and said, "find a seat boys and make yourselves at home." No time was wasted in conversation once the invitation to start eating was made. Nothing pleased Mom more than to witness these men enjoying their meal.

During these periods of harvest, everyone talked about the weather, no matter if the sun was shinning or the sky held threatening clouds. A short thunderstorm or a light sprinkle could put a stop to the harvesting process in nothing flat.

Hay and grain needs to be dry to process and store in the barn, so a daytime shower was not always welcomed. Wet hay, straw, and grain stored in the barn can cause combustion which could start a fire that could burn the barn down.

So, if all this work was not enough to ruin the day for the farmer's wife, what could be worse than to have a big meal half-way cooked, a thunderstorm descending, and every man leaving the day's work and heading towards his home.

Once the harvesting season was over in the summertime, the farmers' wives gave a finishing party. In some areas of the county all the families would gather on a selected evening for fun and lots of good food. Ice cream could be counted on, plus as many cakes and pies as could be baked!

These days, Mom can vision the scenes on the farm as she thinks of the neighboring homesteads and the carefully planted corn and grain fields. The pasture fields with cattle so content can lead to making one homesick. And the sight of the sun dropping in the western sky behind South Mountain is one sight that's hard to forget. The mountains loom just outside the kitchen windows and provide a peaceful scene that no artist can capture or duplicate. Then too, the Middletown Lutheran Church steeple stands tall over the hills towards town and will always be remembered. On a calm, silent day one can hear the strike of the old clock housed there.

Not only will Mom and her family never forget these scenes, but the details, like a soft breeze through the trees will always be with us. The church chimes ring through the valley to the tune of old hymns, so sweet and peaceful. Oh, home sweet home it is!

Mom had menus she used when preparing special meals on the farm. Here are two we found tucked in her cookbook on the original scraps of paper. Christmas Day Dinner included fried oyster pats, roasted turkey, sauerkraut with fresh pork, gravy, mashed potatoes, candied sweet potatoes, bread dressing, oyster plant casserole, creamed lima beans, buttered corn, cole slaw, cranberry sauce, a variety of gelatin salads, cheese and crackers, Letha's mincemeat pie, Letha's light fruitcake, white cake with fresh coconut on icing, a variety of Christmas cookies, fresh fruit plate or butchering day fruit salad.

The butchering day menu included baked country ham, roasted chicken, sauerkraut with fresh pork, mashed potatoes, candied sweet potatoes, gravy with floating saltine crackers, green beans with ham broth, creamed lima beans, bread dressing, buttered corn, oyster plant casserole, stewed tomatoes, cole slaw, orange cranberry relish, butchering day fruit salad, home-canned pineapple and stewed prunes (purchased in 25 pound boxes and Mom canned them to use at a later time), home-grown celery sticks, rich cherry cake, red devil's food cake, angel food cake, fresh banana cake, Letha's light fruitcake and mincemeat pie.

Mom needed good standby menus to use when preparing meals for the harvesters, since it was not unusual for the men to be at the farm during the busy seasons for an entire week.

Eggs Over Potatoes

4 eggs, slightly beaten
1 cup whole milk
salt and pepper, to taste
5 cups cooked and sliced potatoes
(NOTE: Potatoes must be cooled for a few hours in the refrigerator. Freshly cooked potatoes will fall apart.)
3 slices of bread, broken or crumbled into pieces
2 tablespoons butter, for frying

1. In a mixing bowl beat the eggs with a fork. Add the milk, salt, and pepper. Set aside.

2. Heat the butter in a skillet on low heat. Add the potatoes and when they are hot add 3 slices of broken bread pieces.

3. Pour the egg mixture over the potato and bread mixture. Turn with a spatula while frying slowly to prevent scorching. Use low heat.
(NOTE: Do not overcook; mixture should not appear dry.)

Serve for breakfast or supper.

Yield: 6 servings.

❧   ❧   ❧

I tell you, stout and hearty may be the words to describe fried onions. They taste good with home-fried potatoes and green leafy vegetables or with breakfast foods. Before it was popular to have exhaust fans installed in the kitchen, the house reeked with the smell of onion after preparing this dish.

Old-Time Fried Onions

4 cups sliced raw onions
1/4 cup of hot water
1 teaspoon granulated sugar, if desired
salt and pepper, to taste
1 to 2 tablespoons butter, for frying

1. In a heavy skillet heat the butter until melted and add all the ingredients.

2. Cover the pan with a lid and cook until tender. Remove the lid and fry until lightly browned.
(NOTE: Watch carefully--onions will burn quickly.)

Yield: 4 servings.

&ea;   &ea;   &ea;

Scalloped Potatoes are a popular dish with folks of all ages. In the early 1920s, on Monday mornings Dad hitched the horse to the spring wagon and headed to Myersville to deliver milk and butter from the farm to his mother, Flora Wiles. She lived across the street from George Bittle's general store, the Bittle's bank and Bittle's home. Stanley and Mae Kline presently own the Bittle's Store. They make their home there and operate Kline's Wood Works in the old store front. The old bank building is owned by C. Basil Grossnickle Insurance.

Back then, Flora Wiles' neighbor on the north side was Robert Ridgely and on the south side lived John Kinnerman. John operated a telephone exchange and shoe repair business. At a central telephone exchange an operator connected all calls manually by a switchboard. The very first phones did not use a switchboard because only a pair of wires were used. This method provided service for just two phones. As more telephones came into use, each one was connected to all the other phones. This required manual manipulation so a telephone exchange was set up and most often in the operator's home.

George Bittle's store carried food staples and hardware items, such as nails, buckets, men's work clothing, and shoes. It was a genuine country store. Some of my older sisters and brothers remember riding along with Dad into Myersville, and upon arrival they tied the horse to the old iron hitching posts that were fixed along the street. If Dad was planning to transport a heavy load of farm supplies or grain either way on the trip, he used two horses hitched to the wagon. Most wagons offered the ability to switch between one-and two-horse hook up. Dad thought why should one horse struggle to pull the load when two horses could be used, eliminating a strain on either one. Most often, when Dad went to town the other horses were at home, just standing and waiting for his return. Always, while on these trips, Dad would walk across the street to Bittle's to purchase a few supplies that Mom needed from the store.

Scalloped Potatoes

Bake at 350 degrees.

5 to 6 medium potatoes
3 tablespoons all-purpose flour
salt and pepper, to taste
parsley and onion, if desired
butter
cheese, American or cheddar
whole milk

1. Wash, peel, and slice about 6 raw potatoes. Place a layer of sliced potatoes in a greased baking dish. Plan to make about 3 layers.

2. Sprinkle with a tablespoon of flour, salt and pepper. Add onion or parsley, if desired.

3. Dot with butter and place a layer of your favorite cheese on top.

4. Continue making layers.

5. From the edge of the dish, pour enough whole milk to cover potatoes.

6. Bake in the oven for about 1 hour or until potatoes are tender.

Variation: Little extras can be added to this recipe, such as a few tablespoons of sour cream, different cheeses, seasoning, and bits of bacon to enhance the flavor.

Yield: 6 servings.

ða   ða   ða

Sometimes Mom misjudged when preparing mashed potatoes so she used the surplus and made potato cakes for the next meal. As I write this recipe for potato cakes, I am reminded of baking slices of raw potatoes on top of the cooking surface of the old wood-burning stove. We called them "tator cakes" and does the thought ever bring back a sweet remembrance of home.

We knew spring would return sooner or later, but still the winters were usually long and hard to endure. On a cold stormy winter day, when Dad finished the morning's barn work and came to the house for a break, we began our fun. We peeled the skin away, then cut thin slices the width of the potato. The slices were placed directly on the black cast-iron stove top to heat until tender and crispy on one side. Quickly we turned them over to the other side. Once cooked, the slices were removed from the stove. We children waited with a plate in hand and quickly doused the slices with butter and salt. What a treat! Of course, half the fun was eating the hot potatoes as soon as they were removed from the stove and before they had a chance to sit and turn heavy. Too bad we don't have the old stove today to periodically use for cooking something special!

Potato Cakes

1 egg, well beaten
2 to 3 tablespoons all-purpose flour
1 teaspoon dried onion flakes
1 teaspoon dried parsley
pepper, to taste
2 cups leftover mashed potatoes
3 to 4 tablespoons butter, for frying

1. In a mixing bowl beat the egg with a rotary beater or wire whisk until light yellow. Add the flour, onion flakes, parsley, and pepper. Mix together.

2. Add the mashed potatoes to the mixture and stir with a spoon until well blended.

3. In a skillet add a few tablespoons of butter and allow to melt. Form potato mixture into patties and place in hot butter to fry over medium heat until crispy and lightly browned.

Serve piping hot.

Yield: 4 servings.

&a   &a   &a

There are hundreds of varieties and methods for preparing stuffed peppers. When my mother was a little girl, her mother made these cold cabbage stuffed peppers from this recipe. She remembers being in the kitchen and helping her mother carry the prepared peppers to the springhouse to place in the cold spring water. She recalls how much her father and brothers enjoyed the peppers.

Some of the same old recipes in this cookbook were used to make food a 100 years ago and served by my grandmother Clara Grossnickel. The social activities of that day were not vacations, or going to a show with dinner, or concerts, but quilting circles and corn husking parties. Oftentimes, their social events were used as ways of getting help to get work done or projects completed.

Hot or Cold Cabbage Stuffed Peppers

8 cups grated raw cabbage
1 cup chopped raw bell peppers
celery seed, to taste
salt and pepper, to taste
1/2 cup vinegar
1 cup granulated sugar
8 raw bell peppers

1. Grate the raw cabbage by hand or in a food processor. Sprinkle with salt and let stand for about 20 minutes.

2. Squeeze any liquid from the cabbage by hand. Add the chopped peppers, celery seed, salt and pepper. Set aside.

3. In a small saucepan boil the vinegar and sugar to a thick syrup. Remove from the heat and allow to cool.

4. Pour the syrup over the cabbage mixture. Stir until blended. Place in the refrigerator in a covered dish to wilt.

5. Cut a thin slice from the stem end of each pepper. Remove seeds, any membrane, and wash.

6. Stuff the raw peppers with the slaw mixture and place in a baking dish.

Syrup Ingredients:

(NOTE: The following syrup is to pour around peppers once placed in the pan.)

2 1/2 cups vinegar
2 1/2 cups water
1 1/4 cups granulated sugar
1/4 teaspoon ground cloves
2 teaspoons salt

7. In a heavy saucepan cook the syrup ingredients until thick and pour around the peppers.

8. When making Cold Cabbage Stuffed Peppers: place stuffed peppers in the refrigerator to marinate. When making Hot Cabbage Stuffed Peppers: bake immediately at 350 degrees for about 30 minutes.

Yield: 6 to 8 servings.

&a.   &a.   &a.

Potatoes, especially mashed, are a must when serving warm cabbage slaw. Dad loved it. Older folks prepared and served cabbage in a variety of ways. Most gardeners planted lots of cabbage plants back then, and the crops were stored in a cool cellar or buried in a ground cave to use in the winter months.

Mom planted cabbage in the early spring and again, later in the season to ensure that there was fresh cabbage in the garden for a longer period of time. She first planted Early Jersey Wakefield cabbage, which produced a small pointed head. The later variety, Flat Dutch, grew a large flat head. It seems today folks consider gardening a hobby, but years ago it was a means of survival.

Warm Cabbage Slaw

1 small head of cabbage
1 teaspoon salt
3 tablespoons butter

1. In a heavy kettle shred a small head of cabbage and cover with salt water. Cook until tender.

2. Remove from heat and allow about 1/2 cup water to remain on the bottom of the pan. Add the butter.

Dressing Ingredients:

1 cup sweet cream
1/2 cup vinegar
4 tablespoons granulated sugar
2 tablespoons all-purpose flour

3. In a heavy saucepan combine the sweet cream, vinegar, sugar, and flour.

4. Boil the mixture for 1 minute while stirring constantly. Reduce the heat and cook until thick.

5. Pour the dressing over the cabbage, stirring slowly and constantly until well blended.

Serve hot.

Yield: 6 servings.

ॐ   ॐ   ॐ

Mom always kept asparagus roots planted along the edge of the garden by the white picket fence. They are usually planted on a mound of soil, then covered with straw to preserve moisture and to help prevent the weeds from growing up around it. When the weather turns warm, the tender sprouts with scalelike leaves, poke up through the ground and grow rapidly. Towards the early fall, if not cut the sprouts will turn to three-foot stalks. At that point the pulp becomes hard, goes to seed and sprouts out a beautiful lacy fern-type foliage.

In the spring when asparagus first starts to come up in the garden and is not plentiful yet, you can stretch the dish by simply adding broken pieces of plain toast to the prepared sauce. I think it improves the taste. I recall Dad telling Mom he had an appetite for a *mess of greens* or a *mess* of whatever in the garden took his fancy. The terminology, *a mess*, is not used as frequently in conversation today.

Asparagus

2 cups asparagus, chopped

Sauce Ingredients:

3/4 cup whole milk
2 tablespoons all-purpose flour
1 tablespoon butter
salt and pepper, to taste
1/2 to 1 cup grated cheese

1. In a saucepan combine the chopped asparagus with enough salt water to almost cover. Cook over medium to high heat until tender.
(NOTE: Do not drain.)

2. In a separate heavy saucepan combine the milk, flour, butter, salt and pepper, to taste. Cook over medium heat while stirring constantly until thick like a gravy.

3. Pour the sauce over the asparagus and reserved water. *(NOTE: Much of the water will evaporate while cooking the asparagus.)*

4. Return the asparagus mixture to low heat. Add the cheese and allow to melt. Add additional milk if sauce becomes too thick.

Variation: Add broken pieces of toast to the finished dish.

Yield: 4 servings.

ã   ã   ã

To me, corn pudding stands up next to a good baked egg custard! When fresh white Silver Queen corn came in season and was available in the truck patch on the farm, you can imagine how many kettles of roastin' ears it took to feed all of us children, plus the adults. We husked a gunnysack of corn for a meal. We never wasted the leftover ears, but cut the kernels from the cob to heat and serve at the next meal.

Corn on the cob has to be eaten while in season. After that, the sweet taste is only a memory until the next year's crop is harvested. If living in Maryland, to mention fresh Silver Queen corn on the cob is the same as to have spoken with a voice of thunder; you will get a lot of people's attention.

Corn Pudding

Bake at 350 degrees.

2 eggs
3/4 cup whole milk
2 tablespoons melted butter
1/4 teaspoon wet mustard
1/2 teaspoon dried onion flakes
2 tablespoons all-purpose flour
2 cups cooked corn or 1 14-ounce can of creamed corn

1. In a mixing bowl beat the eggs with a rotary beater or wire whisk until light yellow.

2. Add the remaining ingredients and stir until blended. Pour into a greased baking dish.

3. Bake for about 30 minutes or until knife inserted into the center of the pudding comes out clean.

Variation: Omit the onion and mustard; add 1 teaspoon vanilla and 1 tablespoon sugar.

Yield: 4 servings.

ès   ès   ès

Numerous recipes in this cookbook require lard, despite knowledge of the harm it can bring to our health. Though there are many substitutes available, the flavor lard adds to many foods cannot be replaced!

Old-Time Fried Cabbage

5 cups shredded raw cabbage
1 1/2 to 2 teaspoons granulated sugar
1 1/2 to 2 cups sweet cream
salt and pepper, to taste
3 tablespoons lard, for frying
(NOTE: Solid vegetable shortening or bacon drippings can be substituted for lard.)

1. Cut or shred the raw cabbage and transfer to a bowl. Salt lightly and toss to distribute over the cabbage. As the cabbage is worked, it will become juicy.
(NOTE: Do not drain.)

2. Melt lard in a heavy skillet. Pour in the cabbage and juice. Fry over medium heat for about 5 minutes. Stir while frying to prevent scorching.

3. When cabbage is tender, sprinkle with sugar, add the sweet cream, salt and pepper, to taste. Stir until blended.

Serve hot with fried or mashed potatoes.

ôª   ôª   ôª

Turnips in Ham Broth is an autumn dish. Each day brought Mom the challenge of deciding what to cook for her large family plus the farm hands who would gather around the table, hungry and ready to eat three times a day. Not everyone enjoyed turnips, but this dish had its turn appearing on the table. It certainly is not elaborate, but turnips will nourish hard-laboring folks. Some foods return to us again and again--this one came every fall.

The summer months on the farm brought feasting on fresh home-grown vegetables, along with the chore of preserving them. It is always a treat to enjoy the ones that have been grown to maturity in the hometown sunshine, not shipped to us from some distant point of the country. Often many days pass between the time those vegetables are harvested and the time they get to your table, which robs them of their fresh goodness.

Turnips in Ham Broth

raw turnips
raw potatoes
ham broth

1. Wash, peel and cut into blocks, equal amounts of raw potatoes and turnips. Reserve the potatoes.

2. Cover the turnips with broth and bring to a boil. Cook for 5 minutes. Add the reserved potatoes and continue to boil until vegetables are tender.

Variation: Omit ham broth. Cook in water and add a few tablespoons of butter, with salt and pepper.

&a &a &a

Oyster plant or salsify is not served as widely in casserole dishes today as years ago. This plant has a long, white, edible root having an oyster-like flavor. It is a little smaller in diameter than the average size carrot. When preparing, the root is scraped clean by removing the outer layer of flesh. Mom always grew rows of this vegetable in the garden in order to have plenty to eat during the late summer and enough left over to can in the fall of the year. It was a special dish served with butchering dinner. Oyster plant casserole is similar to a baked macaroni casserole, but without cheese. Mom topped the dish with saltine crackers dotted with butter. Very tasty!

Oyster Plant or Salsify Casserole

Bake at 325 degrees.

2 cups chopped oyster plant, cooked
salt and pepper, to taste
1 1/2 cups coarsely broken saltine crackers
1 cup whole milk
2 tablespoons butter

1. In a heavy saucepan cover the oyster plant with salt water and cook until tender.
(NOTE: Do not drain. There should be only a small amount of water remaining in the kettle when done cooking.)

2. Season with pepper and add salt, if needed.

3. Break saltine crackers coarsely and add to the oyster plant. Toss gently.

4. Pour the mixture into a greased flat baking dish and cover with the milk.

5. Cover the top with additional broken saltine crackers and dot with butter.

6. Bake in the oven for about 30 minutes or until lightly browned and bubbly.

(NOTE: If crackers brown too quickly, lay a sheet of aluminum foil loosely on the top of the dish. Do not seal. If heating the casserole at a higher temperature than recommended, add crackers on top after dish has been in the oven for about 15 minutes. A buttery cracker can be used on top, in place of saltines.)

Yield: 6 servings.

a.   a.   a.

Stewed tomatoes are nice to serve with bean dishes, but will enhance any menu. This can be considered a low calorie dish.

No matter how cold the temperature or how much snow was crunching under our feet, we knew spring was just around the corner when the Shumway's Seed Catalogs arrived in the mail. We children walked from the farmhouse, up the road to the mailbox to get the daily delivery dropped off by the mailman. Often the mailbox was covered with a late winter's snow when we pulled down the cold metal door to see the catalogs. At first sight, we were so excited we ran to get back in the house, catching our breath, plus trying to be the first one in the door to tell Mom what we had in our chilly little hands. We wanted to give them to her as quickly as possible since we knew how much she enjoyed reading the new issue from cover to cover. After reviewing and planning for a few weeks, she carefully placed an order. In return, the company mailed the seeds to the house, not too early but in time to plant when the freezing winter weather broke and the balmy days returned.

Weeks passed and when the package of seeds arrived with the mailman, he would pull his car in the driveway, honk the car horn as a signal for one of us to run out of the house and take the heavy box. Even on a rainy, cold day we wondered when it would be dry and warm enough for Mom to rush out and plant those tiny seeds in the soil. After a long hard winter, there was an excitement with the thought of planting time. During the winter we did not buy fresh vegetables, other than celery and sometimes lettuce, since we had Mom's canned ones in the cellar to use. But I will tell you, we surely had a longing to bite into a fresh, juicy tomato.

Small envelopes of seeds could be purchased at the local country stores for only a nickel or two when Mom was a young girl. At the same time, no one bought bottled pesticides or dangerous sprays to use for pest control that might endanger their health. Some of the vegetables that grew in Mom's garden were as beautiful as those colored pictures printed on the cover of the seed catalog!

Stewed Tomatoes

4 cups fresh or canned tomatoes
1/4 to 1/2 cup granulated sugar, adjust to tartness of
    tomatoes
1 teaspoon salt
2 tablespoons all-purpose flour
1/2 cup water
1 1/2 to 2 cups coarsely broken saltines

1. In a heavy saucepan bring the tomatoes to a boil. Stir in the sugar and salt.

2. Prepare a thin sauce from the flour and water. Stir into the boiling tomatoes and cook over low heat until thickened.

3. Pour into a large serving bowl. Add broken saltine crackers and push down into the tomatoes.

Variation: Add diced onion to the boiling tomatoes for extra flavor.

Yield: 4 servings.

&a.&a.&a.

Baked squash is simple to make, yet a variety of spices can be added to introduce new flavor. Squash can be prepared in so many tasty ways.

I cannot believe the many times Mom grabbed her sunbonnet from the wall hook in the pantry and literally ran to the garden to spend a few hours hoeing and cultivating the soil. Perhaps the meal planned was quick and easy to serve that day, thus freeing up some time. Maybe the sky looked as if it was threatening rain and she wanted to break the soil's crust that had been baked by the hot sun, allowing the water to soak in quickly.

Each row of vegetables was planted as straight as if she used a plumb bob. Well, she did lay a string line across the garden to mark each row. She used bailer twine tar rope with a stack or corn cob tied on both ends. She shoved the stacks down into the soil at the end of each new row. Now she sowed her seeds or plants by following the twine, and repeated these steps to make the next row. When she finished, the rows were as straight as the stripes in our country's flag. Her garden was along Route 17, and she didn't want anyone to notice a crooked row as they drove by.

Mom took as much pride in her rows of beans, onions or whatever vegetable seed she was sowing as Dad took in planting his rows of field corn. But he couldn't use a string spread across the vast acreage. Instead, from the starting end of the field, he set his eyes on a landmark, either a tree or fencepost, gave the command "giddy up" to the horses and away they went, horses' heads bent from the strain of pulling the corn planter. With Dad's gentle pull on the lines of the horses' gears, old Bob and Kate led him directly to his target. Once those little kernels of corn popped through the soil he could enjoy the efforts and results of his long day's work.

Work from morning to night was a way of life for Mom, Dad, and the family. We knew one hard day of work would follow another. My parents never prayed for fame, but for strength to get through life and to establish a home centered with family.

Baked Squash

Bake at 400 degrees.

squash (any variety)
all-purpose flour
granulated sugar
salt, to taste

1. Cut into 1/4-inch slices the width of the whole fresh squash.

2. Dredge the slices through flour and place in a single layer in a greased flat baking pan.

3. Sprinkle tops of the squash with sugar and salt.

4. Bake in the oven for 20 minutes or until tender. Adjust cooking time to thickness of squash.

Variation: Brown sugar can be substituted for granulated sugar.

&a &a &a

In the springtime, the countryside comes alive with the farmers in the fields working the soil. The farmland turns green with new growth, and everyone has more work plans than will fit into the day that God has made. Dad enjoyed a meal of dandelion greens, boiled potatoes, hard-boiled eggs, fried ham, and homemade buttered bread. He often joked saying the greens were his spring tonic. Our family considers dandelion a food but others consider it the pesky weed that is sure to appear each year. Dictionaries describe the shape of the leaf as the tooth of the lion because of its jagged edge. It is also referred to as a common weed with a long root and edible leaves.

Mom and whoever was available to help would walk out into a field or meadow early in the spring as the first young weeds poked their heads through the ground. With the March wind whipping and hands numb from the chill, we were off on the search for young dandelions, carrying a large kettle to hold the treasured greens in one hand, plus a sturdy sharp knife to cut the plant off at the root in the other. After spotting a patch, on bended knees we plucked out each plant from the muddy spring soil. Carefully we removed any discolored or wilted leaves, then chopped the plant into the kettle. We made certain it did not hold a yellow bud in the center, since at that point of growth the leaves turn bitter tasting.

Dandelion dressing is tasty and can be used on any variety of dark greens that you may enjoy serving wilted style.

Wilted Dandelion Greens

2 1/2 quarts dandelion, chopped

Dressing Ingredients:

1/3 to 1/2 pound bacon, chopped fine
1 egg
2 tablespoons all-purpose flour
3 tablespoons granulated sugar
1 1/2 cups water
5 tablespoons vinegar

1. Prepare greens by washing the leaves in salt water to dislodge the grit. Allow to drain. Set aside in a heavy kettle.
(NOTE: Use only crisp and tender spring dandelions. Do not use ones with yellow flowers. Do not precook dandelions.)

2. Chop the sliced bacon in fine pieces. Place in a skillet and fry until crispy. Set aside in the skillet.
(NOTE: Do not drain fat from the pan.)

3. In a mixing bowl beat the egg with a rotary beater or wire whisk until light yellow.
(NOTE: Beat egg well or it will curdle.)

4. Add the flour, sugar, water, and vinegar to the egg. Stir until blended. Pour into the skillet and combine with the bacon. Bring the mixture to a boil.

5. Place the pan of greens over very low heat. Pour the dressing evenly over greens and toss until wilted. The boiling hot dressing will heat the greens.

Serve greens hot.

❧ ❧ ❧

This recipe is used not only to prepare spring onion tops, but turnip tops as well. So often today, we dispose of the portion from vegetables that houses most of the nutrition. Most vegetable and fruit skins hold lots of vitamins and minerals, only to be lost because we do not enjoy eating them.

Stewed Young Spring Onion Tops (or Turnip Tops)

6 cups chopped young onion tops
1/3 to 1/2 pound bacon, chopped fine
1 egg
2 tablespoons all-purpose flour
3 tablespoons granulated sugar
1 1/2 cups reserved water
5 tablespoons vinegar

1. Cut crisp tender tops from young spring onions. Remove dried or discolored leaves and chop in 1-inch pieces. Wash in salt water to dislodge the grit.

2. Place tops in a heavy kettle and nearly cover with water. Cook until tender, about 5 to 10 minutes. Allow to drain and reserve 1 1/2 cups of water.

3. Chop the sliced bacon in fine pieces. Place in a skillet and fry until crispy. Set aside in the skillet.
(NOTE: Do not drain fat from the pan.)

4. In a mixing bowl beat the egg with a rotary beater or wire whisk until light yellow.
(NOTE: Beat well or it will curdle.)

5. Add the flour, sugar, reserved water, and vinegar to the egg. Stir until blended. Return to the bacon in the skillet and bring to a boil.

6. Pour dressing over onions and stir to cover evenly.

Serve hot stewed onions with potatoes, prepared in any fashion.

Yield: 6 servings.

&a   &a   &a

Marinated tomatoes are quick and easy to prepare. Dad loved Mom serving marinated tomatoes when the weather was hot. He placed the chilled tomato slices on buttered bread, then carefully spooned some of the juice on top. Spreading it with the back of a spoon in a methodical motion until smooth, he was now ready to eat. It was cool nourishment, and it was tasty and pleasing! Whether your fresh vegetables come from your own garden or the market, recipes in this cookbook will be an inspiration for all those who enjoy food that is satisfying and simple.

Marinated Tomatoes

6 large tomatoes
1 cup granulated sugar
salt and pepper, to taste
3/4 cup vinegar

1. Wash and slice ripe tomatoes about 1/2 inch thick.

2. In a glass bowl or flat dish place the tomato slices in layers, sprinkle with sugar, salt and pepper to taste, and drizzle with vinegar. Continue making layers.
(NOTE: Use about 1 cup sugar to 3/4 cup of vinegar. Adjust to the tartness of the tomatoes.)

3. Place in the refrigerator to allow the vinegar to dissolve the sugar and form a syrup.

Serve cold, alone or over a slice of bread.

❧   ❧   ❧

Bread and Butter Pickles

9 cups water
3/4 cup salt
6 quarts of raw cucumber slices, cut about 1/4 inch thick
1 pint onions, sliced

1. In a large bowl or jar make a brine of water and salt.

2. Cut the cucumbers and onions in 1/4-inch slices. Drop into the brine and let stand for 3 hours.

3. Allow the cucumber and onion slices to drain in a colander and then squeeze remaining brine out of vegetables by hand. Set aside.

Syrup Ingredients:

5 cups granulated sugar
5 cups vinegar
1 tablespoon tumeric
1 teaspoon mustard seed
1 teaspoon celery seed

4. Bring the syrup ingredients to a boil and drop in the cucumber and onion slices. Continue boiling for 2 minutes.

5. Fill sterilized canning jars with boiling pickles and seal. Store in a cool place. Pickles may also be stored in a tight container in the refrigerator for several weeks.

ᏴᏴ ᏴᏴ ᏴᏴ

Really, there is no good reason that farm folks should ever need to go hungry. With land to plant seeds, food can be produced, then preserved for using months later.

Mom jumped out of bed in the morning and did not stop until the work she planned for that day was completed at night. She and Dad succeeded on grit and courage. She preserved whatever food she grew in the garden. Her favorite words when we were tired of preserving were, "you never know what size crop we will have next year. We had better not waste."

Watermelon Pickle

5 pounds watermelon rind
4 cups water, reserved
2 cups vinegar
4 cups granulated sugar
2 tablespoons pickling spice
1 teaspoon salt

1. Peel the outer green rind and pink flesh from 5 pounds of watermelon rind and discard. Cut the rind in long or square pieces.

2. In a large kettle cover the rind with water and boil until tender.

3. Transfer to a colander and allow to drain. Reserve 4 cups of water.

4. In a large kettle bring the reserved water, vinegar, sugar, pickling spice and salt to a boil. Drop the pieces of melon rind into the mixture and boil for about 5 minutes.

5. Pour the pickled rind into sterilized canning jars and seal. Store in a cool, dry place. Pickles may also be stored in a tight container in the refrigerator for several weeks.

Serve with a meal or sandwich.

Variation: Use clove and cinnamon oils; 1/4 teaspoon of each in place of pickling spice.

                  es   es   es

Use small firm clingstone peaches for pickling. Mom prepared the spiced pickled cling peaches and canned them in jars with rubber rings and screw-on one-piece zinc lids. She tapped lightly around the edge of the lid with a metal hammer, pressing it down to make an airtight seal against the rubber ring. There was no waste to this process since the jar, the ring, and the lid could be washed and used again. Now we have the modern two-piece disposable lids. We seem to have converted from a save-at-all-cost attitude to a one-time use attitude no matter what it costs!

Mom still has that tiny hammer with a worn four-inch wooden handle and a metal head no larger than a dime. She believes it was purchased at Bittle's Store in Ellerton when she and Dad married in 1916.

Spiced Pickled Cling Peaches

6 peeled whole cling peaches
1 1/3 cups granulated sugar
1/2 cup water
2/3 cup vinegar
1 teaspoon ground cinnamon
1/2 teaspoon ground cloves
(NOTE: Exchange ground cinnamon and cloves for 2 4-inch sticks of cinnamon and 12 whole cloves.)

1. Peel the skin from the whole peaches. Set aside.
(NOTE: Do not remove the pit.)

2. In a large kettle combine the remaining ingredients and boil over medium heat for 20 minutes.

3. Carefully add the peaches to the hot syrup and simmer for 35 to 40 minutes.

Serve hot or cold.

Variation: Use peaches, pears, or apples cut into halves and seeded; adjust cooking time to each fruit. Add food coloring to the syrup to tint fruit to a deep, natural color.

❧   ❧   ❧

Pickled red beets are just right to serve with most meals. Quality beets remain bright red after having been processed. They help cut the taste of rich or fatty foods.

Mom always planted red beet seeds in the garden. I remember her getting herself dressed to go out to sow, hoe or weed. A suntan was not in fashion when she was a young woman! In order to avoid burning the fair skin on her arms, she cut the feet out of a pair of worn-out women's tan cotton knit stockings. Then she pulled that tube over her arms and secured it at the edge of her short dress sleeve with an elastic stocking garter. None of her house dresses had long sleeves. Since she was working in food and the dishpan of soapy water most of the day, she preferred a sleeve that dropped no longer than to the elbows. Mom never wore slacks even when she worked outdoors. No matter what lengths it caused her to go, she always wanted to dress like a lady.

Mom also wore a starched, wide-brimmed small checked gingham sunbonnet to shade her face from the sunshine when spending time outdoors. A ruffle attached to the back of it covered and protected the tender skin around her neck. Mom still has a blue and white checked sunbonnet, but alas no garden to toil in! With nearly a century behind her, plus rich and full memories to remind her of the years of hard labor while gardening, Mom is more than happy to hang up the hoe and enjoy her rocking chair these days.

Pickled Red Beets

18 to 20 medium raw red beets
2 1/2 cups strained beet juice, reserved
2 1/2 cups vinegar

1 cup granulated sugar
2 teaspoons pickling spice
(NOTE: Spices can be adjusted to your taste.)
2 teaspoons salt

1. Remove the tops and scrub the beets thoroughly. In a large kettle cover the beets with water. Cook until tender. Remove the beets and allow to cool.

2. Strain the juice and reserve 2 1/2 cups. Set aside.

3. Slip off the skins and discard. Cut the beets into large chunks or leave whole. Set aside.

4. In a separate kettle combine the reserved beet juice, vinegar, sugar, pickling spice, and salt. Bring to a boil.

5. Return the beets to the prepared juice and bring to a boil once more. Reduce the heat and simmer for 5 minutes.

6. Pour into hot sterilized jars and seal. Beets may also be stored in a tight container in the refrigerator for several weeks.

Suggestion: Do not discard pickled juice once beets have been used, but make pickled eggs. Combine juice with peeled hard-boiled eggs in a tight container and place in the refrigerator. Turn eggs every couple of hours if not completely covered with juice. Soak for 24 hours to pickle.

ॐ   ॐ   ॐ

MEATS, POULTRY,
SEAFOOD & GRAVIES

Whether preparing meatloaf using catsup or tomato juice, cracker or bread crumbs, with or without onions, it doesn't matter, the end result will be tasty and to your liking. The ingredients in this recipe can be altered to fit your desire.

At times Mom still cooks for nine children and expects two or three of us who visit to eat until the dishes are emptied. Believe me, some of us have tried to please her! We still have good appetites, but it seems not to take as much food to fill us as when we were burning all that energy working on the farm.

Mom was never satisfied to set enough food on her table for one serving per person. She hated the thought of someone not having as much as they wanted to eat. She loves to see folks eating and enjoying food. She can often be seen pushed back a bit from the table with a slight smile on her face, just listening to the conversation of her family as they delight in one another and her food. I often wonder what her secret thoughts are during these times!

Here is a mother, 99 years old, still of sound mind and in good health cooking for her children. One might say, why do you allow her to do this or expect this of her? No one expects her to cook for us, but each one respects her desire to do as she pleases. We should be careful not to crush a family member's will to do what they are able to handle with ease. Many times those chores are what makes life valuable to them. When all is said and done, we all want to be useful and be needed by someone. Never forget, *a mother's devotion goes on forever and ever!*

Letha's Beef Loaf

Bake at 350 degrees.

2 1/2 to 3 pounds lean ground beef
1 medium onion, diced fine, or 1 tablespoon dried onion
   flakes
1 cup cracker crumbs
1 cup whole milk
1 egg
1 tablespoon Worcestershire sauce
2 tablespoons catsup
1 teaspoon salt or all-seasoned salt
pepper, to taste

1. In a large bowl mix all the ingredients together. Transfer
the mixture to a flat baking pan and form a loaf.

2. Bake in the oven for about 1 hour or until loaf is done in
the center. Cover loosely with aluminum foil if it becomes
too brown before meat is done.

Slice leftover cold meatloaf and serve between crackers as
a snack.

ða ða ða

Preparing steak or young chicken oven style, is a quick and easy method. Mom always scores beef steak with a sharp butchering knife before placing in the pan. This cuts the grain in the meat, making it tender.

I recall seeing Mom sharpen the blades of the butchering knives on the edge of a small earthenware crock. The exterior was bone-colored with a dark brown interior; it had a smooth raw edge over the top rim, and sat on a pantry shelf when she wasn't cooking. The pot served a dual purpose: a knife sharpener and a salt pot. She kept it filled with salt and would reach in taking a pinch to add to the food she was cooking.

Mom would gather her knives, carry them into the pantry and soon we heard the sound of her drawing the blade across the edge of the crock. Believe me, the sound was easy to identify. She had a knife sharpened in nothing flat. As long as Mom has her favorite salt pot, she doesn't need a new-fangled electric knife sharpener taking up space in her kitchen.

Oven Style Steak or Chicken

Bake at 375 degrees.

steak or chicken
all-purpose flour
all-seasoned salt or regular salt, to taste
pepper, to taste
butter, to dot the steak or chicken

1. Score the meat with a sharp knife. It is not necessary to score chicken.

2. Dredge the meat through flour. Place in heavy shallow baking pan sprayed with cooking oil. Sprinkle with regular salt and pepper or all-seasoned salt, to taste. Dot each piece with butter.

3. Add enough water to half-way cover the meat. Slowly fill the pan at the edge so the flour is not washed from the meat.

4. Bake 30 to 45 minutes or until tender. Baking time will vary with thickness of meat.

Variation: Use your favorite seasoning.

ðŸ€ ðŸ€ ðŸ€

Salmon Cakes

1 14-ounce can salmon, drained and flaked
2 slices white bread, broken in small pieces
1 egg, slightly beaten
1 teaspoon dry mustard
2 teaspoons sweet pickle relish
1 teaspoon dried parsley flakes
1 teaspoon dried celery flakes
1 teaspoon dried onion flakes
1 teaspoon lemon juice
3 to 4 tablespoons butter, for frying

1. Combine all ingredients and form in patties.

2. Melt butter in a skillet and fry until lightly browned.

ðŸ€ ðŸ€ ðŸ€

Fried Beef Steak or Chicken

steak or chicken
milk, to marinate chicken
1 egg
1/2 cup evaporated or whole milk
all-purpose flour
salt and pepper, to taste
shortening, for frying

1. Score the meat with a sharp knife. It is not necessary to score chicken. Place meat in a dish and cover with milk. Marinate overnight. Drain and discard milk.

2. In a separate bowl beat the egg until broken down with a wire whisk. Add an equal amount of evaporated or whole milk to the egg.

3. Dip pieces of meat into the egg and milk mixture. Dredge through the flour.

4. When shortening is hot, add the slices of meat, sprinkle with salt and pepper, and fry over medium to high heat until crispy brown and tender.
(NOTE: Do not cover with a lid.)

5. Remove the meat from the pan and place on paper towels to drain.

6. Drain and discard excess fat from the pan, being careful to reserve the brown bits of crust. Make gravy from the reserved meat crust in the same pan.
(NOTE: Recipe found on page 372.)

ða   ða   ða

Croquettes are a "waste not, want not" dish--or an excellent way to use leftovers! You will be surprised by the pleasing flavor, so be sure to try this recipe.

At mealtime the little children in our family lined up on the bench behind the table. The bench was pushed against the wall to support our backs and to keep us from tumbling backwards onto the floor, and once seated the table was pushed towards us until we could reach comfortably to eat. The younger children's feet hung suspended as our legs were too short to touch the floor. But we could manage to wiggle off when the desire struck. My parents sat at the ends of the table. The hired hands always sat to Dad's left side, next to him and with the older children. Dad made certain the men were served plenty of food and made to feel welcome. The baby sat in the highchair next to Mom.

Our parents had an old handmade wooden Columbus Stottlemyer high chair with a split bottom. Mom lined it with a blanket to keep the rough splits from scratching the tender skin on our legs. The high chair was not modern; there was no tray and body strap to hold the child secure. To keep us from falling out, Mom tied a feed bag towel around our chest and to the back of the chair. All of the grandchildren have had their turn in the high chair, and they were tied in as well!

While growing up, it seemed one of the children regularly got caught slinking down off the bench at mealtime. I know exactly what I, and whoever was joining me, was planning to do. We plotted to crawl out from under the table to free ourselves from a meal we may not have cared for or did not feel like eating. Once in awhile we got by, but most of the time we were asked to crawl back up the way we got down. Mom watched in amazement more times than not. And, I am embarrassed to confess that this scene is as clear to me as if it happened yesterday!

Mom and Dad tried their best to keep us children on the straight and narrow path. One thing I can tell you; they knew the true meaning of forgiveness with love, and they intended for us to learn it as well. Forgiveness to them was *giving up the right to get even or hurt the person who did them wrong.* We need to shake out the rubble in a life and look not to condemn but to find a gem of goodness. We must never forget to offer praise when praise has been earned--*especially to our children.* We need to forgive and shake brotherly hands with those who have plotted against us!

Croquettes

2 1/2 cups chopped fine leftover beef, pork or chicken
3/4 cup cracker crumbs or 1/2 cup cooked potatoes
1 egg
parsley, to taste
salt and pepper, to taste
whole milk to form a pattie
butter, for frying

1. Grind leftover meat.
(NOTE: Makes no difference if meat is cooked or fried. If using cooked potatoes instead of cracker crumbs, grind fine with a food grinder. Cold potatoes that have been refrigerated overnight are best.)

2. Beat the egg until light.

3. Mix together the meat, potatoes or cracker crumbs, egg, parsley, salt, pepper, and milk. Adjust the milk to the dryness of the meat. Add enough to congeal the mixture. Stir until well blended and moist. Form into patties.

4. Melt a few tablespoons of butter in a skillet and fry until lightly browned and a crispy crust forms.
(NOTE: Cooking oil may be used in place of butter.)

Variation: Add onion, mustard, Worcestershire sauce, pickle relish, or horseradish before forming patties.

Yield: 4 servings.

ᐩ   ᐩ   ᐩ

At our home, oyster stew was served during the Christmas holiday season, but it was too expensive for us to enjoy often. Our parents tried to scrape up a little extra cash to purchase the foods for the holidays that we did not get during the year. I prize and hold dear to my heart the ability to retrace the events of bygone holidays.

Oyster Stew

1 pint whole milk
1/2 cup sweet cream
4 tablespoons butter
1/2 cup water
1 teaspoon salt
pepper, to taste
1 pint of oysters and liquid

1. In a heavy saucepan heat milk and cream until scalded.
(NOTE: Do not allow to boil as it will alter the taste.)

2. Combine in another saucepan the butter, water, salt, pepper, and oysters along with their liquid. Cook until they begin to ruffle and curl.
(NOTE: Add additional water if more liquid is desired.)

3. Combine all ingredients and serve.

Serve hot with little oyster crackers.

Yield: 4 servings.

❧ ❧ ❧

I bet it would be hard if not impossible to find hog's maul (referring to the pig's stomach) served in a high-class restaurant, but it was a feast at our house in the early winter after butchering the first hogs of the season. On a freezing cold night, after the evening barn chores were completed, this warm and nourishing meal sustained us through the night. Mom always made certain we were never put to bed hungry. If that ever happened, it was not to her knowledge, but by our choice.

Dad died in 1977 but the family will never forget seeing him come in from outdoors, freshening himself up a bit, then taking his seat at the head of the table to eat the meal in his wintertime striped-denim bib overalls. The pockets over his chest sported metal buttons that read, *Big Mac, Power House, Hercules, or Pay Day*. The name indicated the store brand.

On cold winter days Mom had a pot of coffee perked and waiting on the back of the wood-burning cooking range. Most country cooks used an old enamelware coffeepot. Mom's pot was blue speckled, and she had pie pans, dishpans, roasting pan, basins and buckets to match. Once the enamel on these utensils, was shattered from a hard knock, a leak would soon develop. She often plugged the hole by drawing a piece of wrapping cord through while attached to a needle. It didn't stop the leak when holding liquids, but it certainly was useable again for dry ingredients!

At meals Mom served coffee in large cups on saucers. When the coffee was boiling hot, as it usually was, Dad poured some out into the deep saucer to cool. Then with slow and steady hands he lifted it to his lips, anticipating to drink. Unshaken, he sipped. The empty saucer was then set down on the table just as carefully as if it were full! No thought was given to whether drinking from a saucer was proper manners, it was just the way he enjoyed drinking his coffee. It was an acceptable habit to him no matter who was seated around their table. Dad also liked Mom's fresh homemade bread spread thick with butter and molasses, then folded in half, and dipped deep into the coffee. You see, his home was his castle, to be enjoyed by family and all who entered. Anyone who ate a meal at Mom and Dad's table was always their guest and also considered "old home folks" the next time around. Anyone and everyone was welcome to join him sipping coffee from saucers!

Hog's Maul

Bake at 350 degrees.

1 large hog's maul
2 pounds fried sausage or cooked pork pulled from the bone
6 to 8 medium potatoes, peeled and diced
1 large raw onion, chopped
salt and pepper, to taste

1. Clean and rinse a hog's maul in cold water. Drain and set aside.

2. Cook the meat until tender and drain. Chop in small pieces.

3. In a large mixing bowl combine the diced potatoes, meat, onion, salt and pepper.

4. Fill the maul with the potato and meat mixture. Stitch the opening closed with a needle and heavy white thread or use skewers laced with string.

5. Place the maul in a greased roasting pan and add about 1/2 inch of water in the bottom of the pan.

6. Cover the pan with a tight lid or aluminum foil and place the maul in the oven. After baking for 1 hour, prick the maul with a fork to allow steam to escape and continue to bake covered for 30 minutes longer. Remove cover and bake for 1 additional hour or until potatoes are done and maul is golden brown. Total cooking time will vary but any maul should be done within 2 1/2 hours in a 350 degree oven.

7. Transfer onto a meat plate and slice through the maul to make 1 1/2-inch slices with a sharp knife.

Serve with your favorite vegetable.

≥● ≥● ≥●

I am certain Pig's Feet Souse is not something one expects to be served at a banquet--it is a country, plain folks dish. Why don't you try it? Mom made it when the hogs were butchered in the fall of the year.

Pig's Feet Souse

4 fresh pig's feet
2 cups vinegar
2 teaspoons salt, or salt to your taste
1/2 teaspoon pepper

1. Clean and scrub the pig's feet thoroughly. Place in a large kettle with water to cover. Season with salt.

2. Allowing approximately 4 hours, cook until the meat is tender and falling from the bones. Remove from the broth.

3. Remove meat from the bones and place in a mold. Set aside.

4. Strain the broth. Approximately 2 cups of broth should have formed while cooking the feet. Add the remaining ingredients and boil for about 30 minutes.

5. Pour the liquid over the meat that has been placed in the mold.

6. Refrigerate to congeal. Slice and serve cold.

Store in the refrigerator.

❧   ❧   ❧

This is an old recipe for making the bologna that Mom and Dad first made around 1932. I included it in this collection of recipes because in the country there are some folks who still butcher and use a smokehouse. In the winter of 1997, a young man came to Mom requesting the recipe. After all these years, she still had it tucked away in her hand-written cookbook!

On many occasions, families and friends would like to duplicate special dishes popular from years gone by, only to find ingredients and instructions were never recorded. Finding someone to fill in the gap and provide an identical recipe is most often impossible.

When making bologna you will need cloth sacks that are about 3 to 4 inches wide and 3 feet long. Be sure they are wide enough to accommodate your hand while pressing in the meat. Use cotton muslin fabric and sew the seams with a sewing machine so the stitches will be tight and not break from the pressure of stuffing. The meat needs to be firmly packed to assure bologna holds together when sliced. Bologna should only be made in cold weather. It needs to be sugar cured and smoked in a smokehouse.

Once the fresh meat is sugar cured in the wintertime, it will keep all year long. The smokehouse on the farm at home was always filled with cured pork to serve on the table in the summertime. When someone came in at mealtime and Mom needed extra meat she could always go to the smokehouse and cut a slice of ham. Returning to the kitchen, she fried it and had a meal ready to eat in record time.

The smokehouse is usually nearly airtight and has a sod floor. The fresh meat from butcherings is hung from the rafters by metal meat hooks. A fire is built in the center of the floor, underneath the meat. It is fed with hickory wood and covered with sawdust to create smoke. The fire must be watched carefully so as not to burn out of control. The whole idea is to make lots of smoke with little or no blaze.

Bologna

2 ounces saltpeter
1 pint of hot water
100 pounds ground beef, raw
2 quarts salt
1 1/2 pounds brown sugar
1 ounce ground cloves
1 ounce allspice
pepper, to taste
1 3/4 pints lard

1. Dissolve the saltpeter in the hot water.

2. Spread the raw ground beef on a clean surface. A tabletop works best. Sprinkle with the salt, brown sugar, cloves, allspice and pepper. Dribble the saltpeter water evenly over the meat mixture. Mix the meat mixture by hand until all the ingredients are evenly distributed.

3. In a separate pan melt the lard. Dip cotton muslin sacks into lard before filling with meat.

4. Stuff the meat as tightly as possible into the cloth sacks. Tie the ends closed with cord or make a knot in the cloth.

5. Hang the tubes of bologna in the smokehouse and smoke in the same fashion as other fresh meat.

When cured, cut bologna in thin slices and serve in a sandwich or between crackers.

ɜ   ɜ   ɜ

Mom has prepared fried oyster patties for Christmas Day dinner for all of 80 years but one.

Fried Oyster Patties

oysters
cracker crumbs
cornmeal
shortening, for frying

1. In a large bowl make a crumb mixture of 1 part cornmeal to 1 part saltine cracker crumbs.
(NOTE: Roll the crackers with rolling pin to make fine crumbs.)

2. Gather a pile of crumbs in your hand, place an oyster on top and pile another handful of crumbs on top of the oyster. Press to form a pattie. Lay patties on a tray and refrigerate. Allow to set a few hours to congeal before frying.

3. Fry in a skillet in deep shortening until brown and crispy. Allow to drain on paper towels.
(NOTE: Do not cover with a lid.)

Fried Oyster Patties taste great when served between white crackers.

ɜ   ɜ   ɜ

Mom and other country cooks learned the art of making a variety of gravies by experience. They never measured the ingredients. Instead, they poured in and stirred until it looked right. Their judgement was usually "on the penny."

Crusty bits remain in the pan after frying pork, beef, or chicken. Never remove this since it adds flavor and makes a tasty gravy. Most families enjoy brown gravy served over mashed potatoes, bread or biscuits.

Basic Pan Gravy

4 tablespoons fat, reserved
3 heaping tablespoons all-purpose flour
1 cup water
1 1/4 cups whole milk
salt and pepper, to taste

1. Carefully remove all but 4 tablespoons of the fat from the skillet.
(NOTE: Do not remove the brown particles.)

2. Add flour to reserved hot fat in the skillet, stirring over medium heat until lightly browned.
(NOTE: Be careful--if flour is browned in excess, it will taste scorched.)

3. Pour water slowly into the skillet while stirring and reduce the heat. Simmer for a few minutes.

4. Add the milk, salt, and pepper while stirring and boil for about 5 minutes or until thick. If gravy is too thick, add milk and stir.

(NOTE: Basic ingredients for making gravy are 1 quart broth, made by adding water to the reserved drippings in the skillet used to fry the meat, and 1/4 cup flour. Or 1/4 cup drippings, 1/4 cup flour, and 3 to 4 cups whole milk. Any variety of these ingredients will produce delicious gravy.)

❧   ❧   ❧

Before the day of modern preserving, fresh meats were kept either by the sugar cure and smoked method, or it was canned in glass jars. Our family not only loved the taste of canned beef and pork, but we enjoyed the rich, flavorful gravy made from the broth that formed in the jar during the processing.

Another preserving method Mom used was to fry beef and pork, then pack it under its rendered fat in a earthenware crock. The container was stored either in a cool cellar or in the springhouse in a trough of water. Once the hot liquid fat hardened, it created an air-tight seal and stopped spoilage from occurring. When ready to use the meat, a portion was removed, and the fat was smeared back over what was left in the crock to make certain no meat was exposed to the air. This method of preserving was to be used in the winter months of the year. It was a temporary means of preserving that could not tolerate summer temperatures.

Meat Broth Gravy

2 cups clear broth
(NOTE: Use canned broth or juices from a roast.)
4 tablespoons cold water
1 tablespoon all-purpose flour
1 tablespoon cornstarch
salt and pepper, to taste

1. In a heavy saucepan bring the broth to a boil.

2. While the broth is heating, combine the cold water, flour and cornstarch in a separate cup. Stir until a smooth paste is formed.

3. Reduce the heat under the pan of boiling broth. While stirring, gradually pour in the thin flour paste. Add salt and pepper, to taste. Cook slowly, stirring frequently, until gravy thickens. About 10 minutes.

Meat broth gravy is best served over mashed potatoes or slices of bread.

Variation: Immediately before serving add saltine crackers to chicken broth gravy. Season with lots of parsley.

ॐ   ॐ   ॐ

Mom did not thicken Fried Ham Milk Gravy with flour or cornstarch because our family enjoyed the "thin" style, but it can be prepared. It seems Mom never served fried country ham at a meal without milk gravy. Dad called it *dip sop*. He poured the thin gravy over a slice of homemade bread and enjoyed every bite. Where I grew up it would have been considered wasteful not to use the drippings in the frying pan for seasoning or making gravy. Addiction to creamy, smooth gravy can happen to you in nothing flat!

Mom could make something good to eat from almost anything. Success at cooking, or anything else, requires enthusiasm and energy to go along with plenty of perseverance. With a vision to proceed, as well as confidence in what you are doing, you will no doubt find success as she did. She has been a wonderful cook and still is!

Fried Ham with Milk Gravy

ham slices
whole milk
shortening, for frying

1. In a heavy skillet fry slices of ham in a small amount of shortening. Remove ham from the pan and drain fat.
(NOTE: Do not wash the pan.)

2. Return the ham slices to the pan and pour in milk to cover. Simmer for about 5 minutes.
(NOTE: No thickening is required.)

Serve over slices of bread.

࡚ ࡚ ࡚

Store a supply of chipped beef in your freezer. And any time of the day make a quick meal of chip beef gravy over toast. Makes a great weekend breakfast or a quick suppertime dish.

Chipped Beef Gravy

5 tablespoons butter
1/4 to 1/3 pound chopped dried chip beef
4 tablespoons all-purpose flour
2 1/2 cups whole milk

1. Melt the butter in a heavy skillet over medium heat. Add the beef and stir until it is coated with butter.

2. Dust the meat with flour and allow to brown.

3. Gradually add the milk, stirring constantly, while cooking over low heat. Cook gravy until thick and smooth.

Serve on slices of toasted bread, waffles, or mashed potatoes.

ᴈ   ᴈ   ᴈ

EGGS, DAIRY & SPREADS

Deviled Eggs are a nice addition to any meal. They are quick and easy to make.

Deviled Eggs

6 hard-boiled eggs
1 teaspoon butter, softened
3 tablespoons mayonnaise
1/2 teaspoon wet mustard
1/2 teaspoon celery seed
1 teaspoon dried celery flakes
1/2 teaspoon parsley
salt and pepper, to taste
paprika

1. Cut hard-boiled eggs in lengthwise halves. Remove the yolk and place in a bowl. Set whites aside.

2. Mash the yolks with a fork. Add the softened butter and stir until smooth. Add the remaining ingredients and beat until very smooth.

3. Pile the egg yolk mixture back into the egg white halves. Sprinkle paprika on top or garnish with a leaf of fresh parsley.

Serve deviled eggs cold or use to garnish other foods.

Store in a tight container in the refrigerator.

⁂

To my mother's way of thinking, no book of local interest can be complete without the mention of the late Thomas Franklin Bittle, owner of Bittle's store located in Ellerton. Frank died in 1917 and his son, James Thomas Bittle, ran the business until 1950. The wooden structure is perched at the intersection where Harp Hill Road and Route 17 meet and is believed to originally have been the Wolfe Store. My mother was a little girl in the beginning years of the 1900s and this kind man made such an impression on her with his loving and tender manner that she never forgot him. Even today, after living for nearly a century, she vividly remembers the interior of the store and the items that were stocked on the shelves. The thought of bolts of calico and gingham fabrics, both coffee beans and sugar in barrels, thread, penny candy in the candy case, horehound drops, and kerosene leap to her mind when thinking about the store. She often refers to the Bittle's little black dog that nipped at her heels when he spotted her waltzing down the road with her long dresstail swishing in the breeze. The old store building stands today in good repair. Mom does not see it as simply an old landmark that sits along side the road, but as a reminder that honors precious memories.

There was an abundance of greetings exchanged between Mr. Bittle and Mom. If all the world's eyes had been set on judging their every action, no greater pleasure could ever have been captured than when he passed penny candy to a tiny little girl with a sweet tooth and a big smile!

To my pleasure and surprise, I received a note from Frances Bittle, the wife of the late Thomas Bittle from Gettysburg, Pennsylvania, in 1998. Recently, I received a letter from James L. Bittle, living in San Diego, California. Frances' husband, Tom, and his brother James are great grandsons of Frank Bittle. Their father is the late Thomas Clifford Bittle.

Both were acknowledging their pleasure in reading *So Many Mornings*.

This great grandfather's generous and kind heart is alive in James as he provided this recipe to share with you. To James' knowledge, during his visits in his grandfather's home, the omelet was cooked by Kate Summers and it was considered a favorite dish to the family. It is believed to have been a favorite dish among the early settlers of the Middletown Valley. Please enjoy this breakfast dish, with the Bittle's best regards to each of you!

Please note that the instructions included in the recipe for Bittle Cracker Omelet are those of Mrs. Clifford Bittle when she first married so many years ago and lived on the Bittle farm at Ellerton. This recipe was passed along to James' bride, Ruth, who was taught how to make her husband's favorite dish created by the family's Pennsylvania cook, Kate.

Bittle Cracker Omelet

4 eggs, well beaten
1 1/2 cups milk
1/2 pound crushed saltine crackers
1/2 pound bacon slices
1/8 pound butter

"Fry bacon til browned and crisp, remove to plate, pour off some of the bacon fat from the pan and add the 1/8 lb. butter. Melt the butter then add the crushed crackers to pan and brown, stirring constantly so as to not over brown. Then add the mixture of eggs and milk into the crackers and continue stirring til moisture has been absorbed and the crackers have dried out somewhat. The crackers should be lightly browned and flaky."

Serve with bacon or ham.

Serves 4.

Nelle Bittle

"In the Jim Bittle household we add 1 tablespoon of Worcestershire sauce to the egg mixture, to liven it up a bit."

&a &a &a

Creamed Eggs

2 to 3 hard-boiled sliced eggs
3 tablespoons butter
3 tablespoons all-purpose flour
seasoned-salt, to taste
pepper, to taste
1 teaspoon dried parsley flakes
1 cup whole milk

1. In a heavy pan melt the butter and blend in the dry ingredients.

2. Add the milk and boil for 1 minute while stirring.
(NOTE: Add additional milk if consistency is too thick.)

3. Add the eggs and stir until blended.

Variation: Add bits cooked ham, bacon or cheese.

For a quick breakfast, try making Egg Omelet. Serve between slices of fresh bread or toast as a sandwich for lunch.

Our parents invited more than one unexpected visitor to pull up a chair to their table to eat a bite of food with the family. Often Mom prepared food for a stranger after her kitchen had already been cleaned for the day. She was tired but her kind and generous heart compelled her to stir up something for the unannounced guest or the hungry homeless soul who routinely came by.

Before the gasoline engine became popular, streams of salesmen traveled our rural area with horse and wagon peddling their wares. Some were managing on a shoestring and in need of a bargain! Mom often provided room and board to them. On short notice, she made an omelet to hold them over until Dad and the hired hands came from the field for the meal.

Mom never held formal parties or entertained as such, but she often cooked and served food to a crowd. She has been an example of tireless energy. The attitude one works with is more important than the style. We all need to keep an enthusiastic spirit for doing good deeds! Always let love abound, even though the cost attached will most likely be great.

Egg Omelet

3 eggs
3 tablespoons sweet cream or evaporated milk
1/4 teaspoon baking soda
salt and pepper, to taste
butter, for frying

1. In a mixing bowl beat all the ingredients with a rotary beater or wire whisk until light yellow.

2. Melt a small amount of butter in a skillet and pour in the egg mixture. Cook over medium heat until lightly browned.

Variation: Add vegetables, cheese, ham or real bits of bacon to the egg mixture.

      €   €   €

Mom recalls making Schmierkase, a type of cottage cheese, from scratch. Here is how she did it during her wood-burning stove days.

Allow an earthenware crock filled with fresh whole milk (not processed milk, but milk straight from the cow) to sit at room temperature until sour. Transfer the crock of soured milk to the top of a warm wood stove. Heat to keep the crock warm is all that is needed. Do not put on a hot stove. Let it sit until the whey and curds part after coagulation. Run a knife through and around the curds, just to part and separate. Under favorable conditions, it usually takes one day for the curds to form. Transfer the curds, when soft like a gelatin, to a cheesecloth bag and hang outdoors on a clothesline. Allow about a day to drain dry. Transfer the cheese to a large bowl and add salt, to taste. Beat until smooth and add enough rich sweet cream to come to the consistency of soft butter. I remember Mom making Schmierkase, and it is delicious. If you have never tasted this homemade cheese, you have nothing to compare.

During the time Mom and Dad lived at Myersville on the George Toms farm, one evening she was in the process of making Schmierkase and hung a bag of cheese outdoors on the clothesline to drain. For some unknown reason, the cheese, bag and all, disappeared during the night and she never discovered what happened. Callie Long, who was working on the farm as a day hand at the time, became amused and jokingly said, "Well my land Letha, the dogs beat you to it that time!" Callie did not care for the taste of Schmierkase and was not one bit disappointed in the fact that it had vanished. Callie thought it was unfit for human consumption, but it might just be something a dog would eat, if hungry.

Try making Schmierkase by this easy method. It is delicious to eat as a spread on bread or served in a dish along with fruit.

Easy Schmierkase

1 quart commercial cottage cheese
1 to 3 tablespoons sweet cream

1. Using a blender mix the commercial cottage cheese with the cream.
(NOTE: Add cream until desired consistency is reached.)

2. Blend until the texture is smooth like cake icing.

Store in the refrigerator and serve cold.

Spread a thick slice of homemade bread with apple butter; then add a dollop of Schmierkase on top.

&a &a &a

I thought you would enjoy reading the recipe Mom and Dad used to make apple butter while they were living on the farm at Middlepoint around 1920. Dad traveled with horse and spring wagon to the Grossnickle Cider Mill to have apples boiled into apple butter for the family's use. Instructions are not included since the cider mill attendant knew exactly what to do.

Since water was needed to operate the coal-fed steam boiler, they were always located at a steady flowing creek. The boiler provided hot water that circulated through a hinged copper coil that the Grossnickle's swung over and down into the wooden oak barrel filled with apples. The apparatus provided enough heat through the tubing to boil the mixture of apples, sugar and spices--producing delicious apple butter. The approximate temperature reached in that coil was 250 to 300 degrees and was controlled by a valve. There was a sense of perfection in this procedure as the apple butter did not require stirring to prevent sticking, then scorching and finally burning. Another early-day method of making apple butter was to boil the apples and spices in a copper kettle. This requires constant stirring and results in a tiring task.

There were day-before preparations involved when making apple butter. Most farms had an apple orchard so first apples were picked or the ones that fell to the ground were gathered. The day prior to boiling, they were washed and cored while the spoiled or bruised areas were cut away and the remaining skin preserved. The farmers poured them into cotton cloth flour sacks that were saved and laundered after the flour had been used. Mom gathered the sugar and spices into a box--ready to be packed in the wagon come morning. The arrival at the mill was pleasant--one always met a neighbor or friend to converse with and share the latest news while the butter was boiling. If you lived close by, you drove home and returned later in the day to pick up the order. Dad hauled the finished product back home to the farm in the same barrel it was boiled in. The Grossnickles always draped and tied a white cloth over the top of the barrel to keep any debris from falling into the butter on the journey home.

Meantime, Mom was at home and gathered up the one-gallon earthenware crocks so that when Dad arrived she would be ready to help carry the apple butter into the kitchen. When he arrived, he pulled the wagon close to the house, stood up on the wagon bed, removed the cloth from the barrel, and dipped the butter into the crocks. He carried them into the house, while Mom melted paraffin wax in an old coffee pot on the cookstove. She poured enough wax in each crock to cover and seal the top. When the wax cooled and set firm, she tied newspaper over the top with old pieces of cord that she unraveled and saved from the seams in the bags of chicken feed. At last she carried the crocks to a cool closet to wait until she was ready to use it on the table. An apple boiling demanded many hours of labor, but it tided the family over from year to year with a delicious spread.

I remember the scent of the spices in the apple butter that filled the air when we opened the closet door. During the years gone by, Mom always had a supply on the pantry shelf. Of course, she made jellies and preserves, but apple butter was the old standby!

Recently, I had the pleasure of visiting with Arthur T. Leatherman, the son-in-law of the late Lester Grossnickle, and what a wonderful visit it was! My thanks to this gentleman for sharing regional history firsthand.

Arthur recalls a story of a local man who had arrived at the Frick Company in Waynesboro, Pennsylvania, to select and buy some parts to repair a steam engine like the one at the cider mill. The salesman in the establishment confronted the still young man and asked the question, "What is steam?" I suppose some quick thoughts flashed through his mind, but not the answer the salesman was looking for. So he replied, "I will tell you what steam is: Steam is nothing more than water going crazy over fire."

This handwritten recipe from Mom's cookbook is given as found. It requires ten cents worth of cloves! How much do you think that would be today? You are right--not much. And who has a flour sack to measure the apples? Do not forget this apple butter recipe is from the 1920s and makes 20 to 22 gallons.

Apple Butter

5 bushels of apple snits
(NOTE: This equals 4 flour sacks full.)
1/2 pound ground cinnamon
10 cents worth of ground cloves

&a   &a   &a

Tasty Apple Butter

7 pounds tart apples
(NOTE: About 20 medium apples.)
4 quarts apple cider
2 1/2 cups sugar
1 teaspoon allspice
1 1/2 tablespoons ground cinnamon
1 teaspoon ground cloves

1. Wash, core, and slice apples. Transfer to a large heavy kettle.

2. Add the cider. Cook until the apples are tender and falling apart. Press through a sieve to remove the seeds and skins.

3. Return the apple pulp to the heavy kettle. Add the sugar and spices. Cook the mixture over low heat to medium heat until thick and spreadable, stirring often to prevent burning. *(NOTE: Cooking time will vary with the variety of apples.)*

4. Pour the boiling hot apple butter into sterilized canning jars and seal.

Apple butter will keep in a cool, dark place for months.

ð·   ð·   ð·

BEVERAGES

In the wintertime no taste is so unforgettable as steaming hot cocoa made with fresh rich whole milk that came straight from the cow. Though most of us do not have a cow handy, everyone knows the best cocoa is homemade. Not only does it give us energy for the cold weather, it satisfies the sweet tooth at the same time.

Hot Cocoa

4 tablespoons baking cocoa powder
3 to 4 tablespoons granulated sugar
1/4 teaspoon salt
4 cups whole milk

1. In a small bowl mix together the cocoa powder, sugar, and salt. Set aside.

2. In a heavy saucepan heat the milk over medium heat. *(NOTE: Do not allow to boil.)*

3. Pour about 1 cup of the hot milk into the small bowl of dry ingredients and stir until combined. Return mixture to the hot milk while stirring. Stir until well blended.

Serve piping hot.

Variation: Remove hot cocoa from the heat; stir in a teaspoon of vanilla.

Variation: Place marshmallows in the serving cup and pour in the hot cocoa. Allow marshmallow to melt.

Variation: Drop a dollop of whipped cream on top.

Variation: This drink can be made with a sugar substitute and skim milk, for those who are watching the sugar and fat content of food.

Yield: 4 servings.

❧   ❧   ❧

This grape juice is rich and robust, with the taste of good home-grown grapes picked straight from the vines.

Unfermented Grape Wine or Juice

10 pounds grapes
3 quarts boiling water
granulated sugar, to taste

1. Place stemmed and washed grapes in an enamel pan. Scald grapes with boiling water.

2. Stir and let stand until cool.

3. Strain the grapes and juice through a cheesecloth into a large kettle and bring juice to a boil.

4. Add sugar to adjust tartness. Seal the boiling juice in sterilized canning jars. Store in a cool, dry place.
(NOTE: If juice is too rich, dilute with water.)

❧   ❧   ❧

Talk about lemonade being served in the shade! When hot, tired and thirsty, sipping lemonade made from fresh squeezed lemons will quench your thirst in seconds. It is as reviving as finding a shade tree on the hottest summer's day. When consuming this drink after being outdoors in extreme heat, it is best not to add the full amount of sugar, rather keep it on the tart side.

In the summertime, in order to make cold lemonade for the family, Mom used an ice pick to chip away chunks from the big block of ice in the old-fashioned ice box. Did it ever hit the spot. We are so spoiled today by having ice at our finger tips to use whenever we wish. Ice is considered a necessity and its availability is as common as water from the faucet.

When the sun was the hottest, and the men were in the fields working, Mom sent one of us children out with a fresh drink of water for them. If we didn't hurry, by the time we got to them the water was already warm and beaded from the heat. I remember meeting Dad, and him wearing his straw hat with a wide brim, and the look of his unprotected arms burned red from the long hours in the sun. Just thinking of the hours Mom and Dad have spent doing things the hard way pulls at my heartstrings. They made many sacrifices in order to give us a good home life.

Benjamin Franklin said "we should work as if we were going to live to be 100 years old and pray like you were going to die tomorrow." I tell you, never, never give up: *success may be standing right at the door you are about to close!*

Old-Fashioned Lemonade

6 to 10 fresh lemons
1 1/2 cups granulated sugar
2 1/2 quarts cold water

1. Wash the lemons in cold water. Roll them on a hard surface to break down the membranes and make them soft and pliable.

2. Cut the lemons into thin slices with a sharp knife and place in a glass pitcher. Add the sugar, mash with a spoon to extract the juice. Allow to sit for 15 minutes.

3. Fill the pitcher with cold water and stir until sugar is dissolved. Strain to remove lemon slices after allowing to cool in the refrigerator for 1 hour.

Serve lemonade over ice cubes.

                                  за за за

Homemade root beer is a fun drink to make that does need adult supervision. You would not believe the amount of corks that blew from the bottles that exploded when we made it at home. The chemical reaction is volatile, given the right conditions.

Today a wide variety of drinks are available in the grocery store to satisfy our thirst and desires. Mom remembers, not so many years ago, standing outdoors by the water pump, pumping while holding the long steel handle and trying to get enough water to run through the pipe to allow a fresh cold drink to flow from the spring. All this energy spent for a cool, not ice cold, drink of water! Before the use of the pump, folks learned to fetch water from the cistern or well with a bucket attached to the end of a rope.

When Mom was a child an old tin cup was placed by the outdoor well or spring for the sole purpose of catching a drink! Sometimes it hung from a nail driven into a corner of a nearby building or a wooden fence. Believe me, fresh water was the drink of the day.

Homemade Root Beer

5 pounds of granulated sugar
2 fluid ounces of root beer concentrate or extract
5 gallons of water
1/2 of a .6 ounce cake of yeast
1 cup lukewarm water

1. In a large container dissolve the sugar and root beer concentrate in 5 gallons of water.
(NOTE: Do not use an aluminum container.)

(NOTE: It is best to boil water prior to making root beer. Allow time to cool.)

2. In a measuring cup dissolve 1/2 of a .6 ounce cake of yeast with the lukewarm water. Add to the sugar and root beer mixture and stir until mixed well.

3. Bottle the drink immediately.
(NOTE: Do not use disposable bottles with twist off lids. Use corks to seal glass bottles.)

4. Place bottles on their sides in a 70 to 80 degree environment for 1 to 2 days. Then store 3 to 4 more days in 40 to 45 degree environment.

Chill and serve with cookies or salty treats!

     🍃   🍃   🍃

The local area had been doused with heavy rains, dumping far more water than the saturated soil could soak up, causing creeks to rise to flood levels. It was somewhere around the late 1920s when the mighty current of the swollen Middle Creek washed away the old iron bridge at the intersection of Route 17 and Highland Road.

At the same time Mom and Dad were living back home at Middlepoint. My dad's cousin, Elbert Grossnickle and his family, lived on the farm adjacent to the bridge, now owned by Robert T. Grossnickle. On this day so many years ago, Elbert and his sons Basil and Quentin, along with Emory Lewis, Jack and Clinton Brunner, and my dad with his two oldest sons were standing at the farm on another tiny bridge that leads into the lane.

I recently visited with Quentin and Pauline Grossnickle and they too, shared the story that my dad so often told. Additional details and names were gathered that afternoon to complete the story I write. Quentin expressed the excitement in the air as the men and the boys were standing there speculating if the bridge would withstand the strong force of the racing water. Elbert had often heard the sound of the creek during high waters, but this day it was different. My father having lived on the farm as a lad was familiar with the habits of the creek as well. Elbert was certain he heard the sound of stones falling away from the wall in the creek bed, and he was sure he felt the force ever so gently moving the earth under his feet.

Emory said he believed the bridge was strong and well built and he was going to walk over it and just check things out. The rest of the men tried their best to discourage him, but he was determined, and his mind was set. All eyes were on Emory as he placed a foot on that old wooden plank floor, and Elbert was more than apprehensive since the bridge at this point was beginning to lean a slight degree, but enough to let him know the worse had not yet come. At two-thirds of the way across, Emory suddenly had a change of mind. He quickly turned and walked back to join the other men. Only minutes had ticked away when a tree with its large roots sticking up out of the raging water came floating down the creek. All eyes were on it as it crashed into the bridge collapsing the leaning iron structure. A loud snapping cracking, crushing sound roared above that of the powerful rush of the water and away the bridge washed down the creek, making a violent splash as it hit the water. The men and their sons stood in amazement and I am sure a prayer of thankfulness was breathed as Emory was standing beside them unharmed.

Meanwhile, that day in the Grossnickle home, Elbert's wife, Sally, was busy cooking a meal for the men, some of whom were working at the farm. To this day, her sons recall the strawberry shortcake that awaited on the table. As I have mentioned throughout this cookbook, many memories are linked to good food.

Back then, when a bridge needed to be repaired or replaced, the able-bodied men in the community set aside time to gather and do the work. There were no organized county or state road departments. And if a winter snowstorm brought drifts that covered the roads, the men gathered to manually shovel a path wide enough to allow a horse and sleigh to travel down the road. The local folks were prepared with horse drawn sleds or cutters as well, so shoveling was a last resort.

Without a bridge in place, it was necessary for folks to forge the creek or travel on the same side. Most of the men rode horses or used a horse and wagon. As long as the creek was not swollen too high, they could still get to the other side with little effort.

With the urgent need for a reliable crossing, the men and the big boys gathered to stack rock against rock on the creek bed to ensure the wheels of their wagons and vehicles did not sink. The days that followed the disaster weighed heavily on the minds of the men in the community. Each one was busy with his farming and daily chores, but time was planned for working on the new bridge.

I regret that perhaps the names of those working at the bridge site are not complete, but with the happening occurring so long ago I have few resources. Those remembered being there are my dad and my two oldest brothers, Elbert and his sons, Lee and Aaron Delauter, Ralph Freshour and Nick Green. My oldest brother recalls hitching old Pet to the two-wheel dump cart and going down to the creek to work. He was just a young boy, but he drove the cart loaded with gravel, stone, and rock to the river bed from the site where it had been gathered. When he had a heavy load, he walked along and lead the horse. All the young boys pitched in and helped their families with the work. My brother remembers Basil was assigned the same chore using his father's cart and horse. The tools these men used were manually operated. By no means was bridge building an easy day's work.

Thoughts of pranks pulled on one anther during these hard days of work remain. One told is of Nick Green. He was selected from the group of men working this day to crawl up on the structure to take a measurement. Nick rolled up his pants legs in the event of a fall, hoping not to get himself wet beyond his knees! Elbert and Lee were holding the plank that Nick was to tread on. Lee was a young and jolly man who enjoyed fun, to say the least. Elbert being the older fellow suspected Lee's young heart might be up to mischief. And it was. Just as Nick got to his destination on the partly built bridge, Lee gave just a slight jiggle of the plank and, needless to say, you know what happened to Nick. Down into the creek he tumbled with a splash. A second later Elbert uttered, "Lee, I knew you were going to do that," and down he pushed him into the creek as well. I am told Lee himself told this story, and had many a laugh about this day throughout his life.

My middle brother was a little boy, just big enough to follow Dad when he was working. Often the little boys played by the work site, escaping boredom and all the while learning the tricks of the trade by sight. He recalls trailing down the road to the Middle Creek to play around while Dad helped to rebuild the bridge. While the men where in the process of building, a Coca Cola delivery truck came down the road, and the driver was unaware of the dilemma he was about to meet. He had made a delivery to the local Wolfsville stores and was on his way to Myersville, his next stop. When he finally surveyed the situation, after careful consideration, and I am sure much advice from the local residents, he decided he could drive the truck on the built-up riverbed to the other side. The men thought perhaps he should unload a portion of the cases of Coca Cola and then surely the creek bed would support the weight of the vehicle including its load. They were wrong! Without enough traction and power to make it to the other side, within seconds the wheels were mired and stuck in the Middle Creek mud. My brother recalls the men giving suggestions, then they assembled themselves around the truck, pushing together and trying to free the wheels. Their hope was to get it across the creek and on its way. With a struggle, the men with their horses succeeded. When the wheels of the truck hit dry ground, it sputtered away dripping with water.

The excitement of being there left a vivid impression in my brother's memory. He recollects a case of bottled Coca Cola left sitting in the creek after the truck left the scene. Mom recalls Dad telling her the driver passed out drinks to all the folks who were there helping with the rescue. My brother never had a carbonated drink and was surprised to learn at first swallow what a shock the tiny sharp bubbly fizz brought to his tiny taste buds and mouth!

Quick Root Beer is a quick and easy method of making root beer by the gallon. Unless you are preparing for a special occasion or the holidays, this could be just the right amount needed.

Quick Root Beer

1 teaspoon dry yeast
1/2 cup lukewarm water
2 cups granulated sugar
1 quart hot water
(NOTE: Not boiling.)
4 teaspoons root beer extract

1. In a measuring cup dissolve the yeast in the warm water. Set aside.
(NOTE: It is best to bring the water used in this recipe to a boil. Then cool to the temperatures required.)

2. In a gallon glass jar dissolve the sugar in the hot water. Stir in the root beer extract.
(NOTE: Do not use an aluminum container.)

3. Combine all ingredients and add enough warm water to fill the gallon jar, mixing well.

4. Put the lid on the jar. Set in the warm sun for 4 hours. The root beer will be ready to drink the next day.

Serve ice cold. Don't forget the cookies!

❧   ❧   ❧

COOKING TIPS

Here are a few helpful instructions Mom has gathered while cooking throughout her life, and she felt they were important to write in this cookbook. They may prove helpful to you in your kitchen.

To make cake flour, place 1 tablespoon of cornstarch in a measuring cup. Fill to the 1-cup mark with all-purpose flour and sift into a bowl.

If more salt than required has been added to food, and it tastes too salty, add 1 to 2 teaspoons of sugar to nullify.

Evaporated milk or whipping cream can be substituted for whole milk in most icing recipes. If recipe permits, whip the icing with an electric mixer until light and fluffy. This replacement gives the icing a nice consistency and improves the taste.

When baking chocolate cake, use 3 tablespoons baking cocoa powder and 1/2 tablespoon solid vegetable shortening to replace the 1 ounce of unsweeten chocolate required in the recipe.

Make sour milk or cream by adding 1 tablespoon vinegar to 1 cup sweet milk or cream and stir.

Spread the bottom crust of a fruit pie with butter to help prevent a soggy fruit pie.

With a brush spread melted butter on top of an unbaked pie crust and sprinkle lightly with granulated sugar. This will produce a nicely browned and crispy top crust.

In recipes requiring solid shortening, do not substitute with oil. Its reaction is not the same and your recipe may fail.

Any vanilla cookie dough can be sprinkled with baking cocoa powder to give it a chocolate flavor.

Gather all ingredients and measure before starting to mix a recipe. As a general rule, room temperature ingredients work best in most recipes.

Hard boiled eggs will peel easier when cooked over low heat.

Most cookie dough bakes best when chilled for a few hours prior to baking.

Sift dry ingredients as directed since this will ensure even distribution.

When thickening berries or fruit pies, combine 1 tablespoon of instant clear jell and 1/2 cup granulated sugar. Sprinkle over 1 cup fresh fruit and toss lightly to coat.

DRAWINGS REFERENCE

Drawings in *This Old Cookbook* are by Alison Gregg Dowd and illustrate family photos.

Page *Foreword*, Mom's homestead at Ellerton--presently owned by Steven Leatherman. Also, Letha Wiles baking. Photo 1995.

Page 54, Dad taking a noon break under the shade tree with grandchildren, Bill and Susan. Photo 1959.

Page 150, Bob and Kate, the workhorses.

Page 168, Young Bill, neighbor Wilmer, and Tom in hat with Peggy Sue, his calf. Photo 1958.

Page 208, Cow barn being built by George Wiles' construction crew at the Wiles farm. Photo 1965.

Page 242, Harmony Church of the Brethren. Dad asked Mom out on their first date here. Photo 1995.

Page 258, Dad's Super C Farmall tractor. Photo 1954.

Page 279, Tom pulling wagon loaded with corn for Mom's chickens. Photo 1954.

Page 308, Letha Wiles.

INDEX

411

415

416

My Notes

My Notes

My Notes

My Notes

My Notes